RELIGIOUS LIBERTY IN THE CROSSFIRE OF CREEDS

Edited by Franklin H. Littell

Franklin H. Littell — Robert McAfee Brown
Robert Gordis — James Hennesey
William A. Jones — Janice G. Raymond
Edwin B. Bronner — Jesse L. Jackson
Elie Wiesel — Marc H. Tanenbaum
William B. Ball — John C. Raines
Elwyn A. Smith — Philip A. Potter
Theodore M. Hesburgh — Milton K. Curry, Jr.
Cynthia C. Wedel

ECUMENICAL PRESS
PHILADELPHIA

Library of Congress Catalog Card Number: 78–51911
ISBN 0-931214-01-7

© *Journal of Ecumenical Studies* 1978

Manufactured in the United States of America

Published by the Ecumenical Press
511 Humanities Bldg.
Temple University
Philadelphia, PA 19122

Since this book is being co-published by the *Journal of Ecumenical Studies* and the Ecumenical Press, there is double pagination. The bracketed numbers are the running pagination for the Fall, 1977 (Vol. 14, No. 4), issue of the *Journal*.

Publication has been made possible by a grant from The Barra Foundation, Inc.

CONTENTS

In Memoriam

Melvin Gingerich
Frank S. Loescher

INTRODUCTION

The first proposal that a conference on Religious Liberty be held during the American Bicentennial was made by Dr. Melvin Gingerich. Dr. Gingerich was emeritus professor of Goshen (Indiana) College, and with his wife Verna was resident of the Germantown Mennonite Center; the adjacent church was celebrating two hundred years as the oldest continuing Mennonite congregation in America. Dr. Gingerich called the first committee meetings, rather informal groups, in February and March of 1972. The present writer in the course of discussion was asked to prepare a budget and a conference proposal. This was submitted on April 6, 1972, under the rubric "An International Congress on Religious Freedom."

As then discussed, Religious Liberty was conceived as America's major contribution to the theory and practice of government. With Vatican II under way, the time seemed propitious for an interfaith conference which would review the sufferings of faithful Christians and the Jewish people under totalitarian governments such as the Third Reich and the USSR and affirm the American experiment in liberty and self-government. The first written proposal conceived of an American "Kirchentag," a mass rally such as those in West Germany, bringing together in large number Americans of the most diverse heritages and commitments to affirm our national experiment in pluralism, dialogue, and inter-faith affirmation of First Amendment liberties.

It was appropriate that the first discussions should be held among persons primarily from the "Peace Churches"—Mennonites, Brethren, Friends, Schwenckfelders, since their testimony played an important part in teaching all Americans the value of "soul liberty"—that respect for the tender conscience which has been so important in defining the American experiment and establishing the unique American Constitutional protection of the free exercise of religion and the barrier against any establishment of religion which might violate the rights and dignities of minorities. Moreover, all were convinced that Pennsylvania was the area and Philadelphia was the location for a Bicentennial emphasis of this kind.

As discussion and planning progressed, two important changes in perspective occurred. In June of 1972, a functioning committee for a "Conference on Religious Liberty" was established, with Francis G. Brown, a Quaker, agreeing to chair it. First, it was agreed that the initiative undertaken by the Peace Churches should be expanded to include Catholic, Jewish, and Protestant planning and participation. Monsignor Philip J. Dowling of the Archdiocese, Dr. Rufus Cornelsen of the Metropolitan Christian Council, and Dr. Murray Friedman and Dr. Bertram Korn of the Jewish community were members of the first official committee meetings. There was still some thought that the observances might be based primarily upon colleges and universities in Greater Philadelphia, but the vigorous participation of Catholic, Jewish, and Protestant leadership soon made inter-faith sponsorship more logical than inter-institutional. Second, consultations with the Philadelphia '76 staff (Mr. William L. Rafsky and colleagues) and with the National Endowment for the Humanities (which made two planning grants) led to further broadening of the committee's perspectives. Attention was given to musical and theatrical events, to films, and to other ways of communicating the concern for affirming the importance of Religious Liberty to the community at large. Second, it was agreed that rather than aiming at a mass rally the Conference would seek to win the participation of key delegates from religious communities across the United States.

For a time, it seemed the major part of the Conference budget might be secured from Bicentennial funds being allocated in Washington or from public funds in Philadelphia. It became clear, however, that the risks as well as the initiative must fall upon the religious communities as such. On January 21, 1975, the Judicatory Bicentennial Coordinators composed of Protestant, Roman Catholic, and Jewish representatives voted unanimously "to approve in principle plans for the Bicentennial Conference on Religious Liberty and to recommend its sponsorship and support to the Bishops and Executives Conference." On January 25th the Bishops and Executives Conference representing the Protestant and Orthodox constituents of the Metropolitan Christian Council, the Roman Catholic Archdiocese and the Philadelphia Board of Rabbis (meeting in separate sessions) voted unanimously to "sponsor and support a national Bicentennial Conference on Religious Liberty to be held in Philadelphia in 1976." A Ways and Means Committee was appointed to implement the commitment, consisting of Dr. Frank Stroup, Rabbi Morris V. Dembowitz, Monsignor Charles V. Devlin, and Dr. Rufus Cornelsen. Although the budgetary problems were not thereby eliminated, the commitment of the religious communities to the project guaranteed its coming to pass and also guaranteed a freedom in planning the program which was appropriate to a conference centered in the free exercise of religion.

In developing the Conference program, considerable liberty was shown in presenting a broad range of issues where human hurt is real and where persons of conscience are exercising a prophetic role. At the same time it was kept in mind that the Conference was not equally concerned with all human rights and liberties, nor even with the entire Bill of Rights. The primary focus remained Religious Liberty, its positive expression encompassing the dignity and integrity of the human person and his or her conscience. Religious Liberty in the twentieth century—in the shadow of two World Wars, two major types of totalitarian dictatorship, several cases of genocide, racism, and starvation, and the threat of atomic holocaust—in its positive expression would certainly involve the right to speak prophetically upon a variety of matters affecting the human future.

The Conference was not to be concerned with problems of education as such, but rather with the right of religious communities to exercise their responsibility for the young without harassment. The Conference was not to argue the case for peace vs. war as such, but rather to deal with the claim of high religions to proclaim without restraint or repression the moral superiority of peace to violence, of building homes to building bombers. The Conference was, in short, to be thoroughly rooted and grounded in the guarantees of the First Amendment— and then to exercise that freedom of religion freely, without fear or favor.

The addresses and reports here presented are published as an act in the cultivation of the free exercise of religion. Religious Liberty can wither and die if reduced to the simple negative of resisting government interference in the business of church or synagogue. It will flourish and grow where cultivated by souls that love liberty and consciences that will not be still in the presence of wickedness.

The Bicentennial Conference was no meeting of desiccated antiquarians, but rather a gathering of thinking and feeling users of liberty in the service of truth.

Franklin H. Littell
Temple University, Philadelphia, PA

FOUNDATIONS AND TRADITIONS OF RELIGIOUS LIBERTY

Franklin H. Littell

The High Ground of Religious Liberty

Constitutional authorities tell us that the Bill of Rights is the cornerstone of the Federal Constitution, that the First Amendment is the heart of the Bill of Rights, and that, of the five liberties guaranteed Americans in that basic charter, religious liberty is unique. A strong case can be made, indeed, that religious liberty is the most important American contribution to the science of government.

Over one hundred years ago, Philip Schaff, one of the nineteenth century's greatest scholars and church leaders, lifted the matter to an even higher historical level, when he wrote:

> The glory of America is a free Christianity, independent of the secular government, and supported by the voluntary contributions of a free people. This is one of the greatest facts in modern history.[1]

Had the positive values of pluralism been more apparent in 1857 (rather than the problems of holding together a new nation embroiled in both religious and sectional hostilities and shortly to engage in Civil War), Schaff's generalization might have included Jews as well as Christians, and ethnic diversity as well as diversity among the churches.

In reference to religious liberty, as in any interfaith contact, we must seek to understand the tones above and below the lines as well as the transparent meaning of plain words. We relate best to each other in difficult discussions, not when each suppresses the idioms and metaphors familiar to his or her deepest speech, but rather when each makes a conscious effort to hear—or perhaps overhear—what is really being said. Only so do we turn the Tower of Babel into a Pentecost of mutual understanding. Interreligious dialogue is mere idle conversation, foolishness (*amathia*), unless we allow the partner to use his or her own language and meet him or her in the pursuit of truth. Let that willingness to listen as well as speak, which Robert McAfee Brown and the late Gustave Weigel demonstrated in their classic, *An American Dialogue* (1960), serve as a model for us in this Conference and on this theme!

Caspar Schwenckfeld, who wrote—on the run—some of the finest statements for religious liberty ever penned, and whose spiritual descendants helped to

---

[1]Philip Schaff, *Germany: Its Universities, Theology, and Religion* (Philadelphia/New York: Lindsay & Blakiston/Sheldon, Blakeman & Co., 1857), p. 8.

Dr. Franklin H. Littell is Professor of Religion, Temple University, Philadelphia, PA.

colonize Penn's woods, put the matter on the plane of high religion and sound politics where it finally belongs. Writing an admonition to Jacob Sturm of Strassburg in 1549, he said:

> Civil authority has no jurisdiction over the Kingdom of God; government was divinely ordained for the sole purpose of maintaining an orderly life in human society, but has no right either to influence or to interfere with religious convictions; the individual is accountable to Jesus Christ as the head of the Kingdom of God.[2]

Sturm was officer in a state-church, more tolerant than most, but still coercive.

Felix Manz, a Mennonite leader and the first martyr to Protestant intolerance (d. 1527), asserted by indirection one religious basis for religious liberty—far above the level of mere political expediency—in a hymn condemning persecution:

> They call out the magistrate to put us to death
> For Christ has abandoned them . . .
> To shed innocent blood is the most false love of all.[3]

We are in the area of basic belief, which only those with a sheerly negative view of religious liberty can avoid.

Already some root thoughts are beginning to emerge, and perhaps in fairness to the dialogue of this Bicentennial Conference they should be set forth here and now:

First, religious liberty—and the values that adhere to it, the structures that make it a viable alternative to coercion—is a matter of high religion as well as sound government.

Second, the free exercise of religion is both historically and theoretically prior to the prohibition of any establishment of religion.

Third, the affirmation of ''soul liberty'' (an early Quaker term for what we are talking about), of which religious liberty is an essential positive expression, necessarily involves too an affirmation of the dignity and integrity of the human person in his or her individual and collective existence.

Fourth, in today's world as in the past, in America as well as on the rest of the world map, there are powerful political and economic forces as well as ideological thrusts that neither understand nor contemplate the sacred truths about human persons and their nature and destiny, which form the essential foundation of our First Amendment liberties.

In sum, there are skirmishes and sometimes pitched battles all along our line of march, our exodus out of bondage toward freedom. And religious liberty is not primarily a matter for antiquarians or armchair philosophers: it is a matter which,

---

[2]Cited by Selina Gerhard Schultz in *Caspar Schwenckfeld von Ossig (1489–1561)* (Norristown, PA: Board of Publication of the Schwenckfelder Church, 1946), pp. 311–312.

[3]Leonhard Muralt and Walter Schmid, eds., *Quellen zur Geschichte der Täufer in der Schweiz, 1. Zürich* (Zürich: S. Hirzel Verlag, 1952), No. 202, pp. 220–221.

rightly understood, confronts us with choices between the obvious risks of *Engagement* and the (apparent) securities of expedient compromise or capitulation to the adversary. It is a matter which in the modern period must be coupled in every discussion with the reality of the Church Struggle against enemies without and the fainthearted within.

Confronted by such choice, the nation's founders—the authors of the Bill of Rights—chose the risks of a continuing pilgrimage toward freedom over the known dependability of sacral government and a coercive Christendom. During the colonial period, for most of nearly two centuries, the colonies had been both politically and religiously a peninsula of Europe, in most regions maintaining a coercive and sometimes cruel Christianity. From this ancient pattern our forebears were persuaded to break.

Never before had any society anywhere attempted such a dangerous experiment as separating the political and religious covenants. Church leaders and rulers knew, as they had known for a millenium and a half, that a society could only be held together if there were a common liturgy and a common worship at a common altar. Although in a few European countries a pragmatic program of toleration had replaced persecution of dissenting Christians, and in a very few a beginning had even been made toward granting Jews who had survived centuries of oppression a slender margin of civil status, in most places Christendom was still intact and the wise and experienced state-church experts, both Protestant and Roman Catholic, uniformly predicted disaster for such a reckless undertaking as government based upon liberty and popular sovereignty.

The ruling classes of European Christendom, accustomed for centuries to use religion as a system of psychological and spiritual control of their subjects, and with the rise of the nation-state making use of a doctrine—the so-called "divine right of kings"—even more coercive in its implications than the monochromatic synthesis of the high Middle Ages, quite correctly felt threatened by "republicanism"—and especially by a government that dared to allow religion(s) to pursue their higher calling, and persons of conscience to listen to and obey a higher law than the will of temporal rulers.

Even the most generous toleration, pragmatic and wise, is not the alternative to persecution: it is the other side of the coin. Both toleration and persecution rest upon a claim of government to an authority that our forebears considered presumptuous, spiritually arrogant. Religious liberty is a right and a truth which is not government's to deny or to grant: government may only recognize it and protect it, for it stands upon higher ground. In the view of most of our forebears, a view to which a minority like Patrick Henry and Lyman Beecher came but late—for initially they defended "magisterial Protestantism"[4] and mistrusted separation—the affirmation of a God-given religious liberty freed the churches to fulfil their rightful high calling. That high calling was to proclaim the truth, to

---

[4]Cf. George H. Williams, *The Radical Reformation* (Philadelphia: Westminster Press, 1962), pp. xxiv–xxvii.

prophesy freely, and to live faithfully, and not to be used to shore up ancient power structures.

There was an eschatological note to it: religious liberty, they believed, was the wave of the future. As one preacher put it,

> May we not view it, at least, as probable, that the expansion of republican forms of government will accompany that spreading of the gospel, in its power and purity, which the scripture prophecies represent as constituting the glory of the latter days?[5]

They knew too what they were leaving behind as they moved toward the coming triumph of liberty. As Walter Prescott Webb summed it up in his great book on the westward movement of peoples,

> It is very significant that for 150 years during which the foundations of frontier societies were being laid down in the Americas the prevailing condition in the Metropolis was that of religious wars and unprecedented intolerance.[6]

Today, we have ready recourse to summary statements from Supreme Court cases. In *Davis v. Beason,* the Court said:

> The first amendment to the Constitution... was intended to allow everyone... to entertain such notions respecting his relations to his Maker and the duties they impose as may be approved by his judgment and conscience and to exhibit his sentiments in such form of worship as he may think proper, not injurious to the equal rights of others.[7]

The language in the famous *Cantwell* case goes further:

> The constitutional inhibition of legislation on the subject of religion has a double aspect. On the one hand, it forestalls compulsion by law of the acceptance of any creed or the practice of any form of worship. Freedom of conscience and freedom to adhere to such religious organization or form of worship as the individual may choose cannot be restricted by law. On the other hand, it safeguards the free exercise of religion. Thus the Amendment embraces two concepts—freedom to believe and freedom to act.[8]

We might be tempted, therefore, to consider religious liberty in the setting of fixed positions, social statics, and immovable religious and political landmarks. Although our languages may sometimes differ, there are two convictions that should bring us to stand shoulder-to-shoulder against all enemies of soul liberty: first, the agreement that religious liberty in America is rooted and grounded in

---

[5]Nathan Strong, *On the Universal Spread of the Gospel* (Hartford, 1801), p. 31. I am indebted to Nathan O. Hatch for this reference.
[6]Walter Prescott Webb, *The Great Frontier* (Boston: Houghton Mifflin Co., 1942), p. 30.
[7]133 U. S. 333, 342 (1890).
[8]*Cantwell v. Connecticut,* 310 U. S. 296, 303 (1940).

fundamental religious and ethical understandings and is in no sense to be confused with a mere charitable toleration of differences or political *pax dissidentium;* and second, the perception that religious liberty points to the last things, the things that are final and ultimate, to the coming defeat of tyranny and oppression and the final triumph of righteousness and peace—with the dignity and integrity of the human person affirmed—over the devil's legions of degradation and death.

Religious Liberty and Totalitarian Regimes

The question of "separation" assumes a special form with the rise of modern totalitarian regimes, especially since the official programs of such one-party governments frequently proclaim separation of church and state. Thus the Nazi Party from the beginning (1920 Platform, par. 24) distinguished between the "non-sectarian religion" (called *positives Christentum*) which the Party claimed to stand for and the "particular confessions" and "Jewish materialism" which were negated. Similarly, one-party government in the USSR professed, already in 1936, a constitutional guarantee of separation. In both cases, however, a new ideological establishment functioned as a persecuting state-church, with disastrous consequences for faithful Jews and Christians and other dissidents of conscience. In the Soviet Union today both Jewry and radical Christians are victims of the persecuting policies of an ideological state-church.

"Separation of church and state," in any case a cloudy formula, by itself provides no guarantee whatever of effective religious liberty. In addition to the systematic destruction of the Jewish counterculture in the Nazi Holocaust, what was intended eventually for any churches that persisted in following a different Lord from the *Führer* can be read out plainly in the administrative decrees governing the resettlement of the Warthegau. Approved by Hitler personally and initialed by Martin Bormann, the program for 350,000 new settlers in purged Poland terminated a functioning church life and privatized religion.[9] The admin-

[9]"1. There are no longer established churches, but only religious societies as voluntary associations.

4. There are no longer any relations to groups outside the district, and also no legal, financial, or official ties to the national church.

5. Members can only join on an annual basis by written application . . .

6. All church societies and fraternal groups (youth groups) are liquidated and forbidden.

7. Germans and Poles may no longer live together in one church (*Nationalitätenprinzip*) . . .

9. No special offerings may be collected above the annual dues.

10. The associations may own no property—such as buildings, houses, land, cemeteries—except for meeting rooms.

11. All foundations and monasteries are liquidated, since these are not appropriate to German morality and population politics.

12. The associations may not conduct social welfare programs, which are alone and exclusively the affair of the NSV.

13. In the associations only native pastors from the Warthegau may be active." Paul Gürtler, *Nationalsozialismus und evangelische Kirchen im Warthegau* (Göttingen: Vandenhoeck & Ruprecht, 1958), Appendix Document #8.

istrative decrees issued for Communist East Germany (the *DDR*) are remarkably parallel to the kind of "separation" the Nazis intended generally and, where they could, effected. For example:

1. The church must diappear from public view and be limited to purely church-cultic affairs. The claim of the church to be *Volkskirche,* that is, church for the whole people, is strictly denied.

2. Above all, the church may not carry on any educational and youth work; social service is also denied her.[10]

Under Marxist and Nazi governments, "separation of church and state" has been followed by the establishment of a new ideological state-church, coercive and neo-sacral.

From every evidence, therefore, the totalitarian parties and governments of the twentieth century are as dangerous to "soul liberty" as the most regressive of traditional establishments. All twenty of the governments in the Arab League support Islamic state-churches, and ten of them have the death penalty for any subjects who convert out. Until the *jus emigrandi* was accepted in central Europe in 1555 (and widened in scope in 1648), most of Christendom maintained that kind of political coercion to enforce religious conformity. In countries where Marxist ideological parties control government, the old kind of coercive practices still obtain—albeit with a new face: individuals of independent conscience are harassed and jailed, countercultures are persecuted, public careers and the advanced education of their children are closed to dissenters, and second-class status is the permanent lot of any who cannot pass the test of a required orthodoxy.

Although our primary concern in this Bicentennial Conference is to reaffirm as Americans our devotion to American fundamentals, and particularly to the structures and spirit that sustain and strengthen religious liberty, we say frankly that we long for the day when all men and women shall be free of persecution. We would be unworthy of our forebears if we failed to notice, for instance, that Egypt, a one-party dictatorship, forbids Coptic Christians to attend the colleges of the national university (Al-Azhar) for which they also pay taxes, that the dictatorship of Malawi has recently tortured and/or driven into exile several thousand Jehovah's Witnesses, that the most outspoken living Russian representative of freedom's holy light—Aleksandr Solzhenitsyn—is forced to live in exile, and that one member nation of the United Nations has been for more than a quarter of a century the object of recurring military attacks blessed by religious functionaries.

Certain lessons worthy of further reflection may be drawn from this set of observations:

[10]Joachim Beckmann, ed., "Die Kirchen in der Deutschen Demokratischen Republik," in *Kirchliches Jahrbuch: 1958* (Gütersloh: Gütersloher Verlagshaus Gerd Mohn, 1959), p. 199.

First, "separation" does not of itself guarantee liberty: in addition, there must be a protection of the free exercise of religion and a general good will to give life to the protective clauses.

Second, the disestablishment of historic religion(s) may, unless accompanied by an affirmation of the temporal values of pluralism and open interreligious dialogue, create a vacuum which will be filled sooner or later by a new coercive orthodoxy (whether *positives Christentum,* "progressive religion," "civil religion," tribal cult or other *Weltanschauung*).

Third, religious liberty cannot survive as a negative concept alone: both philosophically and practically its continuance depends upon a certain respect for the dignity and integrity of the human person—in both communal and individual commitments.

Fourth, there are times and places which require of persons of conscience opposition to illegitimate actions by legitimate government; there are other seasons which raise the question of the duty as well as the right of persons of religion to resist illegitimate governments as such. As Americans, enjoying a freedom for religious and conscientious devotion very rare on the face of the globe, we have a special responsibility not only to affirm our devotion to liberty but also to identify and resist attacks and subversion of liberty—whether abroad or at home.

It has often been observed that Americans were singularly fortunate in having separation of the political and religious covenants accomplished by national leaders who were friendly to religion in its voluntary manifestations, rather than suffering—as has happened in many countries in the twentieth century—a disestablishment born of hostility and often followed by a new appearance of repression and ideological establishment. This thought might well inspire in us a new respect for "secular" government, in contrast to regimes either sacral or neo-sacral, and a new appreciation of the importance of vital, voluntary religious communities that conduct their affairs in mutual respect. In their lively pluralism such communities prevent a spiritual vacuum from developing in the society, they provide strong barriers to the rise of dynamic ideological parties which threaten all basic liberties, and they afford the options which make high religion viable.

Writing of a related liberty, a great political philosopher once stated, "With freedom of speech allowed, the secondrate man has his say along with the rest; without, he alone may speak."[11] We may paraphrase: with freedom of religion protected, lowgrade religion may be offered with the rest; without it, lowgrade religion alone can function. In the middle of the last century a great church historian put the matter on its proper plane in affirming:

> ... the principle of liberty of conscience and the repudiation of religious coercion. It must be clearly understood how great is the gulf which divides the holders of this principle from those who reject it, both in faith and

[11]Everett Dean Martin, *Liberty* (New York: W. W. Norton Co., 1930), p. 200.

morals. He who is convinced that right and duty require him to coerce other people into a life of falsehood . . . belongs to an essentially different religion from one who recognizes in the inviolability of conscience a human right guaranteed by religion itself, and has different notions of God, of man's relation to God, and of man's obligation to his fellows.[12]

Our reasons for affirming religious liberty are not primarily political and pragmatic, although it is obvious that a single coercive religion or ideology is today enforceable only by violence against persons. Our primary reasons for affirming religious liberty are derived from high religion itself.

We know that "God wants no compulsory service. On the contrary, he loves a free, willing heart that serves Him with a joyful soul and does joyfully what is right." The man who said that was Claus Felbinger, Anabaptist/Mennonite martyr.[13] We know that "every human being has the right to honor God according to the dictates of an upright conscience." And further, "every human being has the right to respect for his person, his good reputation, the right to freedom in searching for the truth and in expressing and communicating his opinions. . . ." The man who said that was John XXIII, who more than any other pope in many generations communicated good will to persons of other churches and religions and thereby augmented the credibility of the faith he and his co-believers profess. And the related truth is this: "The men of our time have become increasingly conscious of their dignity as human persons."[14]

The "Declaration on Religious Freedom" of Vatican II also lined out the interrelated truths here emphasized: "The act of faith is of its very nature a free act."[15] Religious liberty, if it means anything, certainly means the liberty of devout persons and groups to practice high religion—religion that is voluntary, grounded in honest conviction, and not based on hypocrisy and dissimulation.

Religious bodies also have the right not to be hindered, either by legal measures or by administrative action on the part of government, in the selection, training, appointment, and transferral of their own ministers, in communicating with religious authorities and communities abroad, in erecting buildings for religious purposes, and in the acquisition and use of suitable funds or properties.

Religious bodies also have the right not to be hindered in their public teaching and witness to their faith, whether by the spoken or by the written word. . . .

In addition, it comes within the meaning of religious freedom that religious bodies should not be prohibited from freely undertaking to show the special

[12]Ignaz von Döllinger, quoted in A. D. Lindsay, *The Essentials of Democracy* (Philadelphia: University of Pennsylvania Press, 1929), p. 76.

[13]Quoted in William R. Estep, *The Anabaptist Story* (Nashville: Broadman Press, 1963), p. 143.

[14]*"Pacem in Terris"* (April 10, 1963), ed. William J. Gibbons, S. J. (New York: Paulist Press).

[15]Walter M. Abbott, ed., *The Documents of Vatican II* (New York: Guild Press/America Press/Association Press, 1966), p. 689.

value of their doctrine in what concerns the organization of society and the inspiration of the whole of human activity.[16]

This is the free exercise of religion to which the First Amendment refers.

Roger Williams, along with William Penn the colonial American most clearly perceiving how liberty and highgrade religion are inextricably intertwined, drew the logical inferences of such perception of the truth:

> (1) God requireth not an uniformity of Religion to be inacted and inforced in any Civill state; which inforced uniformity (sooner or later) is the greatest occasion of civill Warre, ravishing of conscience, persecution of Christ Jesus in his servants, and of the hypocrisie and destruction of millions of souls. (2) It is the will and command of God, that...a permission of the most Paganish, Jewish, Turkish or Anti-Christian consciences and worships, bee granted to all men in all Nations and Countries, and they are only to be fought against with that Sword of God's Spirit, the Word of God.[17]

When the Articles of Confederation failed, and the constitution of a federal union was being debated, Rhode Island was one of two states that refused to join unless a Bill of Rights were included. The resolution passed in the Rhode Island ratifying convention incorporated the two concerns, affirmative and negative:

> That religion, or the duty which we owe to the Creator, and the manner of discharging it, can be directed only by reason and conviction, and not by force and violence; and therefore all men have a natural, equal and unalienable right to the exercise of religion according to the dictates of conscience; and that no particular religious sect or society ought to be favored or established, by law, in preference to others.[18]

As one writer summed up the growing understanding of religious liberty, from Virginia Bill of Religious Freedom (1784–1786) to First Amendment (1789–1791),

> By religious freedom, or soul liberty, is meant the natural and inalienable right of every soul to worship God according to the dictates of his own conscience, and to be unmolested in the exercise of that right, so long, at least, as he does not infringe on the rights of others; that religion is, and must be, a voluntary service; that only such service is acceptable to God; and, hence, that no earthly power, whether civil or ecclesiastical, has any right to compel conformity to any creed or any species of worship, or to tax a man for its support.[19]

---

[16]Ibid., pp. 682–683.

[17]Quoted in M. Searle Bates, *Religious Liberty* (New York: International Missionary Council, 1945), p. 427.

[18]Jonathan Elliot, *The Debates on the Federal Constitution* (Philadelphia: J. B. Lippincott & Co., 1881), I, pp. 334–335.

[19]Charles F. James, *Documentary History of the Struggle for Religious Liberty in Virginia* (Lynchburg, VA: J. P. Bell Co., 1900), p. 9.

It should by now be amply evident that the citizens who made this affirmation were concerned for the profession of high religion and not primarily motivated by political expediency.

In the middle of the last century, Gerrit Smith, the great enemy of human slavery, stated powerfully the higher ground upon which our liberties as Americans are based:

> Our political and constitutional rights, so-called, are but the natural and inherent rights of man, asserted, carried out, and secured by modes of human contrivance. To no human charter am I indebted for my rights. They pertain to my original constitution; and I read them in that Book of books, which is the great Charter of man's rights. No, the constitution of my nation and state create none of my rights. They do, at the most, but recognize what is not theirs to give. . . . It is not then to the constitution of my nation and state, that I am indebted for the right of free discussion; though I am thankful for the glorious defense with which those instruments surround that right. That right is, for the most part, defended on the ground, that it is given to us by our political constitutions. . . . Now, I wish to see its defense placed on its true and infinitely higher ground; on the ground that God gave it to us; and that he who violates or betrays it, is guilty, not alone of dishonoring the laws of his country and the blood and toil and memory of his fathers; but he is guilty also of making war upon God's plan for man's constitution and endowment; and of attempting to narrow down and destroy that dignity with which God invested him when he made him in his own image.[20]

In these days of "positive law," when recourse to the Common Law has been excised from federal cases, we will do well to insist again that our basic liberties as Americans derive from no grant of government—no action of legislature, no decision of court, no decree of any executive. They derive—and religious liberty, the most precious of them, above all—from a higher source. In the American system, government agencies are not in a position to affirm that truth, but they are also forbidden to express ideological positions contrary to the truth of the Higher Law.

The implications of this sublime philosophical and historical truth for both religion and politics are clear. Sound government will not only avoid repression: it will also not pretend that such historic expressions of affirmative religious liberty as conscientious objection to war, clergy confidentiality, tax exemption, religious schools, religious social welfare programs, etc., depend upon a "grant of government." No government can "grant" something that is both philosophically and historically antecedent to it.

Let it be said, too, in an age of rising totalitarianism that "soul liberty" casts its mantle of protection over the family. In the Berlin Kirchentag of 1951, with a third of a million Christians gathered to demonstrate their faith in the beleaguered

---

[20]Quoted in Dwight L. Dumond, *Antislavery* (Ann Arbor: University of Michigan Press, 1961), p. 231.

city, a key discussion centered in the query, "To whom do the children belong?" The irreducable answer was given by "Father" Hans Lokies of the Gossner Mission—an alumnus of four-and-a-half years in one of Hitler's concentration camps, and bold also to speak the truth in the face of Stalin and his minions:

> They don't belong to the state.
> They don't belong to the party.
> They belong to God, and under God to the family!

We Protestants and Catholics and Jews who believe in the higher law have still some unfinished business on this front in America in making clear to some fellow-citizens who have fallen into pre-totalitarian ways of thinking and acting some of the lessons of the conflict between high religion and twentieth-century lowgrade politics, some of the lessons of the twentieth-century "Church Struggle."

Religious persecutions and violent assaults on conscience were wrong before any constitution recognized liberty's truth, and they are wrong when practiced by ideological agencies that have substituted new tyrannies for older despotisms. The knowledge that more than three-fourths of the governments represented in the United Nations have neither knowledge nor experience of either liberty or popular sovereignty is sobering. The great majority have either repressive religious or ideological establishments. Even those that have a tolerant though privileged religion are a small minority. Those that understand the essentials of "soul liberty" are fewer yet. Awareness of this fact should make us rejoice in the Bicentennial Year of the American experiment and also make us doubly alert against those whose bad politics and lowgrade religion (or *Ersatzreligion*) make them a threat to the republic and to our churches and synagogues.

Before the enactment of the Virginia Bill which directly preceded the First Amendment, James Madison commented:

> During almost fifteen centuries has the legal establishment of Christianity been on trial. What have been its fruits?... Pride and indolence in the clergy, ignorance and servility in the laity: in both, superstition, and bigotry, and persecution.[21]

Religions in America are today both sounder and more secure for the emergence of government which is secular, which neither manipulates religions nor is manipulated by any religion or ideology. Having come this far along the path of developing liberties, having freed true Christians, devout Jews and others to practice highgrade religion, we do not propose to muffle our hostility to spiritual tyranny—whether Marxist or Muslim, "Christian" or Hindu, Buddhist or Shinto, fascist or communist. Where there are Americans who would justify such repression and coercion, whether private citizens or office-holders sworn to

---

[21] Quoted in Ronald E. Osborn, *The Spirit of American Christianity* (New York: Harper & Bros., 1958), p. 31.

uphold the Constitution of the United States of America against all enemies, foreign and domestic, they represent regressive politics (even if falsely called "progressive"). More important, they represent the kind of bad politics and lowgrade religion that has made the twentieth century—from the slaughter of the Armenians in the dying throes of "the Holy Muslim Empire" through the murder of 6,000,000 Jews in the heart of a declining Christendom to the present butchery of Christians in Uganda or Kurds in Iraq—the Age of Genocide.

A few months ago the Mennonites of the Lancaster Conference in Pennsylvania spoke a pointed warning to their members which we, in a season of a (happily) declining imperial presidency, may overhear with profit to our souls: "We call upon all our believers to render unto Caesar honor and respect, but not reverence; gratitude and loyalty, but not worship."[22] That is high religion, and as long as the Constitution is loyally enforced by those sworn to uphold it, that belief and practice will also be respected as sound Americanism.

The Future of "Soul Liberty"

For all of our love of our liberties in this history, we know that liberty is not the ultimate. Liberty is penultimate: the end is truth. The substantial case against coercion and repression is not that they do not work, nor even that they make bad politics, but that they point toward hypocrisy and dissimulation and death.

In spite of the dire prophecies which most Europeans and many Americans directed toward the disestablishment of preferred religion at the end of the colonial state-churches, with the recognition that government should get out of the religion business and stay out, voluntary religion has worked very well in America. Although today there is a temporary slackening, over two hundred years of the history of the American republic there has been a tremendous growth of membership, participation, and support. As would happen in any area where disestablishment is risked, the membership lists shrank drastically with disestablishment (1786–1833). But over generations the religious communities developed their own uniquely American methods for holding their own and winning new adherents—especially by mass evangelism in Protestantism, parochial schools in Roman Catholicism, and charitable agencies among the Jews. The statistics tell the story: in 1776, five percent of the population held membership in religious communities; in 1800, 6.9%; in 1850, 15.5%; in 1900, 35.7%; in 1926, 50.2%; in 1970, just under seventy percent.[23] And when asked, ninety-six percent of the American people claim religious affiliation.

Although a church leader cannot help but wonder about that twenty-six percent who claim affiliation but show up on no church rolls, the situation is certainly more favorable to religion than those areas of established churches

---

[22]Reported in the *Philadelphia Inquirer*, September 20, 1975, p. B1.

[23]With sources in Franklin H. Littell, *From State Church to Pluralism* (New York: Doubleday & Co., 1962; rev. ed., 1971), pp. 31–32.

where ninety-eight or ninety-nine percent are officially on the books, but from one-fourth to one-third will vote communist in the next election, or where church taxes are paid, but church participation is limited to the rites of passage (3.4% in Lutheran Sweden, sixteen percent in Anglican England, thirteen percent in Catholic Bavaria, fifteen percent in Catholic Spain). We do not attempt here to assess the true spiritual condition under religious or ideological duress, such as that in Syria or the USSR, where only the occasional outcries of suffering minorities give us some inkling of what might happen to the establishments if the peoples had freedom of choice, and the alternative worldviews of humanity, history, and life's meaning have to compete freely for human souls.

Although religious liberty "works," the fundamental argument for it is not pragmatic but theological, indeed eschatological. It has to do with the human future, with the things that are ultimate, and with the way highgrade religion conducts itself in this intermediate period (*Zwischenstadion*) which is our present human history. In sum, it is the style of highgrade religion to win its way on its merits, just as surely as it is the style of lowgrade religion to bless persecution, crusade, and genocide.

The scriptures sacred to both Jews and Chrsitians pour curses upon the heads of worldly rulers who forget the nature of their stewardship and, puffed up in self-importance, launch their prideful ventures over the bodies of the common folk. When the day of the oppressor ceases and the whole earth breaks forth again in song, the judgment of the Most High against the persecutors and oppressors shall stand:

> Is this the man who made the earth tremble,
>   who shook kingdoms;
> Who made the world like a desert,
>   and overthrew its cities,
> Who did not let his prisoners go home? (Is. 14:16b–17)

Such a one, who purposed oppression for others, shall in God's good time be brought low. Let us take heart—the future is on the side of amnesty, and not with the small-minded and mean-spirited!

The eschatological nature of the fight for liberty can be symbolized negatively, too. Among the awful apparitions which whirl before us in the nightmare seasons of the twentieth century, we are haunted by a number of apocalyptic faces—the disloyal general, the sadistic surgeon, the faithless professor, the apostate preacher, the religious renegade, the lawless policeman, the commissar without a conscience—and the persecuting prelate.

When we affirm liberty, our penultimate goals have to do with life and love, with a principled fight against the necrophiliac engines of economic and political control that treat the human person with contempt.

> We see that every man has the right to life, to bodily integrity and to the
> means which are necessary and suitable for a proper development of life.

And he has the right to be informed truthfully about public events. (*Pacem in Terris*)

The imperative connection between our present affirmation of liberty and the coming victory of truth is also carried by the words of the Passover prayer:

May this season marking the deliverance of our ancestors from Pharaoh arouse us against any despot who keeps men bowed in servitude. In gratitude for the freedom that is ours, may we strive to bring about the liberation of all mankind.

The other side of the equation is of like potency: as black Christians in America still remember, those who were determined to preserve the cruel and debasing system of chattel slavery at any price had finally to legislate against teaching slaves to read the Bible. For the word of God is a powerful explosive which, rightly planted in living minds and souls, springs the structures of oppression and shatters the engines of death. We are moved inexorably from celebration of this present and tangible liberty, guaranteed to Americans in the cornerstone paragraph of our charter of constitutional existence, to rejoin the line of march out of social statics toward the final triumph of love, mercy, justice and peace.

In the background to our meditations and study seminars, we hear the song of those who walked a path bloody and watered with tears—

We have come—over a way that with tears has been watered,
We have come—treading our way through the blood of the slaughtered ...

And amidst it all, we remember with those who remember the passage through the Red Sea, the Emancipation Proclamation, the time when the waters did not part (the *Shoah* in Central Europe), the cries of the helpless in so many places in this very hour. We remember that the Spirit of liberty is the Spirit of truth.

Our immediate purpose is the reaffirming and strengthening of American religious liberty. In the fight that is today raging in America against very real and wrong-headed enemies of liberty, we say with the poet:

... I am waiting
for the American Eagle
to really spread its wings
and straighten up and fly right

And I am perpetually waiting
for a rebirth of wonder...[24]

Our ultimate goal points us toward the rising sun, the sun of the New Day heralded in song by James Weldon Johnson, the day of promise to all human persons—

[24]Lawrence Ferlinghetti, *A Coney Island of the Mind* (New York: New Directions Paperback, 1974), p. 49.

Good news to the poor,
Healing to the broken-hearted,
Release to the captives,
Sight to the blind,
Liberty to the bruised.   (Is. 42)

There are those to whom religious liberty is a purely negative thing: the prohibition of any establishment of religion. And there are times and cases when we must stand solidly with them against the establishment of any peculiar religious rite or doctrine. But the affirmative, the free exercise of voluntary, high-grade religion is the priority affirmation. It is the affirmation which throws its protective mantle over dissenters and sceptics, "heretics" and "atheists," believers and unbelievers, for the sake of that joyful and willing service which alone is pleasing to God.

The pilgrimage we are entered upon, the exodus out of bondage through liberty toward the Promised Land, forbids us to worship present idols, to bow down to any gods of place, tribe or nation. When the time is fulfilled—and it can only be fulfilled in a spirit of broadening liberty—we shall hear the Lord's song resound unto the ends of the earth; to the sea and all that is therein; the isles, and the inhabitants thereof.

Helmut Gollwitzer, an expert in the Church Struggle and a prominent opponent of Nazi repression from the Barmen Synod of May, 1934, and of Communist repression from the founding of Berlin's Free University (1948), summed up the promise of liberty in this way:

> The *form* of freedom is this: to be able to decide for one's self. The *secret* of freedom is this: to be without anxiety for one's self. And the *meaning* of freedom is this: Love. This is the exact meaning of the beautiful old saying upon which we cannot meditate too often: *Deo servire summa libertas.* "To serve God is the highest freedom."[25]

Martin Luther King, Jr., Christian martyr, hated and lied about by enemies of American liberty both within and outside government, also knew how freedom and concern for justice necessarily interact if devotion to either is to be kept alive and moving forward. On August 23, 1963, he preached at the site of the Lincoln Memorial to the largest assembly ever gathered there the greatest sermon preached by an American in this century: "I have a dream. . . ." And when the wicked slew the dreamer, sneering at his vision of a land of human solidarity from sea to shining sea, he escaped their net into the presence of the Author of Liberty:

[25]Translated in Franklin H. Littell, ed., *Sermons to Intellectuals* (New York: Macmillan Co., 1963), pp. 84–85.

Free at last, free at last,
Thank God: free at last!

"Soul liberty," as William Penn long ago discerned and affirmed in this very city of Philadelphia, is an arrow pointing toward the final triumph of truth and love—victorious over denial, degradation, and even death itself.

THE PROTESTANT TRADITION OF RELIGIOUS LIBERTY

Robert McAfee Brown

Both the greatness and the limitations of the Protestant tradition of religious liberty can be encapsulated in the comment of an anonymous seventeenth-century writer: "I had rather see coming toward me a whole regiment with drawn swords, than one lone Calvinist convinced that he is doing the will of God."

I

The *greatness* of this tradition is that the one who believes that God's will is being done through him or her is indeed freed up, liberated, to take risks, even to the point of death, for the sake of the convictions that inspire the action. No power, whether of the state, the church, or the conspiring forces of fate, need daunt such a person. Success or failure is not the ultimate test; the ultimate test is fidelity to God's will, whatever the consequences. "The Christian," as Christopher Fry has somewhere remarked, "is one who can afford to fail." The will of God *will* be done; freedom of expression and of action is given to the "one lone Calvinist," who acts not for the sake of self but *ad majoram gloriam Dei*.

The *limitations* of this tradition are perhaps more readily apparent to non-Calvinists than are the advantages. The freedom the Calvinist has is not something the Calvinist easily grants to others, and the assurance of being the purveyor of God's will can lead to an arrogance and intolerance that history has recorded with balefully complete documentation. The "one lone Calvinist," in fact, has sometimes called upon the "whole regiment with drawn swords," as a way of persuading others that he or she is not only the instrument of the divine will, but that others had better acknowledge that instrumentality or be prepared to pay the consequences. Not all the heretics were burned in Catholic Spain.

When the "one lone Calvinist" is, in fact, the doer of God's will, that one can still pervert that will by the unGodly way it is exercised. And there is always the possibility (sometimes hidden from the Calvinist) of only *thinking* he or she is the doer of God's will, while actually expressing nothing but his or her own will, which he or she seeks to clothe with divine authority. If a Calvinist in full posession of the truth could summon fear, the Calvinist in error was positively terrifying.

The greatest danger in such a position is that those who believe themselves in possession of the truth will feel justified in imposing that truth by force upon those less fortunate, and will be unwilling to make the relationship reciprocal. Calvinists and Lutherans were not notable champions of religious liberty for others.

Dr. Robert McAfee Brown was Professor of Religion at Stanford University, and is now on the faculty of Union Theological Seminary, New York, NY.

Much of the recognition that such liberty belonged to all, and not just to a few, came from the small, so-called sectarian groups, the Left Wing of the Reformation, who had the added incentive that being in the minority made it a matter of self-interest for them to insist on the right of religious liberty for those in the minority. A principle when compounded with a survival impulse is a powerful principle indeed. So one must not try too neatly to create a case for historic Protestantism as the vehicle on which religious liberty rode into the arena of modern civilization. Indeed, as Rabbi Gordis has argued elsewhere,[1] religious liberty is more a gift of the secular tradition than of the religious one, and this is a salutary warning against claiming too much for one's own tradition, particularly when the latter (whether Protestant or Catholic) has been studded with instances of intolerance.

Many today would argue that our modern pluralistic situation is the situation most conducive not only to religious liberty, but to civil liberty as well. Since no single tradition can make exclusive claims for itself, there must be a live-and-let-live attitude on the part of all traditions. Such a foundation is precarious, however, to the degree that indifferentism is hardly a way of building enduring or significant loyalties. Its atmosphere, moreover, paves the way for the intrusion of fresh idolatries that are willing to capitalize on indifferentism and to impose themselves on unsuspecting peoples and nations before the latter are really aware that they have signed away by default the liberties they sought to espouse. The history of modern totalitarian systems is an eloquent illustration of this contention.

II

The above remarks have seemed necessary to introduce a certain healthy circumspection, before proceeding to a discussion of the theological case for religious liberty that can be made from a Protestant perspective. I offer a preliminary comment and a substantive reply.

The preliminary comment is a reminder of what might be called the negative power of Protestantism at its best, i.e., its consistent warning against idolatry. In this insistence, Protestantism has drawn heavily upon the prophetic tradition of Judaism and upon a constant reiteration of the commandment, "You shall have no other gods before me." Whenever an uncritical allegiance is demanded for an institution, an ideology, a person, or whatever, such an allegiance must be disavowed. This is the point Paul Tillich emphasized in his stress on "the Protestant principle"—the assertion that only to God can ultimate allegiance be given. All else can and must be challenged, criticized, attacked, examined, and repudiated if need be. If an institution claims that its structure or its doctrine is an unambiguous expression of God's being or will, the claim must be denied, for the institution is not God. (This is the source of much of the historical Protestant

---

[1] Philip Scharper, ed., *Torch and Gospel* (New York: Sheed and Ward, 1966), pp. 99–133.

vehemence against papal infallibility, though, curiously enough, some of those same Protestants gave allegiance to what could be called paper infallibility, i.e., that a given book, Holy Scripture, was beyond the possibility of error.) This principle serves as a bulwark against inordinate and idolatrous demands of the state, for, as the Westminster divines put it, "God alone is lord of the conscience." The signers of the Barmen Declaration of the Confessing Church in Germany made clear in 1934 that to say "yes" to Jesus Christ meant saying "no" to Hitler.

This means also that one's own statements of the truth, one's own institutional structures, must come under similar scrutiny and judgment, and this is the part of the Protestant tradition on religious liberty that has been most historically flawed. But this can be a self-correcting resource to which appeal from within can always be made, even though those within apparently often need strong nudging from those without.

III

Let us turn now to the more substantive response to the problem. Here I shall use a statement of the World Council of Churches, which, since it includes such a diversity of Protestant and Orthodox groups, has had to deal constantly with the issue of religious liberty. In addition to being an important statement in its own right, the quotation I offer is a safeguard against the "one lone Calvinist" syndrome. At its first assembly in 1948 in Amsterdam, the World Council established various guidelines for religious liberty, on the basis of which discussion continued through the second assembly at Evanston in 1954, leading at the third assembly at New Delhi in 1961 to a clear statement of the theological rationale for religious liberty:

> Christians see religious liberty as a consequence of God's creative work, of his redemption of man in Christ, and his calling of men into his service. Accordingly human attempts by legal enactment or by pressure of social custom to coerce or to eliminate faith are violations of the fundamental ways of God with men. The freedom which God has given in Christ implies a free response to God's love and the responsibility to serve fellow-men at the point of deepest need.[2]

Several things in this compressed statement are worth comment: (1) The case is made in *positive* rather than negative terms. It is not said, "We really have the right to act coercively if we wish, but we will refrain from doing so." Rather, it is said, "Because of certain positive affirmations about how God deals with us, a positive affirmation emerges about how we are to deal with one another." This position is a necessary consequence of the Christian faith, rather than a grudging concession to be extracted from it. (2) The case has *universal* rather than partial application. It is

---

[2]W. A. Visser't Hooft, ed., *New Delhi Report* (New York: Association Press, 1962), p. 159.

not said, "Under certain circumstances, we believe in religious liberty, i.e. when we are too few to be assured of it for ourselves, or when we are so many that we can afford to let the crazies sound off." Rather, it is said, "Under all circumstances, the claim to religious liberty is valid." (3) The case is based on the *central affirmation* about God, rather than on a peripheral theological affirmation. It is not said, "Because items a, b, c, and d are so, there is an inferential likelihood that item e, dealing with religious liberty, can be defended." Rather it is said directly and explicitly, "Since God deals non-coercively with us, we must deal non-coercively with one another." To believe that God's pattern is one of freely offered love and then to seek to communicate that belief by a forced option would deny the integrity of the entire enterprise. If God's will is not imposed by fiat, neither can ours be. (4) The case makes *demands* on those who affirm it. Religious liberty is not only liberty to proclaim, but also "responsibility to serve," and, indeed, to serve those "at the point of deepest need." Arrogance, superiority, and condescension are all ruled out.

This basic affirmation implies certain specific consequences, among which are at least the following:

1. Religious liberty is a fundamental human right that should be universally recognized.

2. The state should not only recognize religious liberty but help to protect it.

3. No group, and particularly no church, can rightfully employ force or violence to propagate its point of view.

4. The right *not* to believe is also a right that must be acknowledged and safeguarded.

5. Each person not only has the right to interior conviction and private worship, but also to public expression of that conviction.

6. Freedom to give corporate expression to one's faith in voluntary public association, and in corporate acts of witness, proclamation, and teaching, must be protected.

7. One must be free to change one's religious convictions, if one so chooses, without fear of social, economic, or political reprisals.

8. The freedom one claims for oneself and one's group is a freedom that must likewise be extended to all other individuals and groups.[3]

IV

Further clarifications of the Protestant tradition of religious liberty are still needed in a number of areas. The first of these is the vexing problem of *limita-*

---

[3]This list is a compilation of themes from a variety of World Council of Churches statements, conferences, resolutions, etc. It appears in the above form in Robert McAfee Brown, *The Ecumenical Revolution,* rev. ed. (New York: Doubleday, 1969), p. 239.

tions to religious liberty. Are there any such? How *much* can one claim as a right, in the name of religious liberty? If my exercise of that liberty involves the infringement of another's liberty, we have a problem. I may not invoke a Markan passage in defense of snake-handling, claiming that the right is inherent in my understanding of revelation, when such an action jeopardizes the life expectancy of those in my immediate vicinity. More importantly, must a society grant religious liberty to a group or individual whose point of view would involve denying religious liberty to others if the group or individual had enough power to do so? (This was an earlier Protestant fear concerning Roman Catholicism that Vatican II has safely put to rest. It may be a more real consideration in the future if the followers of the Rev. Sun Myung Moon continue their present rate of conversion.) How much power should the state have in protecting religious liberty for its constituents, when the state might feel an understandable reluctance to support those who claim that "God alone [and not the state] is lord of the conscience"?

A second unfinished item of business has to do with the *relationship of religious liberty to civil liberty*. Is it enough to say that, if we opt strongly for religious liberty, this will provide an umbrella under which concerns about civil liberty can be guaranteed? To claim the right to speak freely on behalf of Jesus Christ ideally ought to entail the right for someone else to speak freely on behalf of a political candidate or an unpopular viewpoint or a minority cause. *De facto,* of course, that is not always the case, and many in civil society may feel very uncomfortable with such a formulation.

This suggests, therefore, a third item of unfinished business. A basic issue of *theological methodology,* with important practical consequences, may be at stake. Third world liberation theologians, for example, have been arguing forcefully in recent years that theological assertions grow out of engagement in the here-and-now, as "critical reflection on *praxis,*" rather than being initiated by truths somehow handed down from on high. They might be very critical of the W.C.C. statement as starting from the wrong end, and prefer the approach of Vatican II, which in its affirmation of religious liberty appealed first to claims that could be accepted by all thinking people, before stating a distinctively Christian position. Perhaps there needs to be more two-way traffic on this street; statements about guarantees of civil liberties might also buttress claims about religious liberty. In a shrinking world, as more and more cultures and traditions must live together, the widest possible consensus on these issues must be sought.

JUDAISM AND RELIGIOUS LIBERTY

Robert Gordis

The centrality of religious liberty in the democratic worldview in general and the American vision in particular is highlighted by the fact that it is set forth in the opening sentence of the First Amendment, "Congress shall make no law respecting an establishment of religion or prohibiting the free exercise thereof."

Unfortunately, the familiarity of these words has tended to blunt their revolutionary impact, and the concept is all too frequently taken for granted. Many Americans find themselves in a position similar to that of the highly cultured but rather straitlaced old lady who was very well read but had never gone to the theater. Her grandchildren finally persuaded her to see a performance of *Hamlet* on the stage. When she returned, they were non-plussed by her reaction, "Nothing but a string of old quotations." This Bicentennial Conference on Religious Liberty will be performing a highly significant service to the American people, by freshly exploring all the dimensions and implications of religious liberty and indicating the long and difficult struggle that lay behind its being incorporated in the First Amendment.

Religion has been a universal phenomenon, present in every human society since human beings emerged upon this planet. On the other hand, the doctrine of religious liberty has been generally recognized as an ideal only within the last two hundred years. To be sure, there were individual, great-souled believers who had espoused the ideal of freedom of conscience before the modern era. There have also been a few religiously motivated communities which had established religious freedom before the eighteenth century. Perhaps the earliest instance of such societies is the Tartar kingdom of the Chazars in Central Russia, between the Volga and the Don Rivers, which lasted from the sixth to the tenth century. The rulers and upper classes of Chazaria had adopted Judaism as their faith in the eighth century, and they accorded full religious liberty to Christians and Moslems as well. The Dutch kingdom established by William the Silent in the sixteenth century adopted the principle of toleration, though there were limitations on the doctrine in practice. Roger Williams, in establishing the colony of Providence Plantations, or Rhode Island, in the New World, made full freedom of conscience the basis of the commonwealth. The Catholic Lord Baltimore extended the right of worship to Protestants. But these were isolated and exceptional cases.

By and large, the principle of freedom of conscience became widely held and increasingly operative only with the Age of Reason and the spread of the ideas of the Enlightenment. Perhaps the outstanding expression of religious tolerance in

Dr. Robert Gordis is Professor of Bible and Professor of the Philosophies of Religion at the Jewish Theological Seminary, New York, NY.

the literature of the period was Lessing's famous drama, *Nathan der Weise*. The drama, which had a Mohammedan Sultan and a Jewish sage as its protagonists, contained the famous parable of "the Three Rings." These rings, which were identical in appearance, had been fashioned by a father for his three sons, because he could not bear to give his priceless, ancestral heirloom to any one of them. The overt message of the parable was clear. The three rings symbolize the three monotheistic religious of Judaism, Christianity, and Islam, all of which represent an expression of God's love for humankind and of the reverence they owe God in return. Scarcely beneath the surface was another implication—none of the three faiths can reasonably insist that it alone represents the true revelation of God and should therefore be granted a privileged position in a free society.

Elsewhere I have had occasion to point out that because of its secular origin the modern concept of religious liberty suffers from certain weaknesses and limitations.

Today, we need to recall that the concept of religious liberty possesses three distinct yet related aspects. Like so many ethical values, its roots lie in the instinct of self-preservation. In other words, *the first and oldest aspect of religious liberty is the right which a group claims for itself to practice its faith without interference from others*. The extension of this right to other individuals and groups is a great leap forward in both time and insight. Frequently it requires centuries to achieve and too often has remained unattained to the present day. Indeed, even in our age, instances are not lacking of groups in virtually every denomination who define the right to religious liberty as the right to deny religious liberty to those who differ with them. In this respect, religious liberty is no different from any basic right, such as freedom of speech or assembly, which is first fought for and achieved by a group in its own behalf. *Only later*—and often half-heartedly—*is freedom of conscience extended to other groups who differ in belief and practice*. Finally, the third and most difficult stage in religious liberty emerges—and it is far from universal—when *a religious group, dedicated to its belief and tradition, is willing to grant freedom of thought and action to dissidents within its own ranks*.

The Jewish people have played a significant role in the emergence of religious liberty in its first aspect. With regard to the two other aspects, we believe that Judaism and the Jewish historical experience also have some significant insights to offer all people. No other large religious group has as great a stake in the present and future vitality of the doctrine as has the Jewish community.

While it is true that virtually every religious group finds itself a minority in one or another corner of the globe, Jews have been a minority almost everywhere and always. There is, therefore, historic justice in the fact that the people for whom religious liberty is so fundamental were the first to take up arms in defense of this right. The earliest recorded war for religious liberty is the struggle of the Maccabees against the Syrian Greek King Antiochus Epiphanes, which broke out in 168 B.C.E. The Maccabean struggle was inaugurated not for the sake of political liberty, territorial aggrandizement, national honor, or booty. It represented the armed resistance of a group in Palestinian Jewry who were resolved to protect their religious faith and way of life in a world where a determined effort was being made to impose a uniform pattern of Hellenistic culture and pagan religion on the entire Middle East.

Had the Maccabees not fought, or had they fought and lost, the Hebrew Scriptures would have been destroyed, Judaism would have perished, Christianity would not have been born, and the ideals of the Judeo-Christian heritage, basic to Western civilization, would have perished. There was, therefore, ample justification for the practice of the early church, both in the East and West, which celebrated a festival on August 1 called "the Birthday of the Maccabees." It testified to the debt which Christianity, as well as Judaism, owes to these early, intrepid defenders of freedom of conscience. Thus the long struggle was launched for the first and oldest aspect of the concept of religious liberty.

Freedom of religion in an open society today must necessarily presuppose two elements which were less obvious in the stratified societies of earlier days. *It must include religious equality,* for there can be no true religious liberty if the formal freedom of worship is coupled with legal, psychological, or financial liabilities. To be sure, the minority group cannot reasonably expect the same level of importance in society as the majority, but it has the right to demand that there be no restrictions or liabilities placed upon it by the state. In other words, full religious liberty means that the state will recognize the equality of all believers and nonbelievers, even though in society the relative strengths of various groups will necessarily impose disadvantages upon the poorer and less numerous sects.

There is one additional element essential to full religious freedom; *religious liberty is not being truly safeguarded if it is purchased at the cost of religious vitality.* Frequently the position of the Jewish community on questions of church and state is misunderstood, because it is attributed solely to the desire to avoid religious disability for itself and other minority groups. It is true that the position of minorities in regard to freedom of religion may parallel that of secularists who also oppose utilizing the power and resources of the state to buttress the claims of religion. But there is another and at least equally deep motivation for the Jewish position: a sincere concern for the preservation of religious vitality. Here majority groups have as direct an interest as do minorities, for religious vitality is based on *voluntary* commitment and sacrifice.

At times, well meaning and dedicated advocates of religion believe that the provisions of the First Amendment can be safeguarded and the cause of religion advanced by the introduction of "non-denominational" practices into the schools and other arenas of the public estate, such as prayer, silent or otherwise, or Bible reading. They frequently overlook the fact that non-denominational religion is frequently little more than dessicated religion, lacking the specific content, the color, and the warmth of a living religious tradition. Moreover, it places the authority of the state or the public school behind a brand of "official religion," often called "civil religion," that carries the clear implication that the specific practices or doctrines of a given tradition are secondary and may be dispensed with. As anyone genuinely committed to religion knows, there are some ·"nonsectarian" beliefs and practices that are more nonsectarian than others!

We have dealt thus far with the first aspect of the ideal of religious liberty: the right which every religious group claims for itself to practice its faith freely, without restriction or interference from others. With regard to the other two aspects of the ideal of religious liberty—more theoretic in character—we believe the specific Jewish historic experience has significance for other religious groups and for the preservation of a free society itself.

As we have noted, there is, theoretically at least, no problem with regard to the doctrine of freedom of conscience for those who maintain that all religions are equally good—or bad. Years ago, when communism was making substantial inroads among American college youth, the writer participated in a symposium on "Communism and Religion." Among the panelists were a Methodist bishop, a Presbyterian minister, two rabbis, and Earl Browder, then a leading spokesperson for communism in the United States. As the various speakers for religion sought to develop their positions vis-à-vis communism, Mr. Browder turned to us and declared, to the manifest delight of the youthful audience, "The communists are the only ones who can establish peace and equality among all the religions—because we do not believe in any of them!" The history of twentieth-century totalitarianism has demonstrated that religious intolerance is far from impossible under communism and fascism. The crude and brutal persecution of religion by atheistic regimes today makes the classic instances of religious intolerance of the past seem almost idyllic by comparison. In the Soviet Union today, all religion suffers grave disabilities, but Judaism has been chosen for special treatment: no religious education is permitted to young or old, no seminaries for the training of rabbis exist, and Hebrew has the distinction of being the only language the study of which is proscribed within the borders of the communist "paradise." Antireligious bigotry has proved itself second to no other prejudice in its virulence in the Soviet Union.

Nonetheless, it is true that the problem of evolving a theory of religious tolerance and practicing it is genuine and complex. This is a major moral and intellectual challenge for those believers who are convinced that they are the repositories of religious truth and that those who differ with them, whether within their group or without, suffer from a greater or lesser degree of error. In this connection, the attitude of Jewish tradition is highly interesting. It arose within a religion which believes profoundly that it is the repository of God's authentic revelation and that all other faiths possess, by that token, a lesser standard of truth. Since such a standpoint is widespread among communicants of most creeds, it should be useful to examine the theory and practice of *religious liberty within Judaism*—the approach of the Jewish tradition toward dissidents within its own community. Even more significant for the world at large is the unique theory in Judaism of *religious liberty for non-Jews and their right to maintain their own worldview and way of life.*

The key to the Jewish attitude toward religious differences within the community is to be found in the historical records. Judaism was always marked by a vast variety of religious experience, which is given articulate expression in the pages of the Hebrew Scriptures. The Hebrew Bible contains within its broad and hospitable limits the products of the varied and often contradictory activity and thought of priest and lawgiver, prophet and sage, psalmist and poet. It reflects the temperaments of the mystic and of the rationalist, of the simple believer and of the critical seeker after ultimate truth. All are part of Holy Writ, being, in the language of the Talmud, the words of the living God.

This characteristic of the Bible set its stamp upon all succeeding epochs in the history of Judaism. It is not accidental that perhaps the most creative era in its history after the Biblical era, the period of the Second Temple, was the most "sect-ridden." Even our fragmentary sources disclose the existence of the Pharisees, the Sadducees, the Essenes, and the Zealots—to use Josephus' classic tabulation of the "Four Philosophies." The Pharisees, the dominant group in number and influence, were divided into various groups which held strongly to opposing positions. The Talmud, which had its inception during this period, is a massive monument to controversy, with two thousand individual scholars differing and debating hundreds of issues. Although much less is known about the Sadducees, the same variety of outlook may be assumed among them. With regard to the Essenes, the discovery of the Dead Sea Scrolls has indicated that the term "Essenes" is best used of an entire conspectus of sects who differed among themselves passionately. The Samaritans were also a significant group of dissidents, highly articulate in their divergence from a Jerusalem-centered Judaism. It was in this atmosphere that the early Jewish sect of Christians first appeared, adding to the charged atmosphere of vitality and variety in Palestinian Judaism. There were also countless additional patterns of religious nonconformity in the various Diaspora communities.

In the Middle Ages a variety of factors combined to counteract this latitude of religious outlook in the Jewish community. The constantly worsening conditions of exile and alien status required, it was felt, a greater degree of group-homogeneity. Secondly, most of the earlier dissident viewpoints disappeared. Thus, the standpoint of the super-nationalist Zealots was totally meaningless after the loss of national autonomy. Similarly, the outlook of the Sadducees, who centered their religious life in the Temple at Jerusalem, was completely irrelevant to the life of an exiled people. Thirdly, the widespread emphasis on religious conformity imposed by the medieval world on its aberrant sects also proved a model and example. Fr. Joseph Lecler points out in his massive, two-volume work, *Toleration and the Reformation,* that St. Thomas Aquinas was "relatively tolerant toward pagans and completely intolerant toward heretics." As Fr. John B. Sheerin notes, St. Thomas explicitly stated that "to accept the faith is a matter of free will, but to hold it, once it has been accepted, is a matter of necessity."

Nevertheless, the attempt to impose conformity in religious belief never succeeded in medieval Judaism, even when undertaken by so august a figure as

Maimonides. Several attempts were made to expel from the community individuals or groups that were regarded as "heretical." The rite of excommunication, which was essentially an instrument for enforcing community discipline and obedience to the courts in legal and judicial matters, was invoked to this end. None of these attempts proved either successful or enduring. Maimonides, the greatest Jewish thinker of the Middle Ages, confidently proposed a set of *Thirteen Principles,* which he hoped would serve as a creed for Judaism. Though his statement attained wide popularity, and was printed in the traditional prayerbook as an appendix, lesser persons did not hesitate to quarrel with both the content and the number of articles of belief in his *Creed,* and it never became an official confession of faith.

An even more striking illustration of the enduring vitality of the right to religious diversity in Judaism may be cited. Uncompromisingly rationalistic as he was, Maimonides declared that to ascribe any physical form to God was tantamount to heresy and deprived one of a share in the world to come. Nowhere is the genius of Judaism better revealed than here. On the same printed page of the Maimonides' *Code* where his statement is encountered, it is challenged by the remark of his critic and commentator, Rabbi Abraham ben David of Posquieres, who writes: "Better and greater men (than Maimonides) have ascribed a physical form to God, basing themselves on their understanding of Scriptural passages and even more so on some legends and utterances, which give wrong ideas." The critic's standpoint is clear. Rabbi Abraham ben David agrees with Maimonides in denying a physical form to God, but he affirms the right of the individual to maintain backward ideas in Judaism without being read out of the fold on that account. The right to be wrong is the essence of liberty. Nonetheless, it is clear that the spirit of medieval Judaism was far less hospitable to religious diversity than Rabbinic Judaism had been in the centuries immediately before and after the destruction of the Temple.

In summary, religious liberty within the Jewish community existed and still exists *de facto.* It is recognized *de jure* by all groups in Reform and Conservative Judaism and by elements in Orthodoxy as well. Undoubtedly practice lags behind theory, but the conclusion is unassailable that the nature of Judaism, buttressed by its historic experience, makes the freedom of religious dissent a recognized reality for virtually all members of the community *de facto,* even by those who would not recognize it *de jure.*

What is the attitude of Judaism toward religious liberty for those professing other creeds? It is frequently argued that with the appearance of Judaism intolerance became a coefficient of religion. It is undoubtedly true that, in a polytheistic world view, tolerance of other gods is implicit, since there is always room for one more figure in the pantheon, and the history of religious syncretism bears out this idea. On the other hand, the emergence of belief in one God necessarily demands the denial of the reality of all other deities. The "jealous God" of the Old Testament who forbids "any other god before me" therefore frequently became the source of religious intolerance. So runs the theory.

It sometimes happens, however, that a beautiful pattern of invincible logic is contradicted by the refractory behavior of life itself. An apposite illustration may be cited. The French Semitic scholar, Ernest Renan, declared that the monotony of the desert produced a propensity for monotheism among the ancient Hebrews, whereas the variety in the physical landscape of Greece, for example, with its mountains and hills, its valleys, rivers, and streams, necessarily suggested a multitude of divinities indwelling in them. This plausible theory enjoyed considerable vogue until it was learned that the pre-Islamic nomadic Arabs, who inhabit the vast stretches of the Arabian Desert, possessed a very luxuriant polytheism, and that all peoples of Semitic languages whose original habitat was the same desert, also had very elaborate pantheons. Thus the list of gods in the library of King Ashurbanipal contains more than 2,500 gods, and modern scholars have added substantially to the number from other sources.

Now it is true that Judaism was strongly exclusivist in its attitude toward paganism. It insisted upon the uncompromising unity of God and refused to admit even a semblance of reality to other gods. Nonetheless, biblical Judaism reckoned with the existence of paganism from two points of view. Though logicians might have recoiled in horror from the prospect, the fact is that Hebrew monotheism, the authentic and conscious faith in the existence of one God, did accord a kind of legitimacy to polytheism—for non-Jews. In part, this may have derived from a recognition of the actual existence of flourishing heathen cults. In far larger degree, we believe, it was a consequence of the particularist ethnic emphasis in Judaism. Dedicated to preserving the specific group character of the Hebrew faith, the Jewish tradition was led to grant a similar charter of justification to the specific ethos of other nations, which always included their religion.

Whatever the explanation, the fact is clear. No book in the Bible, not even Isaiah or Job, is more explicitly monotheistic than Deuteronomy: "You shall know this day, and consider it in your heart, that the Lord is God in heaven above, and upon the earth beneath; there is no one else" (4:39). Yet the same book, which warns Israel against polytheism, speaks of "the sun, the moon and the stars ... which the Lord your God has assigned to all the nations under the sky" (4:19, compare 29:25). Thus the paradox emerges that the particularist element in Judaism proved the embryo of a theory of religious tolerance.

The second factor that helped to grant a measure of value to non-Jewish religion is one more congenial to sophisticated religious thinkers. A broadminded exponent of monotheism would be capable of recognizing, even in the pagan cults against which Judaism fought, an imperfect, unconscious aspiration toward the one living God. Perhaps the most striking expression of this insight is to be found in the post-Exilic Prophet Malachi: "For from the rising of the sun to its setting, My name is great among the nations; and everywhere incense is burnt and pure oblations are offered to My name, for My name is great among the nations, says the Lord of hosts"(1:11).

This is not the only instance of universalism in our biblical sources. The human sympathy of the author of the Book of Jonah, who exhibits the pagan sailors in a far more favorable light than he does the fugitive Hebrew prophet, the warm compassion of the Book of Ruth, and the breadth of view of the Book of Job, which pictures the Patriarch not as a Hebrew observer of the Torah, but as a non-Jew whose noble creed and practice are described in his great *Confession of Innocence* (chap. 31), all testify to the recognition in Judaism that it is possible to maintain the unity and universality of God, while reckoning with the values inherent in the imperfect approximations to be found in the pagan cults.

Thus the two apparently contradictory elements of the biblical worldview—the emphasis upon a particularist ethos and the faith in a universal God—served as the seedbed for the flowering of a highly significant theory of religious tolerance in post-biblical Judaism. To this concept, known as the Noachide Laws, we shall return.

Nonetheless, it was self-evident that a universal God who was Creator of all humankind deserved the loyalty of all people. A steady and unremitting effort was therefore made to counteract the blandishments of paganism and to win all people for Jewish monotheism through the use of persuasion. The biblical *Deutero-Isaiah,* the Apocryphal *Sybilline Oracles,* the life-long activity of Philo of Alexandria—indeed the entire apologetic literature of Hellenistic Judaism—were designed to win the allegiance of everyone for the one living God of Israel.

Holding fast to their conviction that Judaism alone represents the true faith in the one God, the Prophets had looked forward to its ultimate acceptance by all people: "For then will I turn to the people a pure language, that they may all call on the name of the Lord, to serve Him with one accord" (Zeph. 3:9). "And the Lord will be king over all the earth; on that day shall the Lord be one, and His name be one" (Zech. 14:9).

The Apocryphal Book of Jubilees, written before the beginning of the Christian Era, could not conceive of untold generations before Moses living without a divine Revelation. It therefore attributes to Noah, who was not a Hebrew, a code of conduct binding upon all men:

> In the twenty-eighth jubilee, Noah began to enjoin upon his son's sons the ordinances and commandments and all the judgments that he knew and he exhorted his sons to observe righteousness and to cover the shame of their flesh and to bless their Creator and honor father and mother and love their neighbor and guard their soul from fornication and uncleanness and all iniquity (7:22).

This injunction is elaborated in the rabbinic tradition under the rubric of the Laws of the Sons of Noah. According to this rabbinic view, all human beings, by virtue of their humanity, are commanded to observe at least seven fundamental religious and moral principles. These commandments include the prohibition of idolatry, sexual immorality, murder, and theft; the avoidance of blasphemy and of cruelty to animals by eating the limb of a living creature; and the establishment of a government based on law and order. When these principles, upon which all civilized society depends, are observed, Judaism regards the non-Jew as worthy of salvation, no less than the Jew who observes the entire rubric of Jewish law. Hence, there is no imperative need for the non-Jew to accept the Jewish faith in order to "saved."

These Laws of the Sons of Noah, it may be noted, seem to be referred to in the New Testament as well: "But that we write unto them, that they abstain from pollutions of idols and from fornication, and from things strangled, and from blood . . . That ye abstain from meats offered to idols, and from blood and from things strangled and from fornication: from which if ye keep yourselves, ye shall do well. Fare ye well" (Acts 15:20, 29).

This doctrine of the Noachide Laws is extremely interesting from several points of view. It represents in essence a theory of universal religion which is binding upon all people. Characteristically Jewish is its emphasis upon good actions rather than upon right belief as the mark of the good life. Ethical living rather than creedal adherence is the decisive criterion for salvation. Its spirit is epitomized in the great rabbinic utterance: "I call Heaven and earth to witness, that whether one be Gentile or Jew, man or woman, slave or free man, the divine spirit rests on each in accordance with his deeds" (*Yalkut Shimeoni* on Judges, sec. 42).

Many contemporary religious thinkers are now seeking a theory which will combine complete loyalty to a specific tradition with accepting wholehearted adherence to the postulates of a democratic society which is committed to pluralism as a reality and to religious liberty as a good. The issue is one which profoundly agitates Americans in our day because of its obvious practical importance for government and politics, as well as society as a whole.

There is more than academic interest, therefore, in this rabbinic adumbration of a theory of religious tolerance resting upon a concept of "natural law." This doctrine of the Noachide Laws, be it noted, was not the product of religious indifference. It arose among devotees of a traditional religion who not only loved their faith, but believed that it alone was the product of authentic revelation. Yet they found room for faiths other than their own, as of right and not merely on sufferance.

The attitude of Judaism toward religious liberty may now be summarized as follows: (1) Judaism insists on total freedom of religious belief and practice for itself, which will include full equality before the law and no attenuation of vital religious commitment freely given. (2) Judaism accepts the existence of differences within the Jewish community and accords to dissidents the right to their own viewpoint and practice, at least *de facto*. (3) Judaism recognizes the existence of other religions among humankind and their inherent right to be observed *de jure*.

Albert Einstein once declared, "I thank God that I belong to a people which has been too weak to do much harm in the world." But more than mere incapacity inheres in the Jewish attitude toward religious liberty. The balance between the universal aspirations of Judaism and its strong attachment to the preservation of its group-character have impelled it to create a theory that makes room in God's plan—and in the world—for people of other convictions and practices.

Moreover, the deeply ingrained individualism of the Jewish character, its penchant for questioning, and its insistence upon rational conviction have made dissent a universal feature of the Jewish spiritual physiognomy. As a result, all groups within the Jewish community have achieved freedom of expression and practice. Efforts to limit or suppress this liberty of conscience have not been totally lacking and undoubtedly will recur in the future. But such attempts are invariably accompanied by a bad conscience on the part of the apostles of intolerance. Thus they reveal their weak roots in the tradition that they are ostensibly defending and betray their sense of predestined failure to achieve their ends.

Finally, the millennial experience of Jewish disability and exile in the ancient and medieval worlds has strengthened this attachment to freedom of conscience. In addition, the modern world has demonstrated that the material and intellectual position and progress of Jews, individually and collectively, is most effectively advanced in an atmosphere of religious liberty.

Thus all three elements—tradition, temperament, and history—have united to make religious freedom, for both the Jewish community and the larger family of humankind, an enduring ideal and not merely a temporarily prudential arrangement. Undoubtedly Jews have fallen short of the lofty standards of their tradition in this as in other respects. Yet it remains true that, by and large, they have maintained their loyalty to the ideal of freedom of conscience for themselves and for all people.

AN AMERICAN ROMAN CATHOLIC TRADITION OF
RELIGIOUS LIBERTY

James Hennesey

I have twenty minutes. I am not, therefore, going to discuss Boniface VIII and *Unam Sanctam,* the Inquisition, Tomás de Torquemada, Proposition 55 of the 1864 Syllabus of Errors, or divorce laws in Italy and Spain. I propose instead to outline an American and authentically Catholic tradition in the area of religious liberty.

The American Catholic story of religious liberty began in post-Reformation England. It was brought to Maryland on the *Ark* and the *Dove* in 1634. It made its most dramatic international impact in the Declaration on Religious Liberty adopted by the Second Vatican Council on December 7, 1965. It developed between 1634 and 1965 in the history of the Roman Catholic community, first in English America and then in the republic born in 1776. It is a pragmatic story, shaped in reaction to circumstances. But it is not a story, as some have wanted to claim, of opportunism. It has been a story of deeply-held convictions stemming from the concrete historical circumstances of life on this side of the Atlantic.

We begin in sixteenth-century England. The process of religious reformation had begun under Henry VIII. By the time of the reign of his daughter Elizabeth I, England was Protestant, and the increasingly tiny Papist remnant could not accept that their political sovereign has authority over them in matters of religion. There was a radical disharmony with which they had to struggle. The disharmony was not only with the dominant political and religious climate, but also existed within the English Catholic religious community. The continental exiles grew ultramontane. They saw as solutions to the disharmony acts such as those of Pope Pius V, excommunicating Elizabeth and attempting by fiat to deprive her of her crown in 1570, and of Pope Gregory XIII, supporting the landing of a Spanish army at Dingle Bay in 1580. They welcomed Pope Gregory's alliance with England's enemies, and in so doing they gave countenance to the charge that loyalty to Rome meant treason to England.

But there were other English Catholics who remained at home, suffered the penal laws, and gradually evolved the stance that what was in question was the right of freedom of conscience. In 1601, while Elizabeth was still on the throne, William Watson and the priests involved in the "stirs at Wisbech" declared that they were "thoroughly persuaded that Priests of whatever order ought not by force of arms to plant or water the Catholic faith." In other words, in religious matters, men and women have the native right to be free from physical coercion. As the seventeenth and eighteenth centuries came along, the conviction grew

The Rev. James Hennesey, S.J., was president of the Jesuit School of Theology in Chicago, and is now Professor of Church History at Boston College, Boston, MA.

among English Catholic laity and clergy that there must be clear delineation between religious and political loyalty, that, on the one hand, in matters of conscience sovereigns and laws were incompetent, but that religious affiliation could not, on the other hand, be used to command political commitment. In England this eventually led to the late-eighteenth-century Cisalpine movement, which in turn contributed much to the eventual Catholic Emancipation of 1829.

Maryland began out of this climate. Lord Baltimore's 1633 instructions to his colonists stressed that religious discourse should be muted. In a mixed colony of Anglicans and Papists, governed by Catholics, "no scandal nor offense" was to be given to Protestants; there was to be a climate of mildness, favor, and above all justice—a recognition of rights. As Maryland historians Matthew Page Andrews and William Hand Browne and American historians such as George Bancroft have freely admitted, Maryland under Catholic auspices exhibited a sense and practice of religious toleration until then unmatched elsewhere in the seventeenth century. In his *Religion in America,* Robert Baird put it well when he wrote:

> Think what we may of their creed, and very different as was this policy from what Romanism elsewhere might have led us to expect, we can not refuse to Lord Baltimore's colony the praise of having established the first government in modern times in which entire toleration was granted to all denominations of Christians.

It all ended with the coming of the Puritans in the wake of Cromwell's Revolution. Their influence was already evident in the restrictive clauses of the 1649 Act Concerning Religion. But a tradition had been established which, sometimes battered and bruised, persisted in the American Catholic community until it found its theoretician in our own time with John Courtney Murray and its place in the Declaration *Dignitatis Humanae* of 1965, which states baldly, "The Vatican Council declares that the human person has a right to religious freedom," and founds this right "on the very dignity of the human person as known through the revealed word of God and by reason itself."

A detailed history of subsequent turnings and twistings is patently impossible here. There were the Carrolls—Charles of Carrollton, signer of the Declaration of Independence, and his relative John, first Bishop of Baltimore. Charles was outspoken in his condemnation of religious repression wherever found, whether in Catholic France or Spain, or under James II, or in the English Protestant empire in which he lived. Bishop John Carroll was frequently moved to express what reads like an ecstasy as he wrote of the religious toleration which spread in the wake of the American Revolution, which he declared to be "the genuine spirit of Christianity," of which he boasted as an American contribution to the world.

America and American history changed drastically during the nineteenth century. Thirty million immigrants wrote *finis* to the homogeneous, eighty-five-percent-British America which had made the Revolution. Odd-looking, odd-smelling, odd-acting, and odd-speaking, the immigrants turned the United States into a multi-racial, multi-cultural, multi-religious society, and the melting-pot really never succeeded in melting them down completely. There were conflicts aplenty as Native Americans reacted to the intrusion and were reacted to in turn. As Horace Bushnell put it, "Barbarism" was the first danger; "Romanism," the religion of too many of the "barbarians," next. Old fears were rekindled. Pitched battles were fought on both sides of us here, in the Kensington and Southwark districts of Philadelphia, with muskets, cannon, and arson. The wars of the 1840's, the ecumenical dialogue of the time in Philadelphia and elsewhere, turned on issues such as the Roman Catholic refusal to accept Protestant public schools, suspicions of divisive loyalty to a foreign prince—the pope, the concentration of property and power in the hands of bishops, and the speedy enlistment of immigrants in the ranks of urban political machines. The mother superior of the Ursuline nuns in Charlestown, Massachusetts, whose convent school was set afire in 1834, did not help when she proclaimed that the Catholic Bishop of Boston had 20,000 Irishmen ready to come to her assistance; nor did Bishop John Hughes of New York, when he threatened that New York City would be turned into "another Moscow," burned to the ground, if a single Catholic institution were attacked. It is interesting to read in this context the pastoral letter of the bishops at the 1837 Council of Baltimore affirming political loyalty to the United States, and rejecting "any civil or political supremacy, or power over us, in any foreign potentate or power, though that potentate might be the chief pastor of our church."

A distinctive American attitude, continuous with that of the early Marylanders, developed. American bishops were appalled when in 1853 an Italian archbishop, Gaetano Bedini, was sent to the United States in hopes of establishing formal mutual diplomatic relations between the Holy See and Washington. They were equally disturbed by promulgation in 1864 of Pope Pius IX's Syllabus of Errors. Archbishop Spalding of Baltimore found the Syllabus "evidently intended for the standpoint of European radicals and infidels," but a misfire when applied to the United States, where "our fathers acted most prudently and wisely in adopting, as an amendment to the Constitution, the organic article that 'Congress shall make no law respecting the establishment of religion or prohibiting the free exercise thereof.'" As Spalding understood it, the First Amendment declared all religions "equal before the law." It laid down "the sound and equitable principle that the civil government, adhering to its own appropriate sphere of political duty, pledged itself not to interfere with religious matters, which it rightly viewed as entirely without the bounds of its competency." There are other examples, such as that of Archbishop Purcell of Cincinnati, informing the fathers of the First Vatican Council of 1869–70 that what American Catholics asked in religious matters was "a free field and no favor." In the latter part of the century, spokespersons such as Isaac Hecker, John Ireland, James Gibbons, and Denis O'Connell defended the traditional American themes.

But the nineteenth century was in Europe an age of papal centralization in reaction to European political and intellectual developments. The American religious experiment was misunderstood, and conservative Catholics reacted violently against it. In 1895, Pope Leo XIII wrote the letter *Longinqua Oceani,* in which he praised the growth and success of the Catholic Church in the United States, but could not bring himself to admit that it was precisely the American climate of religious freedom which had fostered that growth and success. He still thought it better that the church be protected and supported by the state. Pope Leo's 1899 condemnation, in the encyclical letter *Testem Benevolentiae,* of theological "Americanism" revealed further the dichotomy between European and American understandings.

Independent American Catholic thought withered in consequence of these developments and the subsequent Modernist crises which came to a head in 1907, so that in 1922, John A. Ryan, surely one of the great social progressives produced by the Catholic Church in the United States, felt compelled to allow religious liberty on the American model only as a pragmatic adjustment to the multi-religious American scene, but falling short of some abstract "ideal." Al Smith, to his own great confusion, felt the backlash of that in 1928, just as did John F. Kennedy in 1960. In the 1940's and 1950's Catholic University theologians Joseph C. Fenton and Francis J. Connell labored under the same difficulties as Ryan and wrote of the American system as akin to heresy if it were considered as anything but a pragmatic acceptance of what could not be changed. The old Maryland and mid-nineteenth-century tradition had come on hard times. It seemed to be forgotten.

Historical developments are rarely, if ever, the work of one person. Resurrection in Roman Catholicism of a theory of religious liberty informed by the American experience is no exception. It was the work of many, and it was not a solely American affair. But the outstanding American contribution to what would ultimately be Vatican II's Declaration on Religious Liberty was clearly made by John Courtney Murray, painfully following labyrinthine theological ways in the 1940's and 1950's and eventually contributing to the elaboration of the Council's Declaration of 1965. He accepted as a basis for religious freedom the theological-ethical principles of the free human person and that person's obligation to follow his or her conscience. He also developed a political-juridical theory founded in historical consciousness according to which "the personal internal forum is immune from invasion by any powers resident in society or state." "It is contrary to the nature of civil law," Murray wrote, "to compel assent to any manner of religious truth or ideology." For Murray—and here he was attacking the common nineteenth-century European understanding—"no ideal realizations are possible in history." History is concrete, not abstract. Religious freedom is based on "the concrete exigences of the personal and political consciousness of contemporary man—his demand for religious freedom, personal and corporate, under limited government." The state is limited to "a care for the religious freedom of the body politic." Its only competence is to "promote the religious freedom of the people." Its only limiting power on religious expression can be "when such forms of public expresion seriously violate the public peace or commonly accepted standards of public morality, or the rights of other citizens." This general statement is to be specified in "continual dialogue between the public powers and the personal and political consciousness of the citizenry."

It was not a long step from these propositions of John Courtney Murray to Vatican II's declaration that:

> ... the human person has a right to religious freedom. This freedom means that all men are to be immune from coercion on the part of individuals or of social groups or of any human power ... in matters religious no one is to be forced to act in a mànner contrary to his own beliefs. Nor is anyone to be restrained from acting in accordance with his own beliefs, whether privately or publicly, whether alone or in association with others, within due limits.

The right to religious freedom, the Council said, was a basic civil right, founded in the very nature of humanity. It is, in fact, inalienable.

The Maryland colonists, the Carrolls, Purcell, Spalding, and the others would approve. Their contributions have not been lost.

FREEDOM OF CONSCIENCE—THE BLACK EXPERIENCE IN AMERICA

William A. Jones

I am both solicitous and deserving of tremendous sympathy this morning. Dr. Shetler mentioned my circuitous travels to this place. I thought until last evening that Philadelphia was a major city. A major city is defined as one that you can get to without serious difficulty. I preached in Chicago last evening, flew to New York (that is a major city), landed at 1:30 this morning, went to my home, slept for 2½ hours, caught the 6:30 Metroliner to Philadelphia; and here I am, what's left of me that is, so I'm sure that I have your sympathetic concern this morning. I am appreciative of the invitation to share in this significant gathering. I must confess that I did have some misgivings when the invitation was first extended, but no misgivings about this Conference per se.

My mind went back to an experience, a rather ironic experience of twenty-seven years ago in my native Lexington, Kentucky. In that year (I was fifteen years of age), the American Legion sponsored an essay contest. High school students throughout the city were asked to write essays on the subject, "Our Great American Heritage—Liberty". I won first place in that contest, but, because of the prevailing situation at that time, I had to receive my prize at the Nathan Caulder American Legion Post, which was the black branch of the American Legion in Lexington. I'm sure that can't happen here, because no prizes will be awarded when this is ended.

On the outside wall of a Cathedral in Barcelona, Spain, there is a bronze plaque with an interesting engraving. It is a scale, a pair of balances, with an eagle on one side and a turtle on the other. Upon seeing it, I asked my guide what it meant. What was the symbolism? He answered, "It is the symbol of justice. Justice should be as swift as the eagle, but it's as slow as the turtle." Such a statement sends the mind of a Black American at once, not to some political theory or to some philosophical treatment of the idea of justice, but to America, to the American dilemma, to the American promise yet unoffered. In a quick moment, the years are traversed and mind races back to that period of human slavery with its awful agony and affliction. Segregation, discrimination, the struggles for basic freedoms, the sweat, the blood, the tears—all of these come into sharp focus at once.

The history of humankind from Eden's flaming gate to the Iron Curtain, and on to the bloody battlefields on either side of the Bamboo Curtain, is a catalogue of human sin against one another. Injustice is tragically akin to the human pilgrimage. It almost always emerges from the desensitized consciences of people who deem themselves better than others. It is the Pharaoh ideology at

Dr. William A. Jones is pastor of Bethany Baptist Church in New York, NY.

work, born out of a master race ethos which has been properly described as the eternal joke played on conscious culture at the expense of unconscious biology. A gravestone in a cemetery in Japan bears the inscription, "Here lies a black man who fought the yellow man for what the white man took from the red man". Simply and succinctly, that inscription depicts the American trinitarian formula of capitalism, racism, and militarism.

Frederick Douglass in his celebrated Fourth of July speech in Rochester in the year 1852 remarked, "For revolting barbarity and shameless hypocrisy, America reigns without a rival. America is false to the past, false to the present, and solemnly binds herself to be false to the future." The passing of more than a century has not significantly altered that appraisal. It is the prevailing barbarity and the continuing falsity that produce the swelling chorus of dismay and discontent.

The nation historically has been long on promise and short on performance. The promise contained in the Declaration of Independence is probably the most humane, outside of Scripture, ever reduced to human language: "We hold these truths to be self evident, that all men are created equal, that they are endowed by their Creator with certain inalienable rights, that among these are life, liberty, and the pursuit of happiness." The promise imbedded in those words is theologically correct and anthropologically sound. The democratic ethic represents the ideal with respect to historic social experiments. It is rooted in religious realism. It is grounded in the Judaeo-Christian doctrine of humanity. Reinhold Niebuhr's famous epigram puts it well: "Man's capacity for justice makes democracy possible, but man's inclination to injustice makes democracy necessary." Man has the capacity for justice and injustice, for creativity and destructivity. In America, necessity has perennially outweighted capacity. The democratic ideal has yet to flower. Irrespective of Constitutional guarantees, Congressional acts, Presidential pronouncements, and denominational proclamations, America must be seen through the lens of microscopic realism, rather than the lens of telescopic idealism.

This was to be that land under the sun where freedom's flag waved in the interest of all—but! How bright with promise was the nation's beginning—but! What a glorious harvest her springtime promised—but! Every attempt to articulate the nation's glory serves only to dramatize its shame. A simple surface diagnosis reveals a sick sociology, based on a faulty anthropology, which emanates from a false theology. The attitude of one toward others reflects the nature of his or her ultimate values. When sin becomes systemic and inequity is institutionalized, the resultant arrangement is ineluctably wicked and nefarious, for it denies others access to the tree of life. This, my friends, is the continuing tragedy of America. And the victims are altogether correct when they speak of the nation in terms of the "System," for they properly address themselves to that power arrangement in society based on wealth and whiteness, which prevents the gap between the needy and the greedy from closing.

In a pointed, poignant book, titled *Unyoung, Uncolored, Unpoor,* Colin

Morris, a British cleric, talks about that ruthless triumvirate which rules this world. Says Morris, "They can at will reverse the miracle at Cana and turn wine into water. They are so decadent as to make ancient Byzantium seem like the new Jerusalem and yet so decent that even when they are clubbing you to death you feel impelled to apologize for spilling blood on their carpet." He goes on to say, "Freedom is what they mean by freedom; democracy is what they mean by democracy; and they have the power to make their definition stick." The System is racist to the very core. So deep and so pervasive is the reality that its bitter fruits multiply without cultivation.

Now, to be certain, the programmatic aspects of racism are not as overt as they once were. The apartheid of the pre-1863 era is non-existent, the de-humanizing features and symbols of the period of segregation such as separate restrooms, separate water fountains, segregated transportation, and "Niggers not allowed" signs are no longer present. However, the absence of overt expressions does not spell the demise of covert realities. If relationships are determinative in evaluating the social or human posture of people, the racist label appropriately applies to America. For relationships, you see, have to do not only with psycho-social attitudes, but with the sharing of resources and the distribution of power. We stand this day 113 years on the bright side of slavery, and Black Americans have freedom without finance, access without assets, and that is tantamount to existence devoid of equity.

Reporting on the results of an experiment titled, "White Racism by Design," Robert W. Terry wrote, "By being a normal every-day citizen, by doing business as usual, racism flourished. To be anti-racist meant confronting the basic arrangements and norms of American life. Although a painful learning, the group realized that to be anti-rascist was subversive of the presently practiced American dream." The logical conclusion is obvious. To be anti-racist is to be anti-American. American racism is predicated primarily on color differences, and color is a condition that blacks cannot alter, one which they do not desire to alter. Annihilation of the race problem by amalgamation is not on the black agenda. Racism is regarded by blacks as "white sickness," and is, therefore, essentially a white problem.

The Kerner Commission reported more than a century after emancipation that the nation is rapidly moving toward two increasingly separate Americas. That is true and at the same time it is untrue. Two Americas already exist. Polarization is no new phenomenon, it is as ancient as the slave system itself. In spite of the death-blow that has been dealt legal segregation, the basic institutions of American society remain sharply segregated with respect to power. White super-ordination and black sub-ordination is the norm in white-black relations as far as the majority of whites are concerned. The hard brutal realities of the racist ethos touch and affect the lives of all Black Americans. It is the root cause of their common afflictions and of their pain predicament.

Now racism is decidedly more than a social aberration. Racism is demonic, a spiritual perversion. It is the demon which ruined Egypt, Babylon, Greece,

Rome, England, and Germany, and which threatens to destroy this nation. Racism can never exist without foundations and underpinnings. To be exact, it requires a doctrine of human nature that in turn produces a value system. In other words, the racist posture is anthropological in its overt expressions, and theological in its covert presuppositions. It says something about a segment of the human family and predicates it on conclusions regarding the ultimate nature of reality. When stripped to a state of attitudinal nudity, the racist ascribes to God a posture of partiality predicated on pigmentation, and then assigns to human beings, on the basis of pigmentation, their permanent places under the sun. The racist creates God in his or her own image, and the creation eventuates in divine racism; once the scheme is designed and developed, heaven is expected to honor it. angels are asked to applaud it, and white people are called into service by the Eternal to promote and preserve it. So demonic is the diatribe that the iniquity is visited upon the children of all the generations following. Its effective transmission is tremendous testimony to the power of an oral tradition.

By way of contrast, the biblical revelation holds that to sin against any segment of humankind is to sin against God. To deny or to even question another's personhood is sinful. To exclude on the basis of blackness is to call something evil which God has already called good, unless, of course, there is a dichotomy between blackness and humanness. If blacks are non-human, or even sub-human, whites are guilty of no sin.

The black person's relationship to God was the cause of great debate during the early years of American slavery. Questions were raised such as: Does a slave have a soul? Should the gospel be preached to slaves? The dilemma was complicated and confounded by the very nature of the servitude. It was chattel slavery. Slaves were primarily property and secondarily persons. And slavery, you remember, was basically a Christian enterprise, the first massive program of Christian-sponsored genocide. During the sixteenth and seventeenth centuries, two-and-a-half million black Africans were transported westward to labor on plantations. It is estimated that by the late nineteenth century, fifteen million slaves had been brought alive to the Americas, and that some thirty million had died in the capturing process and in the ordeal of the middle passage.

Such a massive program of peddling and destroying human lives could not have developed without the approval of churches on both sides of the Atlantic. "From the beginning," says Pierre Burton, "it was the church that put its blessing on slavery and sanctioned a caste system that continues to this date." Being pious religionists, the church leaders tailored their theology to fit their sociology. The preachers, many of whom were slave owners themselves, sought theological justification for the damnable institution, and the voices that prevailed made a rather simplistic deduction—"Blacks are children of Ham; Ham is forever cursed of God to an existence of servitude; therefore, slavery is of God, and whites are pre-ordained for mastery."

But even this perverted interpretation of Scripture did not give a total solution to the problem. No biblical basis could be found for denying slaves access to the

Gospel. The debate subsided, slaves had the Gospel preached to them and were baptized into the body of believers. Though regarded as chattel, the slaves did not receive the Gospel without critical evaluation and analysis. Their religious outlook, stemming from the African worldview, enabled them to see the biblical revelation as consonant with their traditional understanding of the great High God. They took the biblical testimony given by the slave masters and gave it a utilitarian twist. In spite of their limited learning, they saw clearly the evils of the System. They saw the dichotomy between faith and practice, between Christian ethics and social policy, and they did an interesting thing. They began to de-mythologize and personalize the moving stories of Scripture. They heard the Exodus story and started singing, "Pharaoh's army got drowned one day." They learned of Daniel in the lion's den and sang, "Didn't my Lord deliver Daniel, then why not deliver poor me." They sensed that judgment was real, and they rang out, "My God's gonna move this wicked race and raise up a nation that shall obey." The Negro spirituals were a prophetic response to a crisis predicament, and they had both an existential and an eschatological dimension. They described in forceful language the slave's dreadful existence, but they also pointed to an ultimate arrangement wherein justice would reign without a rival.

The slaves took their new understanding of God, based on the biblical revelation, and created a new faith, a new salvation history. Parallelisms between the Israelite experience in Egypt and the black experience in America were often used. Blacks considered themselves God's new Israel and such a self-image called for a new Exodus. How did slaves look upon the religious foundation which gave the slave system sanction and support? They had the deepest abhorrence for the religion of their masters. The Rev. Henry Highland Garnett, a slave preacher, wrote his fellow slaves in 1848 saying, "If a band of Christians should attempt to enslave a race of heathen men and to entail slavery upon them and to keep them in heathenism in the midst of Christianity, the God of Peace would smile upon every effort which the injured might make to disenthrall themselves," and he added, "The humblest peasant is as free in the sight of God as the proudest monarch that ever swayed a scepter. Liberty is a spirit sent from God and like its great author, is no respecter of persons." There were many slaves—the Rev. Nat Turner is a striking example—who revolted in the name of the Lord. The slaves were clear in their understanding of where God stood on the question. They also knew by virtue of a kind of sixth sense (that God always gives to oppressed people) that only persons estranged from God would engage in such barbaric behavior.

Frederick Douglass, who escaped from slavery in 1838, described his view of the slavemaster's religion. Said Douglass, "We have men-stealers for ministers, women-whippers for missionaries, and cradle-plunderers for church members. . . . The warm defender of the sacredness of the family relation is the same that scatters whole families—sundering husbands and wives, parents and children, sisters and brothers, leaving the hut vacant, and the hearth desolate." The slaves were bound, but only in physical bondage. No slave master could touch the soul, the essence of being. Their minds and their spirits were free, free to pray and to plot, free to dream and to despise, free to rebel against the most vile and vicious tyranny ever experienced on these shores. In the midst of slavery, there emerged rather naturally two separate and distinct views of God and humanity, that of the masters and that of the slaves, and the two were irreconcilable because of the oneness of God's will for humankind. Black religion and white religion were inherently antithetical.

Racism demands separatism in both church and culture. A segregated society based on a separatist theology resulted in a segregated church. Kyle Haselden is correct when he writes, "Long before the little signs 'White Only' and 'Colored Only' appeared in the public utilities, they had appeared in the church." The signs are now gone, but the scars remain; and, worse still, racism remains a potent presence within the white church. The white church and white culture are united in unholy wedlock. The similitude is not simply strange; it is striking. The white church is not free to declare the truth because it has not yielded to that truth which frees people from pride and sinful presumption.

Many white clergy are mere puppets rather than prophets. I guess that explains why a book can come rolling off the press titled, *The Empty Pulpit*. It is not literally empty; there is someone standing in it, but it might as well be empty because nothing is being said. The white church historically and presently is an instrument of the American system, sanctifying its sins and giving inspiration to its iniquities. It has never, in collective manner, assaulted the prevailing power arrangement in the name of God who has "made of one blood all nations of men to dwell on all the face of the earth."

The white church by its capitulation to culture has provided fuel for the revolutionary fires that are sweeping the world. The revolutionary spirit is rooted in the desire to be free, to experience and to enjoy equity, and it is grounded in the ineluctable urgings of the human spirit. Men and women bound by oppressors cry out all over this world, "I want to be free." Something deep down inside of me, something in that mystical something called the soul, something good and God-like within me prods and pushes me and demands of me that I break out of any unjust confinement to which sinful mortals confine me. Regardless of any derogatory interpretation given to the revolutionary spirit by the "up" people, a genuine trust toward personhood and peoplehood should be regarded as sacred. Biblical narratives cite instance after instance where people were more concerned about the state of their souls than the well-being of their bodies. Non-cooperation with evil is fundamental to the liberation of any people. It is the noblest and purest expression of conscience, for it affirms a dignity which is divinely derived.

Finally, freedom of conscience is essentially a religious posture. The nurture thereof is therefore a religious responsibility. Black Americans have received this nurture primarily from the black church. All across the perilous pathway of our pilgrimage, the church has been the connecting rod between black history and black hope. It is the largest center of numerical strength. It is the only free institution in the captive community. It is the one place where the vision of a nobler life is constantly lifted up. It views life as perennial struggle by people in pilgrimage, and because of its non-dependence on the larger society, it is free to be prophetic.

Better than thirty years ago, Richard Wright declared in *Twelve Million Black Voices,* "Our churches are where we dip our tired bodies in cool springs of hope, where we retain our wholeness and humanity despite the blows of death from the bosses." Well, the blows of death continue to come. The "bosses" of the System must be confronted with the demands of the Creator. The autocracy of pleasure must be replaced by the democratization of pleasure and pain. There can be no genuine reconciliation in the absence of justice, for reconciliation is always the postlude to justice. As they say in Mozambique, "A luta continua," which means "the struggle continues." If the struggle ends with the oppressor and the oppressed living in a climate of reconciliation, let God be praised. If not, let God still be praised, for God is on the side of the victimized masses, and through their conquests in God's name, the kingdom will come on earth as it is in heaven.

There is a word in Scripture which declares, "One with God shall chase a thousand; and two shall put ten thousand to flight." If that be true (and it is), it poses the query, "Is anybody running?" Better still, "Are we chasing anybody?"

WOMEN'S HISTORY AND TRANSCENDENCE

Janice Raymond

There were many women who participated in the founding of this nation and, more specifically, who played a historical part in the nation's evolution of religious liberty. Until recently, these women have been almost buried in the annals of patriarchal history. There was, for one, Anne Marbury Hutchinson, leader of the "Antinomians" in Boston, banished from the Massachusetts Bay Colony, and generally referred to by the Puritan "orthodoxists" as a woman out of place. Or Ann Lee could be cited. Mystic, seeker, and founder of the Shaker society, she believed in equalitarianism and the rights of conscience, both of which make her a likely candidate for examination at this conference. Another example is that of Sojourner Truth. Ex-slave, abolitionist, and reformer, she traveled the eastern and western parts of the country preaching and speaking her message of black rights and women's suffrage. The list is much longer, of course. Yet all of these women essentially adhered to a Christian framework, albeit an unorthodox and often-branded "heretical" version of Christianity.

My commitment to speak at this conference, however, does not include any passion for fitting such women into the mainstream of patriarchal religious history or even into its rebellious left-wing. This has been and will be eminently done by others in this time of bicentennial absorption. There will be many events, celebrations, and writings which will attempt to say that women were really *there,* that women did their part too, and that it is time "we" recognize (assimilate, legitimate) their religious dissent. Patriarchy has burned its Joans of Arc, only to canonize them when history needed to be adjusted.

I have no heart for this task, since I do not wish to fit any woman into her now-designated "appropriate" place within patriarchal history. Performing cosmetic touch-up jobs of this nature can only lend support to a historical affirmative action program in which women and other excluded groups, at best, fill in the gaps and, at worst, are given the illusion of inclusion.

Since the recent wave of feminism, the *illusion of inclusion* has become a sort of sophisticated science, largely due to tokenism. As Judith Long Laws has demonstrated, tokenism is an institution in itself, "... a form of patterned activity generated by a social system as a means of adaptation to a particular kind of pressure."[1] However, since the token is the person or group assimilated under the dominant group's own terms, the token is always destined for "permanent marginality." Women who are now being included within men's history, within men's institutions, are destined for this same marginality—never *real centrality.*

---

[1]Judith Long Laws, "The Psychology of Tokenism: An Analysis," *Sex Roles* 1 (1975): 51.

Professor Janice G. Raymond is Assistant Professor of Women's Studies and of Medical Ethics at Hampshire College, Amherst, MA.

The token can only be central as the *exceptional* woman, the woman who made it in spite of the obstacles. Thus what becomes central is her having "made it." Such a focus becomes obscene, because by fixating upon the uniqueness of the woman who made it by surmounting her difficult milieu, it leaves that obstacle course intact while shifting the focus away from its oppressiveness.

Realizing the futility of the token-inclusion approach, many feminist scholars are beginning to think and write about a gynocentric theory of history and society. In spite of all the academic quibbling about the use of words such as matriarchal, matrilineal, and matrilocal to describe such woman-centered societies, alternative views of history are beginning to emerge which go far beyond fitting women into patriarchal spaces. Many historians will attempt to discredit such theories and will argue that they are based upon the doubtful foundation of the historicity of myth. Take the notion of the historical existence of Amazons, for example. The actual historical facticity of Amazons is unprovable, but it is not beyond the realm of possibility that exclusively-female societies existed. Herodotus alludes to them, as does Homer in the *Iliad,* as does Plutarch in the *Life of Theseus.* Legends (or history) abound about their fighting capacity and the many Greek male warriors who matched strength against them. Representations of such battles, as Sarah Pomeroy has pointed out, appear frequently in the visual arts. These portraits, called Amazonomachies, were scattered throughout the Greek world.[2] However, as Emily Culpepper has remarked,

> ... there is another way in which Amazons really exist in addition to the open question of possible "factual-historical" existance. And that is the direct truth that we know about Amazons. Ask almost anyone. They've heard the word. They may even have a specific image they could describe. Someone may tell you she is one.[3]

The point of all this is to say that new images and symbols are arising out of feminist culture which may well be a mixture of *historie* (scientific history) and *geschichte* (story). There are good precedents for such a view of history. *Geschichte* has had a predominant place in the formation of western civilization. Judaeo-Christian religion has been built upon the historicity of myth. Hebrew Bible scholars have constantly debated the distinction between *historie* and *geschichte.* For many biblical theologians, most notably von Rad, the important thing was Israel's *geschichte,* its story, not its scientific history. Thus we have the term *heilsgeschichte,* or salvation history. Many biblical commentators have been extremely skeptical about the factual-historical reliability of Israel's traditions but have nevertheless proceeded to develop Jewish and Christian history based upon the faith and credos of a people who *believed* in *their* history.

---

[2]Sarah Pomeroy, *Goddesses, Whores, Wives, and Slaves: Women in Classical Antiquity* (New York: Schocken Books, 1975), p. 25.
[3]Emily Culpepper, "Female History/Myth Making," *The Second Wave* 4 (Spring, 1975): 16.

Likewise, New Testament scholars and other theologians have constantly debated the actual existence of Jesus Christ in delineating between the historical Jesus and the Jesus of faith. Tillich, for example, states that "Historical research has made it obvious that there is no way to get at the historical events which have produced the Biblical picture of Jesus who is called the Christ with more than a degree of probability."[4] Yet Tillich concludes that "Faith can say that the reality which is manifest in the New Testament picture of Jesus as the Christ has saving power for those who are grasped by it, no matter how much or how little can be traced to the historical figure who is called Jesus of Nazareth."[5]

Yet there is a curious double standard where women are concerned. Feminist research about earlier woman-centered societies, about goddess images and worship, about Amazon representation, and about the witch movements in Europe and America is often trivialized and dismissed as non-historical. Perhaps the real reason behind this dismissal is the male fear that such images and events will generate a more authentic *salvation history* for women which will burst the bonds of traditional patriarchal frameworks. On a deep level, this *is* what is happening for many women. Many of us see these above-mentioned events and images as having revelatory power, as intimations of transcendence which, aside from grasping the female mind on an investigative level, are creating a community in which these intimations can express themselves in feminist culture and social action.

Female myth has always been accepted as salvific and/or as historical when the myth has been sufficiently patriarchal to warrant its acceptance—i.e., when it can be easily accepted into patriarchal tradition. Thus the Virgin Mary became incorporated into Catholic Christianity as an acceptable female presence. In contrast, the witch was at worst burned and, at best, blamed for her own fate. This Bicentennial Conference on Religious Liberty began by commemorating the six million Jewish martyrs of the Holocaust. But there is another holocaust which very few memorialize. What happened to thousands of women in Europe from the fifteenth to the seventeenth centuries has been historically dispensable. The lowest estimate of witches burned in Europe during these years is 30,000; the highest estimate is nine million. Salem disposed of twenty. Moreover, in Europe, witches were persecuted just as fiercely in Protestant territories as they were under the Roman Inquisition and Counter-Reformation. Where has this history gone?

On the one hand, the reality of the witch has been trivialized and transformed into the popular stereotype of the witch. Less harmless descriptions project her as the woman on the broom, the old hag who has provided Halloween material for youngsters. More recently, witchcraft has come to be associated with repulsive black magic and the occult. History has summed up the witch's personhood and

---

[4]Paul Tillich, *The Dynamics of Faith* (New York: Harper & Row, 1957), p. 87.
[5]Ibid. p. 88.

activity by portraying her as harmless yet hysterical, and thus provoking her own persecution. Most recently, the young girls who accused the Salem witches of diabolical deeds are said to have suffered from convulsive ergotism, an LSD-like agent. The "show" at the Salem witch museum enhances these perspectives. In this year of bicentennial travels, many people will visit the Salem witch museum. What they will see will be a photographic and artistic representation of the witch as hysterical and her accusers as irrational young girls. Thus the witch and her female accusers become objects of psychopathological interest. As Thomas Szasz notes, in this way medical and psychiatric historians have come to treat the witches as proof of the transhistorical and transcultural "reality" of mental illness.[6]

Thus, once more "history" distracts attention from the oppressors and turns it on the victims. Patriarchal history has deleted the judges and church leaders of medieval and Reformation Europe and of seventeenth-century Salem almost completely from the picture. It is hard to imagine the Jews who were persecuted and killed during the medieval inquisition, the Russian pogroms, and the Nazi era being represented in history as hysterical, and therefore as eliciting their own oppression.

If Margaret Murray and other scholars of the witch-movement in western Europe are correct—and there is good evidence to show that they are—the reason that witches were persecuted so systematically by both Catholicism and Protestantism is that they constituted a *religious* threat to Christianity and offered a woman-centered religion specifically. Murray concluded, from examining the legal records of the witch trials and the writings of the Inquisitors, that the witches of western Europe were the remnant of an earlier pagan religion that was female in origin.[7] What the witches incarnate, in patriarchal recordings of history, is the false naming of women by men, specifically the false naming of female religious power and energy. The religious reality of witchcraft was defined by the Christian victors. Thus, as Murray notes, divination, when done in the name of the deity of an established male religion, is called prophecy. When done in the name of a pagan god or goddess, it is called witchcraft.

Although there are many women today who are working within Judaeo-Christian religion, many others feel that there can be no essential integrity to this. What many women are saying is that there were earlier woman-centered religions which have been lost to our memory. The point is *not* to romanticize goddess worship or the witches or to return to these earlier forms—but to realize that *they were there—and are there*.

Bicentennial time commemorates, memorializes, and remembers. This Bicentennial Conference calls to memory traditions of religious liberty in this country. But religious liberty has consistently meant freedom to worship a male

---

[6]Thomas Szasz has an acutely perceptive analysis of witchcraft and its modern counterparts in *The Manufacture of Madness* (New York: Dell Publishing Co., Inc., 1970).

[7]Cf. Margaret Murray, *The Witch-Cult in Western Europe* (London: Oxford Press, 1921).

god. Religious liberty has often meant the domestication of women's energy by false inclusion. Religious liberty never included autonomous woman-centered religion where the whole framework has essentially changed.

This month I participated in the First National Conference on Women's Spirituality held in Boston. Two thousand women were in attendance from across the country. Some of them had at one time adhered to Judaeo-Christian tradition. But it became clear, in the various sessions, that many of these women had been non-believers; i.e., non-believers in both western and eastern androcentric religion. The conference was not a camp meeting, although it had genuine enthusiastic and revivalist dimensions. There was no fixation upon prophets or gurus who uniquely manifested the divine. Nor, in this time of social and political retrenchment, was it a retreat into pseudo-mysticism and the cult of personality. Many of the sessions during the conference made profound connections between spirituality and politics, pointing out that the basic power of the social and political institutions and patterns that have oppressed women has been its "religious" ability to grip us at ultimate levels of power and worth.

It is significant that the conference took place during the bicentennial year. It is also significant that no session of the conference directed itself to patriarchal religious traditions, western or eastern. Many feminists perceive the oppression by patriarchal religion and culture as a battle with "principalities and powers." There is no other adequate way of explaining the hatred of women by men that has permeated such religion and culture and which has, in turn, generated the rape of our bodies, minds, and wills.

What many women are beginning to realize is that a profound religious vision is needed to exorcise the social and political demons of patriarchy. The National Conference on Women's Spirituality and much recent feminist literature are demonstrating that the religious dimensions of the Women's Movement are beginning to surface. Many women are recognizing that without such a vision the radical potential of our movement is cut off. Many of the major movements for social justice in modern times have been anti-religious, and legitimately so. In part, they have exposed and opposed other-wordly religions which distracted their members from concrete social oppression. Yet none of these movements, until the Women's Movement, opposed religion precisely as patriarchal. Thus none has gotten to the roots of the religious problem.

The loss of transcendent energies in our society and the secularization of culture over the past two centuries have hardly been experienced as losses at all. Rather, they have been viewed as historical necessities which enlightened people regard as marks of evolutionary maturity. What is emerging, however, in the Women's Movement is a spiritualization of vision which goes beyond opposition to and loss of patriarchal religion (Antichurch) to more genuine religious consciousness—what Mary Daly has called "Sisterhood as Cosmic Covenant."[8]

[8]Cf. Mary Daly, *Beyond God the Father: Toward a Philosophy of Women's Liberation* (Boston: Beacon Press, 1973); especially note Chapter 6, "Sisterhood as Cosmic Covenant."

Many women are finally realizing that "the destiny of the spirit is the destiny of the social order," and that it is profound religious energies which will generate the genuine politics needed for liberation. As Nelle Morton has said, patriarchy will not admit that it had a beginning and therefore cannot admit it might be transcended.

CONTEMPORARY AMERICAN EXPERIENCE OF CONSCIENCE AND DISSENT: THE PEACE TESTIMONY

Edwin B. Bronner

As we commemorate the bicentennial of the American Revolution, we should not forget that there were a goodly number of religious objectors to the War for Independence. A testimony against involvement in war and violence, based upon the New Testament, was an important article of faith and belief in several churches, and most of the members of these denominations supported a pacifist position. So far as I know, the descendants of these sturdy opponents of military action have not yet created a social organization called the Descendants of Revolutionary Pacifists, or DRIPS, comparable to the DAR or the Sons of the American Revolution.

Two centuries ago pacifists were almost entirely limited to members of the German-speaking pietistic "sects," such as the Mennonites, Dunkers or Brethren, Schwenkfelders, and Moravians, and to the Religious Society of Friends or Quakers. While the different "sects" expressed their opposition to the American Revolution in various ways, they all took a stand against bearing arms, and many of their members suffered from the government and from their neighbors. Some were cast into prison, many paid heavy fines, and those who refused to pay fines had their property and goods seized by the authorities.

Some of the new state governments understood that the issue of religious liberty was at stake, and made efforts to respond to the consciences of the pacifists, but others were so caught up in the war that they ignored the rights of religious minorities. It was easy to confuse non-cooperation with disloyalty, and the pacifists who attempted to keep from being involved in the struggle were frequently labelled "Tories."

Members of the various sects, called collectively "the Historic Peace Churches," made efforts to aid their fellow humans during these years. They were not content with merely opposing war. Some were active in nursing the sick and wounded, and the Quakers, aided by the German-speaking "sects," sent money and supplies to relieve the suffering of the people in Boston during the British occupation. The Quakers were also involved in efforts to find a solution to the crisis between Britain and the colonies, until negotiations were abandoned in favor of violence and talk of war. Generally speaking, the practices followed by the states during the American Revolution were continued by the national government in succeeding wars. When members of the Historic Peace Churches took a stand against participating in war, the government made efforts to recognize the rights of religious minorities by offering some concessions. There were

Dr. Edwin B. Bronner is Librarian and Professor of History at Haverford College, Haverford, PA.

always a few pacifists who were unable to accommodate themselves to the government's policy, and such persons suffered fines and imprisonment.

Between the wars various peace movements sprang up. Some of these organizations grounded their pacifism in religious beliefs, while others were secular in spirit, basing their position on natural rights and humanitarian grounds. Although the latter movements were often more radical than the former, they shared one common characteristic: they tended to fade away in wartime. It was not until World War I that we see some sign of continued support for the peace testimony, even in wartime, outside the Historic Peace Churches. Three organizations which came into being during that period have made important contributions to the peace movement for more than half a century. The Fellowship of Reconciliation, created in England early in the war as an organization for Christian pacifists, was paralleled by the War Resister's League which tended to draw together pacifists outside the conventional religious movements. The Women's International League for Peace and Freedom, founded like the others on the European side of the Atlantic, sought to unite women from all backgrounds, including the Historic Peace Churches. A vigorous peace movement developed between the two world wars, rallying large numbers of persons in organizations far greater than these three. But after the invasion of Poland in 1939, and especially after Pearl Harbor, the mood of the country changed, and pacifism became extremely unpopular once more. It has been estimated that approximately a half-million persons, or less than one-half of one per cent of the American people were committed to the pacifist position during the war years.

The efforts of the pacifists in the American Revolutionary period to prevent the outbreak of that conflict, and to provide for the victims of war were continued by the Historic Peace Churches and later by other pacifist organizations. The Quaker leader George Fox set an example for others when he said in 1651 that he ". . . lived in the virtue of that life and power that took away the occasion of all wars." The efforts to deal with the causes of wars, as well as the devastation caused by them, were institutionalized by the creation of the American Friends Service Committee in 1917. The Mennonite Central Committee and the Brethren Service Commission were formed in the following years, and similar bodies have been organized by members of other religious faiths.

The relief and reconstruction work of the various service bodies is well known, and would not need to be enlarged upon here except for one issue. Pacifists have refused to distinguish between the two sides of a conflict; they have helped the suffering on both sides. During the war in Vietnam, peace groups repeatedly had trouble with the government of the United States over providing medical supplies and other relief goods to suffering civilians of both South Vietnam and North Vietnam and the latter's National Liberation Front allies. The unauthorized sailing of the *Phoenix* for Haiphong in 1967, loaded with medical supplies, drew worldwide attention to the conflict between the conscientious concern of pacifists for all humanity, and the policy of the state. A similar confrontation between the American Friends Service Committee and the

U. S. government over sending relief goods to North Vietnam took place as recently as November, 1975.

Pacifists have also been active in attempting to "take away the occasion of wars" through a variety of efforts. They have organized conferences to discuss particular issues, especially the Diplomats Conferences for junior-level diplomats from various countries. On many occasions they have formed missions to go to a troubled spot to explore the issues and to help in seeking solutions. Working parties have spent months studying conflict situations, and they have published their findings in books such as *Speak Truth to Power* (1955), and *A New China Policy* (1965). Such projects are part of a conscious effort to say something constructive, and to do something useful to help avert war and violence before it occurs, instead of waiting to bind up wounds afterwards. Today pacifists struggle with the dilemma of how to change exploitive, despotic societies by non-violent means. For example, they are looking at conditions in Latin America and elsewhere which cry out for revolutionary change, and they seek to find creative, non-violent solutions.

Nor do those who endeavor to put their peace testimony into practice turn their backs on evil in American society. The areas in which work is being undertaken include education, environment, race relations, and individual freedom. Pacifists today, like those of other generations, are caught up in a whole list of social concerns and seldom limit themselves to the issues of militarism and war. The American Friends Service Committee is currently undertaking a project called "Government Surveillance and Citizen's Rights" which is aimed at protecting the rights and privacy of individuals. Even though Quakers are reluctant to go to court, they have joined where appropriate in lawsuits against the F.B.I., the C.I.A., and other government agencies.

The Atomic Age, now in its fourth decade, has brought about a decisive change in the peace movement in this country and around the world. Ever since the bombs were dropped on Hiroshima and Nagasaki in 1945, countless human beings have sought ways to end the armaments race and to create an enduring peace. The proliferation of nuclear armaments has intensified the desire to persuade governments to lay aside both nuclear and conventional armaments and to develop a community of nations. Non-violent direct actions at experimental stations and at testing sites have in these years drawn crowds of demonstrators and large groups of supporters. The National Committee for a Sane Nuclear Policy (SANE), and the Committee for Non-Violent Action (CNVA) were two of the organizations which sprang into being as people sought ways to make their feelings known. Civil disobedience, as a powerful way to express opposition to government policies, including nuclear testing, became more common than before. When the *Golden Rule* sailed into the South Pacific in 1958, invading the waters of the zone restricted for nuclear testing, the news media around the world carried the story of pacifists defying their government for conscience' sake.

The war in Vietnam was a unique experience in the history of the United States; it created a series of new issues, intensified some old ones, and continues to generate difficulties long after our involvement has supposedly ended. Because the war was unpopular with a majority of the American people, the climate in which the peace movement operated was entirely different from anything the nation had ever experienced. All sorts of peace organizations sprang up, many more radical than the older, established bodies. Following the pattern created during the protests against atomic weapons, hundreds of thousands of persons gathered on a single day for demonstrations in Washington, New York, or San Francisco. Millions of letters were written to Members of Congress, to the Defense Department, and to the White House. Dozens of members of the Senate and House openly denounced government policy in Vietnam, a far cry from World War II when Jeanette Rankin was the sole Member of Congress to vote in opposition to that conflict.

Traditionally, pacifists had only broken the law when they felt compelled to take such action by a "higher law," the law of God, and they were prepared to accept the punishment meted out by the government for their action. Because this was the case, many found it difficult to understand young men opposed to conscription, who resisted the military by disappearing into the underground or by migrating to some other country. They disagreed with those who argued that an immoral government, fighting an illegal war, had no right to make claims upon them. Nor could traditional pacifists condone the policy of avoiding taxes on the grounds that an individual need not feel obligated to pay an immoral tax which was levied to cover the costs of an illegal war. They were often critical of those who perpetrated acts of violence while expressing their opposition to the war. The tactics used by some war opponents, such as physical attacks upon persons and property, drew censure from others. When a few resisters resorted to bombings, some of them fatal, members of the peace movement felt called upon to disassociate themselves from such actions.

Where there had been a few thousand conscientious objectors to World War II, there were hundreds of thousands of men who resisted being drawn into the war in Vietnam. While a large proportion of the C.O.'s in the 1940's were willing to do alternate service, now the vast majority refused to cooperate in any fashion. Draft cards were returned to the government, or they were burned, often at public occasions, as men from many walks of life refused to serve. Tens of thousands deserted from the armed forces once they had been enrolled, and many others undertook to obtain recognition as conscientious objectors by legal means. There is no agreement to this day on the number of young Americans who deserted from the armed forces, who failed to register for the draft, or who refused to appear for induction; nor do we know how many fled from the United States to avoid involvement in the war.

While many in the peace movement agreed that the government of the United States needed to be changed, needed to be made more responsive to the citizens and less beholden to powerful special interests, they were not ready to tear down the existing government and enter a condition of anarchy. Neither were they prepared to support the North Vietnamese and their N.L.F. allies, the stance taken by some radical opponents of the war. Pacifists did recognize, however, that the seeds of anarchy, of near treasonable support of the other side, were to be found in a wicked war, waged by an evil government, with the acquiescence of a sick society.

If some war resisters resorted to illegal actions in their efforts to oppose the war, it is also true that government officials sometimes broke the law. They often violated the rights of persons seeking to protest in a peaceful manner. They used various illegal means to accumulate information about both individuals and organizations opposed to the war. The government tended to confuse opposition to the war with disloyalty, and the fact that a few war resisters appeared to favor North Vietnam heightened this feeling. Pacifists sometimes felt that their treatment at the hands of the government was reminiscent of conditions during the American Revolution two centuries ago.

After the Vietnam agreement had been signed, most of the persons who had joined in the protests turned to other issues such as ecology and the protection of natural resources, to political reform through such agencies as Common Cause, or to the struggle against poverty and racial discrimination. The peace movement shrank back to something like its normal size, namely quite tiny. Today it finds that most Americans do not hear what it is trying to say, and have no desire to listen. The public is tired of hearing about the dangers of an atomic cataclysm, and nothing which anyone can say about this danger seems to make any difference. The proliferation of atomic weapons in the hands of more nations would seem to increase the probability of catastrophe, but few heed the warnings. Suspension of the draft in 1973 took most of the fire out of resistance to conscription, and the announcement that a new registration would not take place in March of 1976 was another step in the same direction. Some effort against the volunteer army continues, as does opposition to the creation of junior ROTC units in the high schools, but these projects elicit little public support.

A spirit of internationalism has always permeated the peace movement, and one important manifestation of this spirit is support of the United Nations. In a period when there is much criticism of the U.N. for a variety of reasons, most pacifists continue to support this international organization as a step in the right direction, despite its weaknesses. The American Friends Service Committee, which has maintained a strong U. N. program for a quarter century, has just issued a new publication, *The United Nations and Human Survival,* in an effort to explain what the U. N. is accomplishing, especially in non-political areas, and to rally public support.

A few pacifists still refuse to pay that portion of their taxes which go for the military program, and the government has continued its campaign to bring tax violators before the federal courts. But tax refusal has never caught on with very many persons; most who regard themselves as pacifists continue to pay, albeit reluctantly, and the average citizen has never really understood the position of tax resisters. There has been an increase in the number of persons who decided to oppose the system by moving into life centers or communes to live the simple life as a testimony against the extravagance, the waste, and the selfishness of the contemporary scene. While one can honor such persons for their intentions, it seems clear that they are not succeeding in persuading many others to join them.

Those who have long held firmly to the peace testimony continue to call for amnesty for war resisters, and this is one area in which they have some chance of success. Even though pacifists did not always agree with the actions of many of the war resisters, I believe that they are united today in demanding that they be given amnesty. It is obvious that many have suffered a great deal for their stand, and it is also clear that no positive good can be achieved by refusing to grant them amnesty at this time. The granting of amnesty is an American tradition. The Tories of the American Revolution were granted amnesty, and many settled back into their old patterns of life; some returned from exile in Canada or Britain. President Washington was quick with offers of amnesty after the Whiskey Rebellion in 1793, and both Lincoln and Andrew Johnson offered amnesty after the Civil War. The government has not been as generous in granting amnesty after World War I and World War II as it had been earlier.

The limited program of clemency and "earned reentry" offered by President Ford in 1974 looked grudging indeed, compared with the magnanimous pardon extended to Richard Nixon a few weeks earlier. Nothing more has been accomplished in this direction, although we have had a great deal of discussion about the issue. There have been nineteen bills introduced in the 94th Congress, but debate has concentrated upon H.R. 9596 introduced by Representative Robert Kastenmeier of Wisconsin. While this bill does not go far enough to satisfy all amnesty groups, it is fairly liberal and has a chance of being passed. Other bills, providing general and unconditional amnesty, have been introduced by Representatives Bella Abzug and Ronald Dellums and by others. Most of the major religious groups have issued statements on this vexing issue, but, as one would expect, the positions taken by various bodies differ in content. However, all of the statements recognize the need to settle the amnesty question as soon as possible, because as long as up to one million men live under a cloud created by the war in Vietnam, the nation will not be able to put that traumatic period behind it. If this Conference feels ready and able to issue any statements at the conclusion of this week, it might well consider a resolution calling for a general amnesty.

The men and women who proclaim their support of the peace testimony are faced with many challenges and look forward to future years of effort to persuade their fellow citizens and their government that the way of non-violence is the only and best way. They continue to oppose the great military budgets, and especially the new projects such as the B-1 bomber. They continue to defend the rights of individuals against a powerful state. They continue to believe that human beings are capable of living in harmony with one another through the power of the Divine Presence. Like their spiritual ancestors of 200 years ago, they are working to bring about the Reign of God on earth as quickly as possible. Faced with some of the dangers which threaten humankind, they can do no less.

References on the Peace Testimony

American Friends Service Committee, *In Place of War* (New York, 1967).

Beerits, Henry C., *The United States and Human Survival* (Philadelphia, 1976).

Brock, Peter, *Pacifism in the United States . . .*(Princeton, 1968). (Quaker chapters published separately under the title, *Pioneers of the Peaceable Kingdom.*)

————, *Twentieth Century Pacifism* (New York, 1970).

Calvert, Robert, ed., *Ain't Gonna Pay for War No More* (New York, 1971).

Encyclopedia Britannica Book of the Year, "Peace Movements," 1963–1974; "Pacifism and Non-violent Movements," 1975.

Ferber, Michael, and Staughton Lynd, *The Resistance* (Boston, 1971).

Gish, Arthur G., *The New Left and Christian Radicalism* (Grand Rapids, 1970).

Habenstreit, Barbara, *Men against War* (New York, 1973).

Jack, Homer A., ed., *Religion and Peace* (Indianapolis, 1966).

————, *World Religions and World Peace* (Boston, 1968).

Lawson, Don, ed., *Ten Fighters for Peace* (New York, 1971).

Lieberman, Mark, *The Pacifists, Soldiers without Guns* (New York, 1972).

Lynd, Alice, *We Won't Go, Personal Accounts of War Objectors* (Boston, 1968).

Marx, Paul, "The Peace Movement: Alive but Not Well," *Christian Century* 92 (December 3, 1975): 1105–1107. "Pacifism Isn't Dying Out," readers' responses to P. Marx, *Christian Century* 93 (March 10, 1976): 227–233.

National Interreligious Service Board for Conscientious Objectors, *A Case for Amnesty* (n.p., n.d. [1976]).

————, *Religious Statements on Amnesty* (n.p., 1974).

Peace and Change, A Journal of Peace Research (Sonoma, CA).

Schlissel, Lillian, *Conscience in America* (New York, 1968).

Tatum, Arlo, ed., *Handbook for Conscientious Objectors,* 12th edition (Philadelphia, 1972).

Walker, Charles C., ed., *Quakers and the Draft* (Philadelphia, [1969]).

Wittner, Lawrence S., *Rebels against War . . .* (New York, 1969).

CIVIL DISOBEDIENCE—CONSCIENCE/SURVIVAL

Jesse L. Jackson

I am honored and privileged to be a part of this religious celebration. I have been in a conflict of conscience about it for some weeks now. On the one hand, I didn't and don't want to speak about the subject. On the other hand, my vanity and something else made me want to come anyhow, and so I chose to try to figure out a way to come anyhow and not speak about the subject; then I politicked the organizers into saying it would be all right since I was already here.

I am concerned that we in this Conference, at this moment in history, attempt to address ourselves in the most profound ways that we can to organize to make a difference in this world. I want to speak about civil disobedience, conscience, and survival.

When engaging in civil disobedience, the weight of proof is almost always on the individual, for the state is a mass of individuals and a more constant and responsible entity. The impersonal nature of the state deprives it ultimately of feelings and thus reduces persons to cogs in a wheel. The state at best is capable of justice but not of love—though a totally sharp line need not be drawn. Primarily, though, we need a balance of *power*. The state at its best serves God-like functions—it distributes justice and mercy, goods and services; protects and shields; produces and provides. Seldom is the state at its best, and usually it is capable of being dispassionate, impersonal, and tyrannical—most people would rather switch than fight.

But the cross—the high hill of conscientious objection—stands between life and death, fear and courage, freedom and slavery, mortality and immortality. Thus, when Christians choose the way of the cross—the way of integrity, involvement, and intelligence (the way of "not my will but thine," the way of a higher calling), they take a cross from around their necks and put it on their backs, and they move from admiring Jesus to following him. Thus a Christian accepts the freedom and assumes the responsibility of conscience. Conscience—the pursuit of higher law, the authority to discern just law from unjust law—a just law being a law made for one group which, when applied, is acceptable to all. It is a just law because it has universal character. The unjust law is made by one group for its advantage, but does not offer the same services or options to others. The sense to discern and the freedom to choose obligates one to the responsibility to bear the cross or pay the penalty until a crucifixion is transformed into a resurrection.

The divine authority by which you speak must help you bear the weight of raising the general consciousness to your level of perception—e.g., Muhatma Gandhi, in India; Dr. Martin Luther King, Jr., in his civil rights struggles; Jesus

The Rev. Jesse L. Jackson is founder and national president of Operation PUSH in Chicago, IL.

Christ on Calvary—the result of civil disobedience; or American Independence—the result of civil disobedience. The belief is that unearned suffering is redemptive, that truth ultimately prevails. A judgment has to be made. There must be a moral relationship between the people and the issues raised. The means by which they live must be consistent with the ends for which they live.

The appointments of government may lead to rebellion for selfish reasons, but the anointment of God may lead to authentic civil disobedience or objection to the state. The laws of convenience lead to collapse, but the laws of sacrifice lead to greatness. The Proverbs remind us to seek this sense of balance and responsibility. The writer says, "Two things I desire—don't give me too much or I'll ask 'who is God?'; but don't give me too little or I'll steal and defame your name."

I conscientiously object to spending all my time discussing conscience and civil disobedience while our movement for liberation has been slowed down by blurred vision and an ethical collapse. Thus, I want to expand my remarks to include the present stage of our struggle and what we must do concretely to overcome the present state of spiritual decadence and despair. The handwriting on the wall of history requires a serious, scientific, and sober assessment of these times. First, we must actually assess and then meet the demands of these particular times.

The first major period for us on these North American shores, for us as a Black people, was a period of "no government." We were denied citizenship rights. It was illegal for us to own land, illegal for us to marry, illegal for us to be educated, illegal for us to vote. We are constitutionally considered three-fifths human. We were in a period of "no government." We call it a period of "no government," slavery, or colonialism. The next state we call "semi-government" or neo-colonialism. This was a period in which we had more rights, but inasmuch as we did not have all of our rights, this period, too, was insufficient. Politically, we always had to choose between two evils. If one dared to smile, we called one "liberal." If one snarled, we called one "conservative." But both belonged to the same church and the same country club and were educated together. However, a smile was so much more pleasing than a whiplash! We gave our support to the coalition.

In the period of "no government," only our brawn or our muscle was considered valuable. In "semi-government," most of our brawn and only a little of our brain were considered necessary. We were able to participate and benefit only to the extent that it was to the advantage and self-interest of our partner in the coalition. Thus, we are pawns in a power struggle and not partners. We played ball, but they coached and owned the team. We went to school, but they ran the administration. We lived in the cities, but they presided. We read the books, but they wrote them. This period of "semi-government" was a period of tremendous contrast with slavery, yet it left us undeveloped and underdeveloped because it did not demand of many of us the sense of responsibility and mind usage that free people must have.

As a result of our marching feet and the creative and courageous leadership of

Dr. Martin Luther King, Jr., we acquired a Public Accommodations Bill and a Voting Rights Bill. However, once these rights were gained, our yearn for freedom was translated into a yearn for power. The fiery flames of Watts and Newark were such symbols. The cries of Black power and the ballot in our hands began to burn away the clouds of inferiority and semi-freedom. We were ushered into a new period called "self-government." This is, by far, the most challenging period. It requires of us the full use of our minds and bodies, our wits and intuition, our feelings and our spirituality. The sum total of our being will be required to hold this mountain and to staff this fort.

Self-government, this awesome new responsibility, demands the pursuit of excellence in every facet of life as the only protection from extinction or a return to slavery. Our only protection against genocide is to remain necessary. This yearn for self-government required our putting together several steps by which we measure where we are. (1) We had to identify the opressor. We identified it as the ideology of racism prevalent in every facet, in every institution, of American life—home, church, school, labor, and management. (2) We had to accept as a challenge to find ways of stopping the oppressor. Thus, we had to struggle. We had to hang. We had to march. We had to go to court. We had to pray. We had to do all of this and more. (3) We had to replace the oppressor. We did it fundamentally through the electoral process. We have today in Washington, DC, a Black mayor, a predominantly-Black city council, a Black school superintendent, a Black congressperson, and virtually, an all-Black city. There we reside in the jaws of jaws, just ten years after the voting rights bill. In a mere ten years, on one level, amazing political progress has been made.

When we went to Selma in 1965, we had only three Black Congresspersons. Today, we have seventeen Congresspersons. We went there with two million registered Black voters. Today, we have eight million. We went there with no Black mayors. Today we have 130. We went there with 400 Black elected and appointed officials. Today we have slightly over 4000—including two lieutenant governors and a U. S. Senator. There is significance in this growth as a direct action movement begins to use the political lever, for it means that we can no longer be discounted, can no longer be publicly insulted—unless someone is willing to pay a severe penalty of defeat or political extinction. In 1960, Kennedy beat Nixon by 110,000 votes. It was an enthusiastic Black vote—because he helped to get Dr. King out of jail in Albany, Georgia—that made the difference. In 1968, Nixon beat Humphrey by 550,000 votes. It was an unenthusiastic Black vote that meant the difference. Dr. King had been assassinated. Robert Kennedy had been assassinated. The war was still raging in Vietnam. In our frustration, we threw away more than a million and a half votes in a futile effort in the California Freedom Party. The point is that the difference between the winning of Nixon and the losing of Humphrey was the lack of an enthusiastic Black vote.

Thus, between 1960 and 1968, two presidents won by less than 700,000 votes. Now what does our having seven million votes mean? It really means that hands that picked cotton in 1966 can pick presidents in 1976. Thus, our options in some measure have changed. On the other hand, just as there are eight million registered, there are eight million unregistered. Just as there was a hopeful and progressive spirit that brought in a relative political and material prosperity, there is a measure of decadence and despair threatening to slow down that Freedom Train.

Lest we forget, no candidate can ignore us now. In 1972, we were 25.7% of the national Democratic vote. Prior to Mr. Carter's "slip of the lip," there was some notion that the Black vote could be ignored. After all, there is not much evidence that Blacks will go Republican en masse. The Black vote is so dominant now in the Democratic party that we can defeat this party: (1) by going Republican, (2) by staying home because of a lack of enthusiasm, or (3) supporting a third party effort. Thus, we cannot be ignored. With this strategic position, no one can say we are impotent. In fact, all must say that we are important. With such a strategic position increasing our chances of self-determination, we must be more effective and more just and provide more service than the previous stages of no-government and semi-government. That is the responsibility of self-government.

If we do not, the fourth stage will set in—the period of counter-revolution backlash. A loss of confidence will follow. We must assess these times. My premise, therefore, is: nobody will save us, from us, for us, but us. Nobody will save us from us, for us, but *us*. Self control precedes community control. We must love ourselves properly before we can love others adequately—but we must know the power of love. For most of us, this adjustment to self-government requires putting new demands on ourselves and on each other. We must not fear the change we seek. If I might give you an example: you must use one strategy going up the mountain, but another strategy is required to stay on the mountain. There was once a long trip from Egypt to Canaan. It only required courage to overcome fear—to identify the oppressor by ethnicity and leave Egypt. But to stay in Canaan required more than ethnicity. It required ethics, internal moral discipline, economics, and education. Pharoah never assumed the responsibility for the development of the escapees or the refugees. That is as true today as it was then. Thus I contend, nobody will save us, from us, for us, but us.

Let us view self-government. In self-government we have the mayor of our choice, our own school principals, our own superintendent of schools, and yet our most precious commodity—the lives of our children—is found weighing in the balance. To save them is our tremendous work. To create a posterity for which all of us can be justly proud is our high calling. The crisis in which we find our children and ourselves is so national, so nasty, and so dangerous that all of us must be involved. It is everybody's assignment.

We can't escape our responsibility through dope, alcohol, sex, philosophy, or religion. We must be involved. Parents, life begins in the bedroom, is developed in the classroom, and is directed from the board room. If, when the physical umbilical cord is cut, the spiritual umbilical cord is not connected, we have failed in the bedroom; the classroom will become a detention center; and, as a result, there will never be power in the board room. All of us must give the best of what each has to offer to this struggle. Parents must supply the spiritual nutrients that no government can offer—motivation, care, discipline, and chastisement, in love. Children must be involved in their own destiny. Children cannot play the game, "you can teach me if you can catch me." Our children must assume their responsibility as well. They must put forth effort, practice, time, and belief in education, as well as have the will to learn. Teachers must engage in rigorous preparation, inspiration, dedication, and the best of instruction. The principal must be the moral authority who demands discipline which results in development. Administrators must justify an adequate budget, set policy, and interpret the system. The media must reward achievement, and the preacher must see education as God's will—as part of our moral responsibility. All must be involved.

Our theme is "PUSH for Excellence." We know we are in a desert, but the challenge is making flowers bloom in the desert. Parents must hew out of the soil and the rock a firm foundation. They must become co-partners with professional educators as architects and designers to build a new creation. There are economic factors contributing to this crisis. There is a national epidemic of failure in our public schools along with a ethical collapse in our civilization. There is the lack of an effective national urban policy, evidence of racism, and the frequent disruptions caused by the struggling against inequities. But there are also non-economic factors contributing to this crisis that cannot be explained away simply by poverty, except the most destitute.

Our problem is that we are living in a state of political decadence. The sum total of a lot of individual decadence has set a political climate. Thus, what once was a solid foundation where people took little and did much is now an acid base, and nothing grows in acid—neither children, nor houses, nor dreams. We must change our attitudinal disposition toward life, toward education and religion. The change must come from the bottom up. No psychological Godfather is going to wake us up and save us one night from this nightmare. No Savior will ascend to the throne in the White House. Nobody will save us, from us, for us, but us.

Ultimately, the only way to stop drugs from flowing in the schools is for children's arms and nasal cavities to cease being a market. This student participation in the drug traffic represents a breakdown in morally sound conduct and rational behavior. My school visits around the nation reveal that there is a breakdown in moral authority, discipline, and thus development. I distinguish moral authority from legal and/or tyrannical authority. Our organization PUSH has as its symbol a pyramid. The left side of the pyramid represents economic generation; the right side, spiritual regeneration; and the base, discipline. With regard to economic generation, our emphasis is on both private and public economic policy. We want houses and jobs. We want the traditional material goals. We want community control, but we know that neither man nor woman can live by bread alone. There is another longing, a need for spiritual regeneration which emphasizes self-control. Discipline, however, is at the base of economic generation and spiritual regeneration.

We know that personal will and sound values are essential to human progress. Even the absence of racism is not the presence of justice. The absence of Wallace doesn't mean the presence of a good candidate, necessarily. The death of ethics is the sabotage of excellence. The death of ethics *is* the sabotage of excellence. The aftermath of our rebellion, like the afterbirth material which follows the birth of a child, must be removed from both the mother and child— lest the germs kill them both. This, too, is true in the aftermath of a successful rebellion. There are remains which must be cleaned up and removed in order for the true purpose of the revolution to be fulfilled.

Extremes have begun to set in. Confusion is too often the result. Many stopped being servile, which was legitimate; but now they don't even want to be of service—and that's illegitimate. The general rebellion against all authority must stop. We must be sober enough to be discriminating. We must distinguish between that which must be revered from that which must be rebelled against in order that our action might have meaning. There is a difference between being mean and being meaningful. Many rightfully stopped working for nothing, but some do not see the value of working for something. Work is important. More than wages, character formation, identity, self esteem, self-fulfillment, and mental stability are all associated with work and achievement. The servant is worthy of his or her hire and the job must afford the worker wages, but we must work. When we are deprived of a job, we lose more than money. We rebelled against tyrannical authority, but now we are rebelling against all authority—parental, educational, moral, and religious. That is unsound.

The value of God-consciousness as a part of the cosmic hierarchy has been slowly removed from the experience of this generation of young people. Thus, some of the sickness that we see manifesting itself is the product of a publicly-Godless generation.

Most of us still live in a three-tier cosmos: there is God's domain, the human domain, and land—a material domain. When we remove God from God's domain and engage in the cosmic domain as though we're self-sufficient, then human beings project themselves into God's domain and play God. We can only *play* God; we can't *be* God. We can put our names on buildings and highways or try to buy or build immortality through some material tangible means. We can fly higher than birds and swim deeper than fish. We can play God for a minute in history. But when we play God, then land and materialism rise up and are valued at the level where man and woman and boy and girl used to be. As a result, we now respect and revere cars and rings the way we used to respect boys and girls. The tragedy of that disruption of the cosmos is that God is not really moved. It's just an illusion. The problem is that human beings move and change, and our illusion never stays. Thus we have no foundation, and without a foundation there is a bottomless pit of degradation.

If a child will not give deference to God—the origin, the Creator of Creation—ultimately, that child will not give deference to his or her parents, teachers, brothers or sisters. If we will not accept God as Creator, there is no basis for accepting each other as brother and sister. God must have a separate domain. In our schools, when prayer came out, pistols went in. When hope came out, dope went in. Choose the God of your choice, but don't play games with the Creator. You can change God's name, but not God's claim: God is God anyhow.

It is fully clear to me that the death of ethics is the sabotage of excellence. What difference does it make if a teacher gives a child homework if the parent does not make the child stay home to do the work? What difference does it make if the child has a new book or an old book if neither is ever opened? What does it matter if the child's classmate is Black or white if the child is anti-social toward both? What difference does it really make if the teacher has a Ph.D. or no "D" if the child ignores both?

There is still something basic (not conservative) about reading, writing, counting, preparation, rhythm, repetition, trial and error. We still must learn the theory, practice the theory, and eventually become masters! These steps to greatness are the same for singers, dancers, preachers, actors, ball players, conservatives, and liberals. The note of greatness is the same key on the universal keyboard. There is no shortcut to greatness. The busing, desegregation, budget, equal representation controversies all have to do with adult power struggles—and very legitimate power struggles. But more basic than that in all schools is the presupposition that there is a *will* to learn and an *urge for excellence*. When that spiritual quality dies, a new school building is no compensation.

On the present acid base, where the desire to be somebody has died in too many instances, racism can't kill us, because cynicism gets us first. We're experiencing a situation where death has changed its name from southern rope to northern dope. Genocide can't get us because homicide, fratricide, and suicide already have. With this present acid base other judgments are premature. How can we judge teachers when they do not even have the climate in which to practice their trade? To judge some of our teachers in this atmosphere of guns, knives, threats, and violence is like sending Hank Aaron to the plate with a popsicle stick or Muhammad Ali into the ring with one glove on and his other hand tied behind his back. Until the rules are set straight and the axis is put back in its joint, everything else is logically out of order.

What do we do? Do we play in a corner and evolve a theology of self-love, self-beautification, and self-preoccupation? Do we go off into our little cubbyhole and start playing and eating grass and apples? Whether we're shouting or being quiet, we cannot remain theologically sound and stay detached from the real problems of this world. We contend that we must organize on a school-by-school basis city-wide councils of students for discipline and against drugs, racism, and violence. We must give them the option to come forward. We cannot do that detached from them. We must also organize city-wide councils of educators for discipline and against racism, drugs and violence—as well as preachers, parents, communicators, and others. Our publicly-licensed radio must stop the glorification of mass decadence. We cannot act in Rome as Romans. We must transform Rome. We must stop the institutional undercutting to exaggerate doubt about educational pursuits in our children's minds. Some ministers naively do this by suggesting: "Get all the education you want, but get Jesus"—as if there were some conflict there! On the other side some educators say: "Shout and be as righteous as you please, but you better learn how to read and write." The fact of the matter is that preachers need to go to school; teachers need to go to church; and parents and children need to do both. The institutional undercutting needs to stop.

At night, it is not enough to tell ABC, CBS, and NBC, "Don't put violence on my television." Parents must be home to turn the television off, whether it is violent or non-violent. They need to be reading from 7 to 10 p.m., developing their academic consciousness. We can't keep passing the buck on everything. We should stop sending report cards home by the children. Parents ought to come to school to pick them up. That is their responsibility. They must get involved en masse.

I was on a program with Dr. Robert Schuller some months ago. He said, "Reverend, you came from a segregated South Carolina, took abuse and humiliation, and went to jail. Why aren't you bitter toward Southern white people? They discriminated against you." I said, "Because I assumed there was something wrong with them, that they were sick. I would not allow them to punish my body *and* my soul. Even in punishment, I had the option of how I would respond to pain. I know it is not your aptitude but your attitude that determines your altitude with just a little intestinal fortitude. No matter what yesterday's strife, today is still the first day of the rest of your life. If you bring all of the burdens, aches, agonies, and history on today's shoulder, you'll be too weighted down to walk into the future even if the doors are wide open. We rehearse and rehearse history until we carefully bear all the burdens of yesterday's wars and lose the capacity to forgive and redeem because we've got too much trash on our shoulders."

Someone said: "What was the high experience for you in education? Was it elementary school or high school? Was it the University of Illinois, North Carolina A. & T., or the University of Chicago Graduate School? Where was it?" As I reflect, it was the first day I started school. My mother took me to school and told Miss Georgeanna Robinson, "This is my boy. I want you to help me develop him. He gets out of hand every now and then; therefore, you might have to chastise him. If you do, send a note home and he'd better bring it. If I don't see you at the PTA because I works at night, I'll see you at church on Sunday." For you see, Miss Robinson taught public school Monday through Friday, but she taught Sunday School on Sunday. She realized there was a relationship between intellectual and character development. She took me down to Mr. Graham's office to reinforce the discipline. They disciplined me to teach me how to discipline myself.

As I reflect in later years, with the home on one end of the triangle—not the house, but the home—we never did have a house made of brick and mortar, but we had a home made of love and prayer and some other kinds of things you can't record on paper. We had spiritual nutrition. With the home, church, and school I was trapped in a love triangle into which not even segregation and barbarism could break. There is the ability to be in the fiery furnace and escape unburned, with not even the smell of smoke—if one has religious immunity, not escapism.

Our public schools have become too informal. There is not the resilence that must exist there. We must have new definitions of men and women. Too many of our young men think they are men if they kill somebody—as opposed to being a man because they heal somebody. We've never struggled to teach non-violence in the schools. Many think they are men because they can make a baby, not because they can raise a baby. Many girls stoop to the distortion of abortion because they are not educated to appreciate life. They walk as hunks of sex and boys fall for the bait and when both panic out of passion, we fail to deal with the ramification of the devaluation of human life. Some even suggest that having babies is a woman's role. Women can't make babies by themselves, nor can men—though they can be irresponsible when they've planted the seed. Life must maintain the highest value in this cosmic order, and when chairs and convenience become more basic than children, even the religious objectors become extensions of the decadence.

We exaggerate conception to birth—nine months. No man can become pregnant. No man can have a baby. No man could stand the pain. Our *great* contribution really begins at birth not at conception. But functional definitions of manhood and womanhood are so messed up that there is no comfortable imagery from birth up to age eighteen—where the real struggle is. The real struggle begins there, because that's where the failures are.

I went to a horse race one time down in Miami, Florida. I was down there with Reverend Jones and some other ministers at a conference. I don't know how I ended up at a horse race except I'd heard about Hialeah and the Bible said "Go ye into all the world." I figured Hialeah was part of the world, so I went there that afternoon to do a little basic observation. While there I was telling some of my friends, "I've never been to a race before." Like a preacher I'm always searching for a sermon in everything. I noticed they had lines in front of little cages—$2 windows, $5 windows, $10, and on up to the $100 window. At the $2 window line was a *long, long* line of people. The $100 window had just a few people. The people who were buying the $2 tickets all had hot dogs, peanuts, and beer and were talking very loudly. The food they had in their hands cost more than the ticket. They were determined to make money at the track. The people at the $100 window were not talking loud. Some of them had cigars in their mouths and binoculars around their necks.

Finally someone said, "It's time for the race to start!" The people with the $2 tickets kept drinking beer, eating hot dogs, chewing peanuts, and talking loudly. Those with the $100 tickets went over near the starting gate, as close as the ushers would allow them. The race was about to start. The people with the $100 tickets took their binoculars out to make certain their horses were not lame and that nothing funny happened at the starting gate. But the people with the $2 tickets were up in the stands by this time—eating hot dogs, drinking beer, eating peanuts, and talking loudly. Then the race started and the horses were off and running. The people with the $100 tickets were up on their tiptoes nervously looking at their horses racing down the track. The people with the $2 tickets continued eating hot dogs, drinking beer, chewing peanuts, and talking loudly.

The horses made the first turn—and the people with the $100 tickets looked as far as their binoculars could see. Finally, you couldn't see because of the hedge bushes. They stood there looking nervous. But the people with the $2 tickets were eating hot dogs, drinking beer, chewing peanuts, and talking loudly. When the horses began to come toward the final turn, those with the $100 tickets were getting nervous, wiping their foreheads, chomping on their cigars, and looking to see what it was going to be like coming into the final turn. The people who were eating hot dogs, drinking beer, and chewing peanuts began to get a little quieter. When the horses came down the final stretch they were very close together. The top four money winners began to emerge because the jockeys who had been riding the horses all the way got low and close and tightened up the bridle with the left hand using the stick on the horse's butt as they came down the straightaway. Those who had been eating hot dogs, drinking beer, chewing peanuts, and talking loud came rushing past the gate, trying to knock over the usher, cussing, and raising hell, trying to find out where their tickets were and trying to snap pictures at the end.

No matter in what state the affairs of political and economic war and peace are, as long as the masses of the people are being avoided by those of us who assume we control the truth, so long as the masses are allowed to sit in the stands drinking beer, eating hot dogs, eating peanuts, and talking loudly, no real progress is going to be made. It reminds me of those school graduations where in September only a few parents are there with their binoculars looking at their children in the starting block and riding those curves with them. Then they come at graduation time, rudely knocking each other over, knocking the teachers over, taking pictures, looking at their little incomplete, half-developed, immoral, sweet little child. Killer, robber, racist—graduates with no information because while the work was going on they were sitting around.

Nobody will save us, from us, for us, but us. Whether we conscientiously cooperate or conscientiously resist, unless that acid is dried up and turned to rock, none can survive. We *can* survive because we serve a mighty God. We *can* survive because we can overcome our cynicism and our negativism, but our analysis must be accurate and sound. Our diagnosis must be true, even if it indicts us, if our future is to be any different.

FREEDOM OF CONSCIENCE—A JEWISH COMMENTARY*

Elie Wiesel

Introduction of Elie Wiesel by Rabbi Bertrand W. Korn, Senior Rabbi of Congregation Keneseth Israel, Elkins Park, PA:

... Today [April 27, 1976] is Yom HaShoah, the Memorial Day for the Holocaust. The Holocaust is one of five or six decisive events in all of Jewish history—from the Exodus through the creation of the State of Israel. It is one of perhaps a dozen turning points in the life of humanity. The Holocaust staggers the imagination, shakes the intellect, beats the emotions relentlessly, and buffets the spirit.

Jewish theologians and philosophers have been essentially unable to grapple with the Holocaust. The only personality capable of confronting the murder of six million of our brothers and sisters, the only personality capable of coping with the Holocaust, of coming to grips with it and being overcome by it, but yet not being destroyed by it, is himself this survivor, a member of the saved remnant, a storyteller, an artist. Elie Wiesel has seen the unbelievable, has heard the unspeakable, has endured the unbearable, has experienced the inexpressible. He is a unique figure of our time—poet of the soul, voice of the martyred, teacher, a rebbe in the truest sense of the word—communicating mind to mind, heart to heart, and spirit to spirit. He is a guardian of an ancient treasure and a guide to tomorrow. It was altogether unplanned that he should speak on Yom HaShoah. And yet here he is in this Conference on Religious Liberty celebrating 200 years of something beautiful in the life of humanity—speaking on this day when we remember something sorrowful in the life of humanity—Elie Wiesel.

It isn't "unplanned," and I do have to tell something to this distinguished audience—to the rabbis and reverends and friends. Had I known that today would be Yom HaShoah, I would not have spoken. Somehow I believe one cannot speak about it. Perhaps one can say a prayer. Perhaps silence would be in order. Perhaps people should only meet and read names. Names. They should perhaps meet and read Jewish names. Names of Jewish towns, Jewish communities, and Jewish children, Jewish teachers. Names. How does one speak? I don't know.

I prepared some notes. But, of course, the day imposes its own meaning, and I believe too much in coincidences. I believe too much in encounters not to yield to the encounter of the person and the date. So I will tell you a story. And the story is a simple, childish story.

Once upon a time—April 1944—a Jewish child, very religious, very pious,

---

*Dedicated by the author to his friend, Robert McAfee Brown

Dr. Elie Wiesel is a Professor at Boston University and an author, living in New York, NY.

extremely taken by God and the Law, was taken away by history. And then history was taken away by the enemy. And this Jewish boy suddenly plunged into a universe of malediction. For the very first time he discovered that humankind is evil, that there is evil in human beings. For the first time he realized that something went wrong with Creation. For the first time he heard the name "Auschwitz." He was young, very young. And it was night, midnight. And as all of the Jews who had come that evening from his town and others were coming closer to a point of selections and flames, inserting themselves in the sky, consuming the sky—suddenly people began coming to him and to those who were with him and began telling him and his father, "You know these flames? These are human beings. Do you know that people are being destroyed here? Do you know that the *akedah* is once more at the heart of Judaism? Abraham and Issac both go to the altar, and both will be consumed." And this young boy turned to his father and said, "I cannot believe it. It cannot be true; it cannot be true that in the middle of the twentieth century people could do such things to other people and the world would be silent." The world was silent.

Eleven years later I wrote a book, my first book in Yiddish. I called it *Und die Welt hat Geschwigen* [*And the World Was Silent*]. When we speak of freedom and conscience, I cannot, therefore, forget what it meant to us once upon a time. There was no freedom, and there was no conscience. The killer killed. The slaughterer slaughtered. And the victims died. And the world was silent.

As a Jew, however, I can fully appreciate the significance of celebrating the Bicentennial, because it means remembering. And to me to be Jewish means to remember. Therefore, to be human means to remember. A Jew who does not remember is neither Jewish nor human. I can understand why our country thinks back with pride of its 200 years of history and pursuit of happiness. But, somehow, as a Jew I view it a little bit skeptically. A history of 200 years, however dramatic, ought not to be compared to my people's history, really, to 4000 years. Four thousand years and two hundred years. But still the emphasis is on memory, and, therefore—since no one has defined himself or herself with more fervor in relationship to memory—we understand and we participate in this celebration, and we do so with great joy but with some misgivings. The misgivings have to do with what America represented to us and what it presented to itself.

Again, I cannot forget that Roosevelt was to us more than a leader—he was a prophet. In my home town, I did not know the name of David Ben-Gurion. I was not a Zionist. I was too religious. I was involved in Jewish studies all my life—as a child, as an adolescent. And political Zionism did not come to my town. But the name of Roosevelt I knew. Roosevelt was the great defender of freedom: the *friend* of the Jews. Only later did we find out that this great man knew everything that took place inside the kingdom of the Holocaust, and yet, he did little to prevent further slaughter. When he was asked by Jewish leaders to bomb the railways leading to Auschwitz, he refused. And, in those days and in those nights, ten thousand Jews would be killed day after day. Hungarian Jews. My Jews.

But still, this is a nation that gave the words "freedom" and "conscience" a new impetus. I think America has taken its mission seriously. After all, it has fought two world wars. After all, it *did* force a President to resign in the name of conscience. It's true, Watergate existed, but it's also true that we defeated the people who incarnated Watergate. It is true that we fought a terribly unjust war in Vietnam, but it is also true that the young students and the young clergy and the intellectuals who began the war against the war *won,* and the war was finished. Therefore, we speak about our past in this country with some joy, and it is justified.

As a Jew I must say that "freedom" and "conscience" are among the words and concepts that have dominated *our* memory, Jewish memory, since its very origins. Having received the Law at Sinai, the people of Israel waited for Moses to expand on its Law. When you study Scripture, you come to a *sedra,* to a portion of the week called *V'eyleh HaMishpatim,* after the portion of *Yithro* where you read about the Ten Commandments. And God says to Moses that these are the Laws that you must share with your people. The first Law is about slavery. Do not hold slaves. Seven weeks before, this people was a tribe of slaves. Seven weeks before, they were in Egypt—owned by Pharoah, *doomed* by their own misfortune. And here, we begin with slaves: owned slaves. Furthermore, we are told that to *be* a slave is as sinful as to own a slave. What does it mean really? The Jews then were told they were forbidden to diminish freedom. They were forbidden to inflict pain. In our tradition, we say that to serve God means to raise the human condition, whereas to serve humanity means to diminish it—hence the punishment intended for slaves who reject freedom, for in doing so they misuse the most precious gift, their inner freedom. One ought to be free in all things, in all areas, in all endeavors. One ought to invoke freedom as the most coveted of ideals, but one must not abuse freedom by choosing to denounce it. One should not do so unless it is for the sake of heaven. But, even then, I am sure that God is not too pleased with such sacrifice. God in our tradition wants human beings to come in freedom—not as slaves who have nothing left to offer anyone or God.

This idea has been illustrated by the Jewish attitude toward the stranger. Whereas in other traditions, societies, and religions the stranger has always been treated with suspicion, resentment, and hate, somehow the stranger has been *welcome* in ours. No tradition has been more generous to strangers, and we all know that. We have never asked a stranger to convert to our faith. Nor have we compelled the stranger to accept our ways, our Law, our language, our customs—quite the contrary: we want the stranger to remain a stranger, for in that capacity he or she can challenge our certainties and shake our complacency. It is as stranger that a stranger can be and is of interest and of help to us, as we are to the stranger.

As an example, let us see how the stranger appears in Scripture. There are three terms that apply to the stranger. The first one is *"ger,"* a stranger who lives in our midst, but who remains a stranger. The *ger* has not converted to our faith, but lives on our land with our friends and *is* a friend himself or herself. And what don't we do for this person! We have to go out of our way to please the stranger, to be charitable, to be generous, to be open—so much so that in the Midrash we learn that Moses became jealous. And Moses asked God: "Why did you give the *ger,* the stranger, the same privileges that you gave the Levites, who after all are here to serve you?"

The second category is a *"nachri,"* also a stranger. A *nachri* come comes from the *nachar,* from abroad, from outside, and is somewhat more hostile to us, and we are somehow a little more hostile to him or her. But, still, we are told in Scripture to share our holidays with the *nachri,* and we are to be *with* him or her.

Then there is the third category, called *"zar."* Toward a *zar* we have to be cruel. *Zar ki yekrav . . .* "A stranger who comes close to the Sanctuary," we are told, "his punishment must be death." Anything bad, somehow, is identified with *zar:* idolatry—*avodah zarah;* pagan thought—*machshavah zarah.* Every-thing is bad, and we are terribly, terribly hostile to the *zar.* You think about it, and you realize that there is really a difference. A *ger* is now Jewish. A *nachri* is not Jewish. A *zar* is. A *zar* is a Jew who is a stranger to self, a stranger to the people, a stranger to the tradition, and because of that, a stranger to humankind. And then we say, "This person is dangerous." One who can deny one's commu-nity and who can be a stranger to one's people when they need one—we are against such a person.

But, then, why not say it: our attitude to a stranger was not shared by others. From *paroah melech mitzraim*—Pharoah in Egypt—to Stalin, most leaders in power use their power to impose their will upon us. Who could survive? Only those Jews who ceased to be Jewish. And in the case of the Holocaust, no Jew could survive at all. And often I wonder—how is one to explain the variety of our enemies? How is one to explain that on the right and on the left, the rich and the poor, the fanatic and the enlightened, you will find in their midst enemies to our people as well. I wonder whether the hate we inspire does not have a secret, a force of its own. And what is more astonishing—is it our collective will to survive or the enemies' continuous desire to drive us to extinction? How is one to explain that they are so different from one another? What unites them is their hostility to the people of Israel. The reactionaries were always against us in Russia and Poland—and they still are. But so are their adversaries today on the extreme left. What would China and Russia have in common were it not for their hostility to Israel?

This phenomenon is not new. We cannot, when we speak today about free-dom and conscience, avoid saying a few words in truth to our non-Jewish friends. Some of you are friends of mine, and we try to do the same thing—in our own fields, and with our own tools. And they know that a true Christian, to me, is more important than a stranger, a Jew. I have much more in common with an authentic Christian than with a Jew who is ashamed of his or her Jewishness. But still the truth must be said. And I certainly do not say it with hate—we are incapable of hate; we didn't even hate the Germans during the War; we couldn't hate—and not even with resentment. I really say it to bring us together, to share and to be open—that what we suffered, what we endured from Christianity for so many centuries, we should not forget. I don't say we should turn it into a source of anger; but we should not forget. And we cannot forget, for instance, that in the beginning Luther was a great man—after all he dared to defy the Pope and open the era of Reformation. The man who dared so much! But on one point he and the Pope agreed—they hated the Jews.

Another example: Marx and Proudhon were bitter adversaries. Proudhon had written a book called *The Philosophy of Misery,* and Marx countered with a pamphlet called *The Misery of Philosophy*. They had *absolutely* nothing in common, except Marx hated Jews, and he wrote a violent pamphlet against them; and as for Proudhon, he said, "All Jews ought to be driven out of France, except those who marry Christians. Synogogues ought to be liquidated; the businesses purged; Jews are enemies of mankind. They ought to be eliminated by fire." And he stated clearly, "What was done to them in the Middle Ages, by instinct, I would like to do to them out of reasoning." Well, how did Einstein put it?— "It's easier to split the atom than to eliminate prejudice." We have to say it: All these hatreds culminated in the Holocaust. If it were not for the education of some Christian books, in some villages and in some towns, I don't think that the Holocaust could have taken place. There would have been an upsurge of conscience in the killers. And the killers did not have an upsurge of conscience. Forgive me if I say something very cruel. We share our history. The Holocaust affected both the Jews and the Gentiles—including you: it affected humankind. It was a watershed. There was a before and an after. And we all feel it, if we are capable of feeling at all, but not all in the same way. If the victims are my problem, the killers are yours. I know it's a terrible thing to say, but I have to say it. The victims are my problem. What made them into victims? Why did they walk to their death? Why were there these nocturnal processions—so many of them?

Sometimes you are haunted by their silence. You read and reread the documents. In Babi Yar they would to to the mass graves in fives, and they would wait for the killer to kill. And then the next five would come up front, and they didn't even cry. What made them into perfect victims? But the same question can be asked of the killer. What made the killer into a perfect killer? How do you explain? This is the question, of course, that our good friend, Franklin Littell, is asking: How do you explain that so many killers continued to remain Christian? And why hasn't the Pope ever excommunicated them? How do you explain that a person could be Christian and a killer of children? One million children. I have no explanation. It must be asked again—not to oppose one another, but to understand what we can do now, one for another. In those days and nights, freedom and conscience were abused.

Freedom to me means to recognize the unique function of conscience as justification for itself and of itself. Without freedom of conscience, it would be nothing but a pale combination of memory and longing, which would offer display of its only hope to stand up and face history. But still this conscience would be that of a slave or of a prisoner. Without conscience, freedom would mean anarchy or tyranny. Is the killer wrong in claiming the freedom to kill? Is the neutral spectator to be condemned for wanting to choose passivity and indifference? We know that in times of crisis, passivity and indifference and neutrality always favor the killer, not the victim. Freedom and conscience must be organically linked—the one to justify and enrich the other. Conscience must by definition be free, just as freedom by definition ought to be exerted in terms of conscience. How symbolic it is, therefore, that we meet tonight on Yom HaShoah, a day that has been written, to use a Talmudic image, with black fire on white fire, in the pages of our memory, in history!

Whenever Jews rejoice, we are told to set aside one moment, one thought, to remember the destruction of the Temple in Jerusalem. Perhaps we ought to learn something from this practice and enlarge it. Whenever you meet, for whatever purpose, on whatever subject, no matter whence you come and who you are—whenever you meet to discuss things relevant to human faith and destiny, perhaps one instant should be set aside to remember what happened one generation ago, when conscience was mute and freedom was mutilated and distorted. Now we know that those events affected more than the victims alone. They affected all people and our vision of our own futures.

Let me, with your permission, therefore, return to the young boy who had left his childhood and mine in April, 1944, to enter the eternal kingdom of the eternal victim. When he left that kingdom in 1945, his disappointment only began. It was much more difficult afterwards than during. The tragedy of the survivors began after the war, when once again they felt unwanted; they felt outcast. Do you know how many hundreds of thousands of Jews remained in DP camps in 1945 because no one wanted them, afterwards, when everything already was *officially* known? In Israel, Palestine was closed because of the British. America had its quota system. And every refugee had to undergo humiliating interrogations to show that he or she was sane, strong, and whatever. For years, they were still kept there, sometimes in the very same places where they had been before—and that was *afterwards*. Afterwards, the survivor felt guilty for having survived. Afterwards, they tried to understand, and so they could never understand. Afterwards, they realized that their disillusionment has no limit—disillusionment with language. He told the story, but he had to tell less in order to be believed. If he had told the truth, they could not have believed him. So he had to tell less and less. Furthermore, he suddenly realized that no matter what, his faith and that of his ancestors must be tested in fire once again. They are religious Jews, because suddenly they understand that this event could not have been without God, nor could it have been with God. It cannot be conceived on any level.

Do you know what it means for a survivor after the war to live with his or her images, with his or her obsessions? I discovered recently some documents written by special people, the *Sonder-kommando*. One of them says: "I wonder whether one day I shall be able to laugh again." Another one goes further and says: "I wonder whether one day I shall be able to cry again." During the war the Jews didn't cry. They simply couldn't cry. Don't say it was mental anesthesia. They didn't cry simply because they knew if they were to begin to cry, they wouldn't stop. How do you teach a person to cry again? How do you teach a person to play again? How do you teach a person to believe in words again? How do you teach a person to walk in the street and *not* to see an enemy in every passerby? How do you teach a Frenchman who was *expelled* by his own nation and given over to the Germans, although his family had been seven or eight generations in France, to believe in France again and fight for France? How do you teach a child eight years old who came out of the fire to believe in culture, to believe in friendship? How?

I remember a Midrash, a beautiful Midrash that I love, that says, "Why has the exile in Egypt ended prematurely?" It was supposed to last 400 years, as you know, but it lasted only 210 years. There are all kinds of answers, and one answer pleased and moved me. At one point the King of Egypt decided that he wanted to build his pyramids with nothing else but living Jewish children. So he gave an order, and Jewish children were caught and buried in the Pyramids. But we are supposed, according to the Midrash, to have a defender in heaven. We are supposed to have an angel, and this angel even has two names. That means two angels performing the same function. At one time he's called Gabriel, and another time he's called Michael. In this case it was Gabriel. And Gabriel caught a Jewish child in mid-air and brought it *lifnay Bet Din shel ma'alah*—he brought it to the Heavenly Tribunal and gave it to God. and God, said the Midrash, looked at the child, already disfigured, already tormented, already dead. And God couldn't take it. God couldn't take the sight of this child, so God decided then and there, "Enough! I shall redeem My People from bondage." I read the Midrash and I was so proud. I was proud of the angel. And I was proud of God. But then I reread the Midrash against the background of the last event. Whatever we do, I believe, must be justifed in our generation against that background. When I reread it, I was still proud of the angel but less proud of God. I said to myself: "*Rebono shel olam* [Master of the Universe]—one child moved God and a million Jewish children did not." And suddenly it chased all the other words, and only a few words remained—"a million Jewish children," "a million Jewish children."

My friends, how do you teach a Jewish father to have a Jewish child today?

Wherever we turned, we found disillusionment. We found that culture had disappointed us. The worst disillusionment, perhaps, has to do with culture. We were used to suffering. After all, we have a long memory, and our memory was a memory of suffering and responses to suffering. But somehow in our memory suffering was linked to pogroms, to savage mobs, to the Crusades, to the pogroms of Chmelnitsky. But never could we imagine that an enlightened person could also be a killer of Jews. And when we discovered that most of the *Einzatzkommandos* (those who really did the killing, physically, in Eastern Europe; one-and-a-half-million Jews were killed in those conditions—Babi Yar, Minsk,

Kharkov) had college degrees, it hit me. Then we discovered how many had Ph.D.'s—believe it or not! Ph.D.'s in divinity, in medicine (like Mengel), in jurisprudence, in philosophy. And a Ph.D. in Germany was not like a Ph.D. in America. It took many, many years of studying, of absorbing books, of reading, of sharing, of deepening. What happened there? They could study Bach and Beethoven for sixteen years and learn Fichte and Schiller and be killers of children? Hitler at one point was afraid that maybe the killing might affect their mental state. Even he was naive. It did not affect their mental state. Very few showed any signs at all of disturbance—not of conscience, but of nervous disturbances. They simply went on slaughtering.

So, our faith in culture, in education, was shaken. Our faith in democracies was shaken. We thought that the free world didn't know what was happening. How naive we were! We were so convinced that if the world would only know, it would do something. Sometimes hundreds of people would organize and sacrifice themselves in order to enable one messenger to get out and reveal the secret. Now we know that everybody knew. I give my students occasional assignments to go to the newspapers—to the *New York Times,* the *Herald Tribune,* the *New York Post,* the *Philadelphia Inquirer.* Read for yourself, and you will see that everything was known. It was reported in full detail. The press fulfilled its function. The reader did not.

On April 19, 1943, the Warsaw Ghetto began its uprising. Two days later, the entire story was in the *New York Times*—in every detail. Was something done? Was a message sent? Nothing was done. When I came to Babi Yar, I thought that we learned about Babi Yar simply because of Yevtushenko. Then I began my inquiry. Not at all! Three months after Babi Yar, the *New York Times* published the full story, in five columns. The world knew. Do you know that there were radio transmitters in Auschwitz? They transmitted the news to London via the underground. Can you imagine? Why did they do it? To tell the world what was happening. The *Sonder-kommando* managed at one point to "organize" a camera. And the camera was brought in. And they took the pictures. You must realize what it meant there—a camera to take pictures. They *took* the pictures. They smuggled the pictures *out.* The pictures reached London, and therefore Washington and the Vatican. And *nothing* was done.

How do you teach a young Jew today to have faith, therefore, in his or her neighbor? How do you teach a young Jew to have faith in any democratic system, in any liberals, in any people who pretend to be friends of the victims?

The most tragic writings are the writings of the *Sonder-kommando.* They were tragic people, more tragic than the others. They served the god of fire. They were chosen to destroy their brothers and sisters physically. The Germans did the killings, but the burning was done by Jews. And usually they lasted two or three months. And then they in turn were burned. Why did the Germans do that? Because, of course, they wanted to erase the traces of their crimes. They wanted to kill the victim a second time. Well, we heard that even the *Sonder-kommando* had kept diaries. But I confess I didn't believe it. I thought, "It's a myth." And I liked the myth. We are all trying to bear witness, and I found it beautiful that these people still had the strength to write and, therefore, display an act of faith, faith in the reader, faith in their own words, faith in history. But I didn't believe it—until we found pages, a few here and there.

And in reading, I came to know the people, the *Sonder-kommando*. I came to know a certain Zalmen Gradowsky who wrote so many introductions called "A Letter to the Reader." "You who read, you won't believe." And then the "Letter to the person who will find these pages." At one point, he wrote: "I have a request to you. I have a request to you who will discover these pages—a last wish, the wish of a man who knows that his last crossroad is near. We are all doomed. Only the date has not been set as yet. Here is the address of my relatives in Brooklyn. Find them—they will know. They will tell you who I am. They have pictures of myself and my family. Publish them together with my testimony. I wish I could think that somewhere, someone would shed a tear for me and my family—for I can no longer cry. I drown in a sea of blood. Waves follow one another. It is impossible to be alone and cry over our common tragedy. But I am unable to shed tears. And yet, at times, I feel my soul so wounded. At times, I hope that one day, one day I will be able to cry." He gave the address and the name of the person, of his relative. And those who found the documents went right away to Brooklyn—to East Broadway, to find him. Indeed, there was a man who had lived there, the very man. He had died a little while before.

There was a man we knew existed, but we called him the Anonymous Writer because he had no signature. All that we had was initials—J A R A. And we didn't know who he was. But we also knew that one of the *kommando* members was a *dayan,* a rabbinic judge. And he was a beautiful man, according to the other testimonies. He was the only one who somehow was spared the work. His colleagues permitted him not to engage in the work. He did not burn the corpses. He was a beautiful man—you sense it from the others. His name was Yehuda Leib Langfoos. Now a Jewish historian, Professor Mark, who died a couple of years ago in Warsaw, deciphered the initials: they meant "Yehuda Aria Regel Arucha," which means "Yehuda Leib Langfoos"! The Anonymous Author suddenly received his identity. I shall read to you what he writes: "I wish that all my descriptions and notes buried once upon a time and signed J A R A be collected." And now listen to the austerity and the dryness of his writing:

> They can be found in various boxes and jars under the courtyard of Crematorium 2, two other comprehensive reports, one of them entitled "The Deportation," which is inside the grave full of bones near Crematorium 1, and a description entitled "Auschwitz," which is under the levelled bones on the southwestern side of the same courtyeard. Later, I rewrote and supplemented it and buried the part among the ashes on the site of Crematorium 2. I wish that all these writings be published together under the title, "In the Nightmare of Murder." We are now going to the zone. We have one hundred and seventy men, the last. We know that we are being led to die.

If ever a person comes close to despair—total, black, irrevocable despair—it is when one reads these documents. And I confess that I find it very hard to read. But I remembered it was Yom HaShoah. And I feel compelled to observe the date in reading. And I said to myself that if he, Reb Leib Langfoos, had the strength to write these pages, surely we must find the courage to read them. These are strange documents. He describes the last phase of the agony; for instance, he describes the people during the last moments in the chambers. Five minutes or three minutes before. Two hundred young Hungarian Jews being beaten savagely before being shot into the chambers; he describes it. He describes emaciated, hungry Jews from Poland, who begged the *Sonder-kommando* to give them bread before being killed. He describes a five-year-old girl undressing her one year-old brother, whispering to him, "Don't be afraid. It won't hurt." He describes Jews from Holland, from Poland, Jews from all over Europe—how they met in the chambers. He describes one young woman who began to make a speech. And the speech: "We shall not really die here. The history of our people will remember us and make us immortal." Listen: I quote:

> This happened to us the end of summer of 1943. A transport of Jews arrived from Tarnov. They wanted to know where they were being taken. They were told: to die. They were already undressed. They looked grave and silent. Then they began to recite the *vidduy*, the last confession before death. Then a certain young Jew, naked, stood up on a bench and asked everybody's attention, and he said: "We are not going to die." And they believed him.

Reb Leib Langfoos describes, and I quote again:

> Passover, 1944. A transport of important Jews arrived from Vittel, France—among them Reb Moishe Freedman of Bayonne, a famous rabbi. He undressed together with the others. Suddenly, he approached an S. S. Obersturmführer, seized him by the lapel of his uniform, and spoke up: "You common, cruel murderers. Do not think that you will exterminate the Jewish people. The Jewish people will live forever, while you murderers will disappear from the world's arena. The Day of Reckoning is near. Our blood will cry for retribution." He spoke, and nobody interrupted him. Then he cried out: *"Shema Yisroel,"* and all the others repeated with him, *"Shema Yisroel* [Listen, O Israel]." And something took hold of all those present. This was an extraordinary, sublime moment—a moment not to be equalled in the lives of men.

Something happened then. Something was unleashed then in history. Hate. Anger, Indifference. Self-destruction. Something happened. And what happens today is nothing but a result. Suffering today is directly and organically linked to that event. Today, we have the impression sometimes that we are witnessing the end of history, the end of times, the apocalypse. In our tradition, there are certain predictions about the apocalypse. And the predictions are beautiful—Hasidic predictions, Midrashic predictions. Women will dominate men. Children will behave like old teachers. Teachers will be terrorized by their pupils. Cold summers and hot winters. People will lose the connection between the parable and its meaning. Words will be in quest of meaning, and meaning will be in search of words. Chaos will be everywhere. And today some of these predictions have come true. Chaos everywhere. We have conquered space and left the streets to muggers. We are obsessed with communication; and yet, like the primitive man who cares, we deal with images. We are about to discover the origins of life— and to achieve the extermination of all life. We don't know where we are going, but we are going there very fast. As Alexander the Great said: "We have conquered everything and possessed nothing."

In politics it's worse—tragic or comical, but not serious. You no longer know who belongs where—in the White House or in prison. We almost had a government not in exile, but in jail. Nixon is popular in China, Ford in Russia. Political definitions and affiliations appear to have been deranged. Conservatives advocate internationalization, while liberals preach isolationism. Politics used to be public and sex private. Now it's the opposite. Many predictions did, indeed, come true. In those days, said my favorite Hasidic master, Rabbi Nachman of Bratzlav: "Fools will be ashamed of their foolishness and imbeciles of their stupidity." This has not happened yet. But, clearly, these are signs to be recorded. Could it really be that we are witnessing the ultimate decline and disintegration of humankind? I'm afraid it is. And I'll tell you why. The world has not yet been punished for what it did to my people. Is this going to be the punishment? Does it take a generation for the punishment to catch up with the crime? Is the absolute weapon to be a result of the Final Solution? I hope not. But I'm afraid. For we know that history has at times entered into madness. It happened more than once that peoples awoke one morning and began slaughtering one another in sheer madness. During the Crusades, 100,000 *children* rose one day and began marching toward Jerusalem to free Jerusalem and the holy places. It was madness.

One generation ago, perhaps humankind was caught in the whirling wind of murderous insanity. Are these winds to blow again? Suppose Idi Amin gets hold of a nuclear missile. Suppose Khadaffi manages to buy a nuclear weapon. I'm afraid not only for the Jewish people; I'm afraid for humankind. As for us Jews, what else can humankind do to us that it hasn't done already? People expelled from society, robbed of our fortunes, and reduced to objects. We were exposed to humiliation, persecution, torture, and annihilation. We were surrounded by walls of fire and fear and pushed to the limits of despair and beyond. Our children were massacred and our sanctuaries profaned, our sages driven to madness and silence. And yet, we took the ruins and we built new beginnings. We took memories and erected new houses of study. As much as humankind has tried to have us give up on its humanity, we go on living it—or at least, we go on working for it. If we chose one generation ago not to turn our back on humanity and society—and our Christian friends—it has a meaning: that humankind is *not* to give up when our fate is at stake. We knew the truth then, and we know it now. In times of need, we are alone or almost alone. We have friends—but they are few. And we are grateful to them. But they are so few! The question we faced then was what to do with our knowledge, what to do with our suffering. This is still the question. What is the answer? I don't know the answer. Perhaps there is none. What we do know is that we shall not imitate the enemy. We shall not attempt to dehumanize people. Quite the contrary, we shall forever attempt to make them more human. For that is the message entrusted to God by this people—not to Judaize humankind, but to make it more human.

Let me read in conclusion a story which is not mine. I love stories. This story is from a book called *Shearith Yehuda,* a book of martyrology in the Middle Ages.

> And it came to pass that somewhere in Spain, in the sixteenth century, a Jewish community was uprooted and sent into exile. It boarded a ship and was then stranded somewhere in Belgium. Among the refugees there was a family of four—a man, his wife, and their two small children. They were hungry and thirsty. So they began to walk, hoping to find a city, a village, a hiding place. They found none. Still they kept on walking and hoping, while hunger and thirst became unbearable. One night they felt too tired to continue, and they decided to rest. They were four as they lay down, but only three awoke—the father and his two small children. They buried the mother and said Kaddish and continued to march from nowhere to nowhere. Then they had to rest again. They were three as they lay down. Only two awoke— the father and one child. They buried the other and said Kaddish. Then they were two as they lay down. Only the father awoke. So he took his dead child in his arms and spoke to God: "Master of the Universe, their mother died of hunger and I said Kaddish. His brother died of hunger. I still said Kaddish. Now he died of hunger, and I know what your desire is. You want to push me, to force me to stop saying Kaddish, to force me to stop believing in you, to stop longing for your Presence. Well, God of Israel, I am telling you now—you will not succeed!"

History has for 2000 years pushed us into such a test, trying to force us to give up faith—faith in God and faith in humankind. And we shall forever, I hope, continue to say "No!" No one will ever succeed—not in this area, which is essential to our people's memory and to our people's understanding of itself.

CONTEMPORARY ISSUES OF CHURCH-STATE RELATIONS

Marc H. Tanenbaum

At the outset, I want to express my deepest personal appreciation to the Christian and Jewish sponsors of this Bicentennial Conference on Religious Liberty. This is not just another conference. It is a work of redemption, an act of moral reparation, in the life of our nation and of all of our people.

The Bicentennial was proclaimed by the last president of the United States as an opportunity to celebrate the remarkable achievement of 200 years of the American experiment in democratic freedom and liberty. Millions of Americans, myself included, were thus led to believe (obviously naively) that the Bicentennial might become an occasion for mature, thoughtful, systematic examination of the values, ideals, and historic forces which have made America the oldest, and in many ways still the greatest, constitutional democracy on earth. We thought too that the Bicentennial observances would enable us to probe deeply the reasons for the current "malaise of our civilization" (Robert Heilbroner) in the wake of Watergate, Vietnam, and the revelations of widespread moral corruption on almost every level of our society. Such a national spiritual and intellectual "retreat" would in fact have been the most appropriate observance in keeping with the highest qualities of our national character. Indeed, that kind of disciplined reflection and self-examination of who we are, where we are, how we get this way, and where we go from here would have constituted a much-needed therapeutic and rehabilitative service of potential hope and moral encouragement to the American people, the American society, the American government, and to the world community at large as we embark together on our common journey into the Third Century of this murky nuclear-space age.

With rare exception, Bicentennial observances thus far have taken the "low road" in American life. The "exceptions," it deserves to be said, are to be found mostly in the programs of the Catholic, Protestant, and Jewish agencies. For the vast majority of Americans, and non-Americans visitors and tourists, the Bicentennial has become an experience glutted with red-white-and-blue gadgets and trinkets, ties, blouses, beer glasses, ball point pens, liberty bells, even toilet seats—in sum, the Bicentennial observance of 200 years of revolutionary independence and liberties has become shockingly trivialized and mocked by advertising hucksterism and commercial exploitation and rip-offs.

That is one of the reasons why this Bicentennial Conference on Religious Liberty assumes, in my judgment, more than conventional significance. We are afforded not only an opportunity, but are faced with the moral obligation, to try

Rabbi Marc H. Tanenbaum is National Interreligious Affairs Director of the American Jewish Committee in New York, NY.

to place the Bicentennial into a perspective that gives insight into its authentic spiritual, cultural, and political dimensions—and their meanings for us today, and possibly tomorrow. And if we do our work well here and elsewhere throughout the country during the months ahead, we may yet be able to succeed in salvaging something of the potential high meanings and creativity implicit in our 200th birthday from the morass of materialism and shockiness, which are but the latest evidences of the hedonism, consumptionism, and paganism that dominate our national value system.[1]

In considering our subject of "Contemporary Issues of Church-State Relations," it would be helpful to keep in mind that the very founding of the American Republic took its primary impetus from a determined search by our Puritan forebears for religious liberty. In many ways American history has been one long adventure in the pursuit of a more adequate and viable set of relationships between church and state, between religion and society, than had existed anywhere else, or anytime before the American experiment was launched. Because so much of the character of American society is staked out on the ways in which we cope with and resolve church-state issues, it is increasingly understandable why debate over these issues continuously evokes such high emotion on the part of Protestants, Catholics, Jews, secular humanists, and others. But precisely because religious liberty was central in the motivations for the founding of America, and also because freedom of conscience is the parent liberty from which derives all our other liberties[2]—free speech, freedom of assembly, the right to privacy—the obligation is all the greater to negotiate our respective communal differences, when they occur, with disciplined restraint in speech and action, with the same respect for the conscience of the other that one seeks for oneself, and with the avoidance of the imputation of bad faith or prejudice which in itself can become an act of prejudice. In short, American democracy is a relatively brief interlude in the history of human freedom, and the experience with genuine religious liberty for all Americans on the level of authentic equality in our pluralistic society is an even briefer chapter. As we have learned from the frightening Watergate nightmare, constitutional democracy with all its superior virtues is still a fragile human invention. Democratic life can and will survive only through the tender, loving care and the creative sympathies, reconciling skills, constructive negotiations of leaders of the state, and most especially interreligious leaders. The resolution of differences on the level of rhetorical street brawls, name-calling, and verbal violence in speech and print will only

---

[1]See Daniel J. Boorstin, *Democracy and Its Discontents* (New York: Random House, 1974), on the role of advertising as the central value-producing agency of our society.

[2]"In the American system, religious freedom is the progenitor of practically all other freedoms. . . . Consider freedom of speech. Today it is generally thought of in terms of political speech; the right to attack the government and condemn its policies. . . . Historically, however, freedom of political speech came late on the scene; it came after freedom of religious speech had been won. The struggle for freedom of speech in England from which we inherited our tradition, was initially a struggle for freedom to speak religiously" (Leo Pfeffer, *Freedom and Separation: America's Contribution to Civilization*).

shock the delicate and intricate system called American pluralism, and if continued indefinitely, could well hammer it to its knees, a victim of group conflict, false pride, and recklessness.

The critical need for these qualities of living mutual respect and accomodation in the face of differences as well as the wreckage that results to social and political systems and to human lives when such interreligious caring and diplomacy are absent are seen all around us—Ireland, Cyprus, Lebanon, India-Pakistan-Bangladesh, Israel-Palestinians, Uganda, Chile, South Africa; the list is tragically long and depressing. In virtually each one of the communal conflicts that now pockmark every single continent of our inhabited globe, religious-sectarian claims are inextricably mixed with economic, social, and political claims. But it is the religious dynamic with its invariable assertion of absolute truth, ultimate and exclusive rights—and in some pre-ecumenical cases, monopolies of salvation—that impart to what might be otherwise conventional group conflicts, that normally would yield to rational negotiation and compromise of differences, an overlay of heightened emotionalism and ideological fanaticism whose outcome predictably becomes the daily massacres and bombthrowings in the streets of Beirut, the pubs and neighborhoods of Northern Ireland, and the supermarkets and tourist buses of Jerusalem. And when you add to that lethal chemistry of religion and politics the insane proliferation of arms and nuclear weaponry that is contaminating every corner of the world community, then you know for a certainty that all of us have a God-bidden responsibility to help find a better way for ourselves and for the rest of the human family of resolving differences, especially when they are real and painful grievances.

Our heritage of religious liberty is complex and ambiguous. While economic and political factors played a significant role in the motivations that led to the great Puritan exodus of 1629 from England to America, there can be no doubt that the chief motive for the founding of the Massachusetts Bay Colony was religious.[3]

Puritanism was essentially and primarily a religious movement; attempts to prove it to have been a mask for politics or money-making are false as well as unhistorical. In the broadest sense, Puritanism was a passion for righteousness, the desire to know and do God's will. Led by country squire John Winthrop and others, the group believed that the only safeguard against the forces of evil—represented in their thinking by King Charles I and his arbitrary and oppressive rule, and the Church of England and its insistence on conformity—lay in establishing a society consisting of a confederation of congregations buttressed by a sympathetic government. This alone, they thought, would cleanse the churches of unworthy ministers and immoral communicants, remodel worship upon the

---

[3]See T. J. Wertenbaker, *The Puritan Oligarchy: The Founding of American Civilization* (New York: Grosset and Dunlap, 1947); and Perry Miller, *Orthodoxy in Massachusetts, 1630–1650* (Cambridge: Harvard University Press, 1933).

biblical model and dethrone bishops. Since this seemed impossible of accomplishment in England, they proposed to bring it about in distant America by founding there a Wilderness Zion. ''We came hither because we would have our posterity settled under the pure and full dispensations of the gospel, defended by rulers that should be of ourselves,'' wrote Cotton Mather in his *Magnalia*.

These Puritans had a definite mission—to establish a community based on the Hebrew Commonwealth of the Bible rather than a mere colony. New England, to them, was a New Canaan which the Almighty had set apart for an experiment in Christian living. They felt, as John Winthrop remarked on the way over, that they were ''a city upon a hill,'' ''with the eyes of all the people'' upon them, an example to prove that it was possible to lead the New Testament life, yet make a living.

One of their first acts upon reaching the site of their new homes was to form themselves into a church by entering into a solemn Covenant with God. For the Covenant, the congregations claimed direct authority from the Bible and direct precedent in the history of Israel. ''The covenant of grace is the very same now that it was under the Mosaical dispensation,'' stated William Brattle; ''The administration differs but the covenant is the same.'' Urian Oakes in his election sermon of 1673 emphasized God's covenant with the Children of Israel and how they were led into the land of promise (*New England Pleaded With*). The Covenant gave to each congregation an independence which would have been impossible had it been constituted by any superior human authority. Thus the Congregational Church in New England happened to be organized on a democratic basis, not because the Puritans were in love with democracy, but because leaders such as John Cotton and Thomas Hooker insisted that the First Church of Boston and the First Church of Hartford copy the exact organization of the First Church of Corinth and the First Church of Philippi, about which they knew very little since the apostles and evangelists did not say much about them.

Congregationalism, because of its emphasis upon localism, would have been hopelessly weak had it not had the full support of civil authorities. Since the failure of the Puritans to gain such support in England was one of the major reasons for the migration, it was natural that in their new commonwealth they would take measures to tie the government with the church.

The relationship of church and state is set forth in some detail in the *Platform of Church Discipline*. ''It is the duty of the magistrate to take care of matters of religion. . . . The end of the magistrate's office is not only the quiet and peaceable life of the subject in matters of righteousness and honesty, but also in matters of godliness, yea, of all godliness. Moses, Joshua, David, Solomon, Asa, Jehosophat, Hezekiah, Josiah are much commended by the Holy Ghost for the putting forth of their authority in matters of religion. On the contrary such kings as have been failing this way are frequently taxed and reproved by the Lord.''

It was the duty of the magistrate to restrain and punish ''idolatry, blasphemy, heresy, venting corrupt and pernicious opinions that destroy the foundation, open contempt of the word preached, profanation of the Lord's Day, disturbing the peaceable administration and exercize of the worship and holy things of God and the like.''

"Church government stands in no opposition to civil government of commonwealths, . . . the contrary is most true that they may both stand together and flourish, the one being helpful unto the other in their distinct and due administrations."

As for religious toleration, the Puritans sought religious freedom for themselves but did not believe in religious toleration for others. '' 'Tis Satan's policy to plead for an indefinite and boundless toleration,'' declared Thomas Shepard, while Urian Oakes denounced freedom to worship as one chose as "the first born of all abominations." After their arrival in New England they insisted upon orthodoxy, and as early as 1631 the General Court passed a law declaring that "to the end the body of the Commons may be preserved of honest and good men . . . no man shall be admitted to the freedom of this body politic but such as are members of some of the Churches." Before the end of the century the freemen, who alone could vote for governor, deputies, and magistrates had become a minority in every town, while those who were not members of churches ("the unsanctified"), but who were in sympathy with the established order, constituted a majority. Those whose religious views differed from the Puritan fathers could suffer imprisonment, whipping, and even hanging.

The religious zeal of the first settlers, Wertenbaker writes,[4] was less apparent in the second and third generations; the ministers who had wielded powerful political as well as moral influence commanded less respect and love; the charter upon which such hopes had been based had been annulled; the unity of church and state in the towns had been disrupted; despite all the efforts to exclude them, strangers had come in who were out of sympathy with the church and government; there were loud demands for the extension of the franchise; in Boston the organization of the Anglican congregation of King's Chapel bore testimony to the break which had been made in the wall of orthodoxy. Before the end of the seventeenth century, the experiment of a Bible commonwealth had definitely failed. The ideals of the founders, however, still exercized a powerful influence upon the minds and hearts of the people—not just in New England, but as well in other parts of the thirteen colonies.

Shortly before independence in 1776, Dr. Martin Marty observes in his study, *The Righteous Empire*,[5] the Americans were still living off a 1,400-year-old charter. The charter went back to the Emperor Constantine, in the fourth century; its theoretical base had been provided by St. Augustine. According to this reading, religion was established by law. Establishment meant official favor and status. The government encouraged one religion and discouraged or persecuted all others. The civil authorities saw to it that somehow there would be fiscal

---

[4]Wertenbaker, *Puritan Oligarchy*, p. 76.
[5](New York: Dial Press, 1970).

support for religious institutions. In turn, the civil powers found that their rule was then blessed by religious authorities. They were able to claim rule "by divine right." In such a combination, Dr. Marty adds, it tended to prevail almost everywhere that Christians were present in any numbers for 1,400 years—the dissenters were either driven out or hemmed in.

After 1776, and certainly after 1789, it was clear that the two-party system of establishment *versus* dissent within the churches was doomed. Here were thirteen small "nations" becoming one out of many. Nine of them recognized official establishments of religion. All of them had a significant number of drop-outs and dissenters. No single church body was strong enough to prevail in the new United States. What some called multiple establishment, official support of several faiths, was soon seen to be unworkable. Only one choice remained. The churches had to be cut off legally and fiscally from support by civil authorities, and many in the churches wanted to prevent the government from disturbing them. The result was the drawing of what James Madison, a committed Presbyterian, called "a line of separation between the rights of religion and the Civil authority."

Madison's text became the basis of the Virginia Declaration of Rights that was a decisive response to the struggle of the Presbyterian and Baptist sects who sought relief from the oppressions they suffered under the Anglican Establishment and the injustices of the Act of Toleration. Before 1776, the Anglican Church was supported by taxation, and enjoyed a monopoly of performing marriages in all southern colonies and in parts of New York. It was disestablished in New York, Maryland, and the Carolinas, and complete religious liberty was adopted in those states during the war. In Virginia, however, it took a ten-year contest, which Jefferson called the severest of his life, to separate church from state. Finally the *Virginia Statute of Religious Liberty,* drafted by Jefferson, passed the Assembly on January 16, 1786. The exercise of religion, it declares, is a "natural right" which has been infringed by "the impious presumption of legislators and rulers" to set up their "own modes of thinking as the only true and infallible," and "to compel a man to furnish contributions of money for the propagation of opinions which he disbelieves," which "is sinful and tyrannical." The statute roundly declares, "No man shall be compelled to frequent or support any religious worship, place or ministry whatsoever." It even warns later assemblies that any attempt on their part to tamper with this law "will be an infringement of natural right." That action formally launched the present epoch of American church-state relations.

As one reflects on that background of the struggle to establish religious liberty in America during the past 200 years, a number of convictions emerge:

1) Far too many Americans, I believe, take for granted the monumental achievement of religious liberty which is the fruit of the First Amendment of our Constitution. Sanford H. Cobb, an expert on the history of religious liberty, claimed that the American pattern of religious freedom was "the most striking contribution of America to the science of government." Indeed, it is that, but for religious people the separation of church and state has also assured the possibility

of the freest expression of the human conscience, described by John Locke in these words:

> Civil power, right, and dominion . . . neither can nor ought in any manner to be extended to the salvation of souls, or can any such power be vested in the magistrate by the consent of the people . . . for no man can, if he would, conform his faith to the dictates of another. All the life and power of true religion consists in the inward and full persuasion of the mind . . . It is one thing to persuade, another to command; one thing to press with arguments, another with penalties. . . . The church itself is a thing absolutely separate and distinct from the commonwealth . . .

If the memories of the persecutions of the Protestant sectarians and the Catholic and Jewish immigrants under the established churches of America's colonies have grown too dim in our recollection, certainly the struggles today for the rights of freedom of conscience on the part of Christians and Jews in the Soviet Union, Poland, Pakistan, Libya, Uganda, and elsewhere ought to strengthen our appreciation of this precious human right and spiritual value.

2) America is the one nation on earth that has not witnessed religious wars. There have been persecutions, harrassments, prejudice, and intimidations. More tragically, there have been massacres of native Americans and enslavement of millions of our black brothers and sisters. But in none of these brutalities—certainly during the past 100 years—has religious ideology, the organized desire to impose one's religious views upon another by force and through the use of civic power, been salient. Even less so has there been a resort to the use of physical force or coercion in relations between the religious groups of our country. Religious liberty has made the difference. The imposition of constitutional limits on the power of government to interfere with religious conviction and on religious groups to interfere with government or to use government as an agency to dominate society has made the difference. All of us who care about the continued preservation of civic peace have a stake in preserving those constitutional principles which have made America a haven of interreligious civility.

3) The disestablishment of the "Evangelical Empire" which dominated America during the first 100 years of our history, and the emergence of voluntarism as the means of identification with religious communities has resulted in an unparalleled growth and vitality in religious life in America today. During the colonial period of our history when churches were established by states, no more than seven percent of our population was identified with religious institutions. Today some sixty-five percent of the American people identify themselves with the Catholic, Protestant, Evangelical, Greek Orthodox, and Jewish bodies. Religious vitality and religious commitment have flourished in freedom.

4) Pluralism and dialogue have resulted in an entire new culture of interreligious relationships characterized increasingly by mutual respect and mutual acceptance. But pluralism and dialogue also obligate all of us to a new set of reciprocal responsibilities. Dialogue, Martin Buber has written, is intended not to

undermine the "other," the partner in the dialogue, but is intended to confirm the other in the fulness of his or her selfhood. Each (religious) self is defined by a group of interests. That implies that to understand one's partner one must reach out to hear and to listen to those matters which are of supreme importance to another. To do less than that is to reduce dialogue to flirtation, and flirtation has been aptly defined as paying *attention* without any *intention*.

Put another way, each one of us—Catholic, Protestant, and Jew; man and woman; black, red, brown, and white—comes to the dialogue table with a particular agenda. Jews come to the dialogue bearing on their hearts their deepest concerns about the welfare and security of their brothers and sisters in need—and today these are the security and survival of our three million brothers and sisters in Israel; the defense of the human rights of three million Soviet Jews and of Jews in Arab countries; and combatting a resurgent, vicious Anti-semitism and verbal violence against Jews and Judaism that is microphoned to the world from the forums of the United Nations by petrodollar-financed Arab governments, the Soviet Union, and some third-world nations in the keep of Arab sheiks. These have been among the primary issues that have genuinely hurt the Jewish people. The sympathetic understanding, response, and identification on the part of millions of American, European, Latin American, and even a goodly number of third-world Christian leaders with Jews in this period of duress has been one of the most heartening developments in recent decades, and I take this occasion to express my deepest personal and professional gratitude for those acts of friendship when they counted. From a Jewish point of view, that outpouring of understanding would not have been possible without the ongoing communication that has been taking place especially during the past decade between Catholics, Protestants, Evangelicals, Greek Orthodox, black churches and Jews in virtually every major city in the United States, and elsewhere in the world. The Jewish community is able to give strong testimony out of these experiences that the dialogue does work when people open up their true feelings and share their fears and hopes with brothers and sisters who care.

But Protestants, Evangelicals, Catholics, Greek Orthodox, blacks, American Indians, Hispanics, and ethnics also have particular agendas, issues that hurt, aspirations that need assistance and collaboration in order to be realized, and above all, they have the same need as do Jews for a sympathetic hearing from someone who genuinely cares about their fate and welfare.

Elsewhere I have written about each of the agendas of the several religious, racial, and ethnic groups I have just referred to. Here I want to address myself to the Catholic agenda, insofar as it bears on our subject of "Current Issues in Church-State Relations." It is my personal feeling that the Catholic community has cause for real grievance against the Protestant and Jewish communities. Catholics themselves, however, are not exempt from responsibility for helping create the very conditions that some Catholic leaders deplore. Let me explain what I mean. The priority issues on the Catholic agenda, as I read them, are abortion and birth control (the right-to-life issues), aid to parochial schools, and such public morality concerns as pornography and censorship. If one studies carefully the programs and actions of the United States Catholic Conference, it is abundantly clear that Catholic leadership is also vitally concerned about a whole range of other serious domestic and international issues which they share with Protestants, Jews, and others.

But abortion, the right-to-life issues, and aid to parochial schools have emerged as the focal issues on the Catholic moral and political agenda; they have in fact been projected to the nation as the Catholic equivalent to what Israel and Soviet Jewry mean to American Jews. The issues, of course, are not the same—the right-to-life issues are profoundly moral theological questions which presuppose a specific theological and doctrinal commitment; Israel and Soviet Jewry are far more human rights and national self-determination issues which do not require theological assent as preconditions for support.

For years, Catholic leadership has publicly advocated the abortion and other right-to-life issues as "Catholic" issues. These have become rallying points involving Catholic identity and in effect the mobilization of Catholic peoplehood. The effect of that formulation of issues is that if they are perceived in the popular mind as "Catholic issues" they need not necessarily be "Protestant" or "Jewish" or "American" issues. The effort to win support for the "Catholic issue" of abortion through the means of civic legislation inevitably will meet with resistance from many non-Catholics and regrettable hostility from others.

When you add to that chemistry the manner in which some right-to-life groups have in their advertising, posters, and press releases literally written a scenario in which the world consists of "angels" (pro-right-to-lifers) and "demons" (anti's), you have assured the alienation of most of the American people from your cause. (Some of the posters showing a foetus with a dagger plunged through its heart, and the inscription, "Don't Join the Murderers," verge, I must confess, on pornography.)

The underlying pathos of this situation is that the reverence-for-life issue is not only a Catholic issue. It is profoundly an issue of biblical morality. And if you scan the world scene today in terms of the growing waves of massacres, tortures, dying by starvation, terrorism, the preservation of human life in all its stages—from womb to tomb—is an overwhelming moral, humanitarian issue that should appeal to the conscience and concern of the most hard-bitten secularist.

And so the first requirement of interreligious leadership, may I suggest, is to de-sectarianize the right-to-life issues and find creative ways to engage thoughtful, caring Americans of all religious traditions in a national dialogue in which I am confident a great many will recognize the moral stake they have in this cause whose ultimate end must be a movement to humanize the human condition—while there is still time.

This is not to say that all Protestants and all Jews must accept unequivocally the Catholic doctrinal position on abortion, birth control, euthanasia, and related issues. But this is an appeal to be far more honest with each other about right-to-life questions than we have been thus far. There is in fact a more extensive pluralism of positions within each of our communities than our official spokespersons are generally prepared to acknowledge. It is not entirely fair nor accurate to suggest to our Catholic friends and neighbors that the organized Jewish community favors legalized abortion on demand, any more than it is accurate to state that the overwhelming majority of the Catholic people are 100% against abortion and birth control. In point of fact, there is a sizeable segment of the Jewish people in our Orthodox and traditional Jewish communities whose views toward abortion, birth control, euthanasia, and related issues are practically identical with those of the Catholic church; and historically, indeed, they precede the Catholic position by centuries. Opportunities ought to be provided in Jewish national life for that position, which is based on firm biblical and rabbinic theology, to get a fair and representative hearing in the organized national Jewish structures. Opportunities should also become possible for coalitions to be formed between those in the Catholic, Protestant, and Jewish communities who share common moral theological commitments to affirm them in the national arena and to get as fair a hearing as do the other prevailing options. A reasoned, serious national dialogue, not a polemic from behind barricades, can only help raise public sensitivity and consciousness about the sanctity of human life, a result in whose benefits all of us have a stake.

Similarly, with regard to aid to parochial schools. In an article appearing in the *Journal of Church and State* (Spring, 1973) by the Baptist scholar, Dr. James E. Wood, Sr., entitled, "The Impermissibility of Public Funds and Parochial Schools," a review is given of the recent Supreme Court decisions (June 25, 1973, *Committee for Public Education v. Nyquist, Levitt v. Committee for Public Education, Sloan v. Lemon*) which have struck down five programs of public assistance to church schools as unconstitutional. Dr. Woods asserts that "the significance of these decisions is that they constitute but one of two instances when the Supreme Court of the United States has rendered decisions on the question of public funds to parochial schools, and they mark the virtual elimination of all presently existing parochial school aid plans for public funds." The article adds that "at least some Catholic leaders and educators still hold out the view of some future plan(s) of public aid to parochial schools. Such persons are quick to point out that the Court has not outlawed all forms of public assistance to parochial schools. They take comfort in what they euphemistically call 'constitutional' forms of government aid to parochial schools, such as real estate tax exemption, bus transportation, health services, textbooks, and school lunch programs." He also notes that proposals are afoot for advocacy of federal- and state-supported education vouchers, and for auxiliary services.

Finally, Dr. Wood notes that Msgr. William Novicky, Superintendent of the Cleveland diocesan schools, declared that he would urge his board to do away with tuition and rely instead on donations to churches, which are tax deductible. Here one is reminded of the tax research study done several years ago by William E. Brown for the volume *Can Catholic Schools Survive?* coauthored with Andrew Greeley. From his research Brown concluded that, contrary to popular opinion, direct state subsidy of twenty percent in place of the present policy of granting tax deductions for contributions to church schools would be financially disadvantageous to the Catholic community.

For both historic and religious reasons which I have tried to outline earlier in this article, I am firmly committed to the principle of the separation of church and state and feel with Justice Powell that the First Amendment and all that it has meant in sustaining religious liberty is "regarded from the beginning as among the most cherished features of our constitutional system." I am equally committed to the support of both the right and the role of church schools, all religiously-related schools, in our free society. Indeed, I am proud of the fact that a president of the American Jewish Committee, Justice Louis Marshall, played a decisive role in the 1928 Court case of *Pierce v. Society of Sisters,* that resulted in the landmark decision that supported the right of Catholic and all other parents to educate their children in parochial schools.

All that has to do with law, with history, and I suppose also the subjective fact that I am a product of the Jewish parochial system to which I owe much of what I am and what I do today. But I am not happy with that stance which for me personally is an inadequate response to the human issues that are raised by the aid-to-parochial-school issues. It bothers me terribly that many good Catholic people, friends and neighbors and parents of children who are friends of my children, feel they are being dealt with unfairly by American society. Many of the Catholic parents I know are middle class people with limited financial resources who are having a difficult time making ends meet in a period of inflation. All of them pay taxes which go to support the public education system, and they carry the additional burden of having to pay added tuition for their parochial schools. There is a sense of having to bear "taxation without representation," and I know from personal experience that the anger and resentment of Catholic parents are real and widespread.

From an ecumenical and interreligious perspective, and for me personally, it is a failure of moral responsibility to be indifferent to these honest feelings of Catholic parents, and simply to continue to say no to them by engaging only in support of amicus briefs that result in denial of any financial relief to these hard-pressed people. For some time now, a number of us at the American Jewish Committee have felt that the time is long past due to take a different stance, namely, that of turning to find what we can do positively to aid our Catholic neighbors and fellow citizens. Under the leadership of Dr. Murray Friedman, AJC director of our Pennsylvania region, the Philadelphia chapter of AJC has taken a position of support of the auxiliary services bill of Pennsylvania. In turn, the national domestic affairs commission of AJC has recently adopted a resolution in support of auxiliary services.[6]

---

[6]" . . . However, benefits directly to the child, such as lunches and medical and dental services should be available to all children at public expense, regardless of the school they attend, provided

Recently, I arranged a meeting with Father Paul Reinert, Chancellor of St. Louis University, to explore how we might collaborate in promoting increased support for church-related higher education. We have determined to join with Catholic and Protestant educators in a coalition in Washington in order to help promote increased federal grants to higher education—private and public.

That action is consistent with a resolution on higher education that the AJC adopted in May, 1965, that declared, in part:

> We endorse the purposes and objectives set forth in the proposed Higher Education Act of 1965 now pending in the 89th Congress, first session, and in particular the comprehensive approach to the needs of higher education today inherent in this proposed legislation.[7]

It is encouraging to read in these last few days in the 1976 report of the National Catholic Education Association on "Catholic Schools in America," and in Father Greeley's latest study that a stabilizing trend has developed with Catholic schools and that the commitment of Catholic parents to their school system remains high. It is a matter for Catholic educators to determine what measures are required to reduce their costs of running their schools and to respond to parental requests for increasing the quality of education offered. But that does not absolve any of us outside of the Catholic community from being concerned for the quality of education and the health and welfare that affects the lives of fifteen million children who happen to be Catholic.

"The salvation of mankind," Alexander Solshenitzyn reminds us in a prophetic utterance, "will depend on everyone becoming concerned about the welfare of everybody everywhere."

---

there is public supervision and control of such programs, while others, educationally diagnostic and remedial in nature, such as guidance, counseling, testing and services for the improvement of the educationally disadvantaged, where offered public school students, may also be made available to all children at public expense, regardless of the school they attend, provided however that such programs shall be administered by public agencies and shall be in public facilities and do not preclude intermingling of public and private school students where feasible."

[7]It continues: "We strongly disapprove, however, of the failure of this federal legislation to provide adequate safeguards against the possible violations of the Constitutional separation of Church and State. We therefore urgently recommend that this legislation be amended to include the following: (1) The usual form of separability provision so that any declaration of unconstitutionality with respect to any provosion of this Act would not automatically invalidate the entire Act. (2) A provision enabling any citizen to secure a prompt judicial ruling as to the constitutionality of any provision with adequate safeguards against a multiplicity of suits. (3) A prohibition against any religiously controlled or operated institution directly or indirectly acquiring new property or expanding existing property unless the same be used for exclusively non-religious purposes. (4) Prohibition against any funds appropriated under any title of this Act being utilized for any religious purpose whatever, whether direct or indirect."

RELIGIOUS LIBERTY IN EDUCATION

William B. Ball

I

One of the famous qualities of Americans in their enthusiasm. Less noticed, perhaps, is the fact that sometimes our enthusiasms for things continue, while the things themselves have become illusions. At Bicentennial time we are enthusing about American things which are both real and good, or becoming so—such as freedom from racial discrimination. But we also continue to enthuse about some things which are not real at all or, being not good now, are threatening to become worse. Perhaps the word "enthusiasm" is precisely *not* the word to use. Enthusiastic expression—the repeating of platitudes, the rote declaring of high purposes, the repeated boasting of achievements—may indeed mask unpleasant truths. Frantic claims of glory may hide poverty of substance. Militancy of insistence may reveal, not an innocent joy, but a grimly deliberate purpose to impose.

The enthusiasm frequently expressed for America's religious liberty in education is a case in point. I do not mean to suggest that the general religious liberty which we enjoy is not a subject for real enthusiasm, and I am hardly fit to say whether or not the enthusiasm which we express for our education is soundly based upon reality. My point is that where religion and education meet we do not have great cause for enthusiasm. The free exercise of religion in education is declining—today constricted in significant ways, and tomorrow threatened with extinction if present trends continue.

I am quite prepared for the fact that this statement may produce some reactions of shock and of anger. Shock or surprise may come from those (they are many) who want terribly to believe that all is really very well in the land, that the market is going to come around, and to whom the only real gravities are Nicklaus in the bunker at the eighteenth or the Steelers with one yard to go in the last five seconds. Today we are largely in that stage of euphoric paganism when we still have some protections derived from our ancient traditions and have not yet entered upon that possible later stage—which is one of violence, chaos, and ultimate slavery. In these still "good times," since great numbers of people are untroubled by religion, they are truly surprised by those few who assert that religious liberty in education is troubled; they are surprised—and understandably skeptical.

Note well also, however, the *angry* response—the response which at once runs to fighting words such as "Irresponsible!" "Hysterical!" "Fear-mongering!" But certainly no one should be angry because someone else com-

Mr. William B. Ball, Esq., is a partner in the law firm of Ball & Skelly in Harrisburg, PA.

plains that an aspect of religious liberty is threatened. Should not the normal response of citizen to citizen then be: "We are sorry to hear of this. Tell us in what way you feel the threat exists. Your concern is our concern." But the instant reaction of anger shows as little commonality of concern as it shows civility. What it shows instead is an *interest,* a jealous zeal for a staked-out order of things, and a willingness to employ harsh, *ad hominem,* and censorial weapons to hang onto its holdings.

Happily, in the face of the apathy of the majority and the anger of some, we are experiencing, on our 200th birthday, a strong, new-born excitement over religious liberty in education. Partly this is due to the times and partly to the quality of people who can test the wind and sense how the sea of these times is moving. Not only because of fear for life but because of love for life they have come to God, to prayer, to a vitally religious sense of being. And they *demand* liberty to educate religiously. From them we find that the threat to religious liberty in education and the struggle to achieve that liberty center upon, first, the public school and, second, private religious education.

II

The public school did not originate as a religionless school. It was a departure from, and yet evolved out of, the sectarian schools of the early nineteenth century. It originated as what would be legally defined today as a religious school. Its students prayed, read the Bible, and knew a moral discipline based on religious norms. The schools were frankly Christian and inculcated a core of those Christian doctrines and values commonly held by Protestants.[1] Thus for decades the common school undoubtedly accommodated fulfillment of the religious liberty of a high majority of the citizens. But not all. In a case in the Police Court of Boston in 1859, a teacher was prosecuted in the following circumstance: an eleven year old pupil, one Thomas J. Wall, upon instructions of his father and his parish priest, refused the order of the common school he attended to repeat the Commandments (such recitation being part of required religious exercises in the schools wherein the Protestant English Bible text was employed). The report of the case states:

> Wall, still refusing, was punished by the defendant with a rattan stick, some three feet in length, and three-eights of an inch thick, by whipping upon his hands. From the time the punishment was commenced to the time it ended, repeated inquiries were made of Wall if he would comply with the requirements of the school. Some thirty minutes time was occupied in the whole.... The blows were not given in quick succession, but with deliberation.

[1]E. P. Cubberly, *Public Education in the United States* 120 (1947); A. P. I. Stokes, *Church and State in the United States* 832 (1950).

The court then entered upon a long discourse on the nature of the common school. Did these religious practices impose on anyone's constitutional rights? Not remotely, said the court, since the practices were not *"sectarian."* The Bible, said the court, "was placed there [in our schools] by our forefathers not for the purpose of teaching sectarian religion but a knowledge of God and his will, whose practice is religion." Moreover, "if the plea of conscience is good for one form of sectarian religion, it is good for another," and the court envisioned chaos in the common schools if the pleas of various religious bodies were to be heeded. As to Master Thomas J. Wall, here is how the court disposed of him:

> The mind and will of Wall had been prepared for insubordination and revolt by his father and the priest. His refusal to obey the commands of the school was deliberate.... The extent of his punishment was left as it were to his own choice. From the first blow that fell upon his hands from the master's rattan, to the last that was given, it was in his power to make every one the last.[2]

We should note the elements that go to make up this case. The central figure is a child of impressionable years. He carries into the public school some sort of religious commitment. This commitment is in conflict with school policy. The school says that its policy is not anti-religious, but neutral (and the court agrees that this is so). And the court says that the common school could not exist if it were forced to adjust itself to every shade of religious belief. And finally there are the roles of the parent and the child's pastor. The child's claim of religious liberty must be discounted, because (although he endured thirty minutes of torture in asserting it) "his mind had been prepared" by his parent and his pastor. We should bear these elements in mind as we now turn to the further unfolding of the story of what happened to religion in public education.

There ensued now a century of tension in this area. Horace Mann, who launched the common school movement, had seen no need for agitation if "sectarianism" were ruled out and common-core Protestant religion kept in.[3] Four decades later, President Grant, in his 1875 address to the Army of the Tennessee, agreed that "sectarianism" was bad and wanted education also to be devoid of "pagan, or aethestical dogmas" (as he put it), but he went a step beyond Mann when he said of religion itself: "Leave the matter of religion to the family altar, the church, and the private school...."[4] In the following years Catholic parents from time to time resisted the public schools' use of the King James Bible and went to court about it. Expressions of Jewish dissatisfaction would not become

---

[2]*Commonwealth v. Cooke, 7 Am. Leg. Reg.* 417 (1859).

[3]Mann's lecture in 1838 on "The Necessity of Education in a Republican Government" concluded with these words: "And, finally, by the term education I mean such a culture of our moral affections and religious sensibilities, as in the course of nature and Providence shall lead to a subjection and conformity of all our appetites, propensities, and sentiments to the Will of Heaven."

[4]"The President's Speech at Des Moines," *Catholic World* 22 (1876): 433–435.

widely heard until after 1950. Perhaps the most insistent agitation in the first half of the twentieth century came from Protestants. Some leaders, as the new century went on, became alarmed, not over Protestant inculcations in the public schools, but over the decline of all religion in the public schools and of religiously-based moral training. The "Protestant practices" were becoming vestigial. They were pretty well boiling down to token religion—dabs of prayer or bits of Bible recitation—totally unconnected with anything else in those vital areas of the child's life relating to the conduct and course of his whole being. That those areas had been religion's old domain in the schools cannot be doubted. Many a public school textbook from the nineteenth century attests vividly to that fact. In the twentieth century all this was becoming changed. We need not explore at length the reasons. Scientism, or the vogue for regarding science as affording all possible keys to existence, was one. The handmaiden of that vogue, skepticism about religion, was possibly another. Undoubtedly also was the factor, in the era of the apex of national self-confidence, of a psychological transfer of affection and reliance from God and churches to Nation and the American Democratic Ideal.

A reaction to what was deemed a growth of secularism in public education began to set in. Dr. Nicholas Murray Butler, in 1940, stated that a "curious tendency" has grown up

> ... to exclude religious teaching altogether from education on the ground that such teaching was in conflict with our fundamental doctrine as to the separation of church and state. In other words, the religious teaching was narrowed down to something which might be called denominationalism, and therefore because of differences of faith and practice it must be excluded from education. The result was to give paganism new importance and new influence...

Dr. Alexander Miklejohn, in 1942, spoke of public education in these words:

> We have torn our teaching loose from its roots. We have broken its connections with the religious beliefs of which it had grown. The typical Protestant has continued to accept the Bible as, in some sense, the guide of his own living. But, in effect, he has wished to exclude the Bible from the teaching of his children.

In the 1930's there had appeared the "three faith" plan, a scheme for elective courses cooperatively developed by representatives of the Protestant, Catholic, and Jewish religious communities which would consist of religious and moral teachings common to all three groups. This encountered, however, the limitation that areas upon which agreement would be found were rather narrow. In 1937, came the "Elgin" plan which called for students to be given religious study in the public school classroom, under certified public teachers, on an interdenominational basis. Still another plan was that for release of children to public school classrooms so that they might there receive religious instruction from their own minister, rabbi, or priest. In 1947, in the *McCollum* case, the Supreme Court of the United States struck down that plan and—by inference—any program for use of public school premises for formal religious instruction.[5] In 1962, in *Engel v. Vitale,* the Supreme Court held unconstitutional a New York-sponsored, non-compulsory program consisting of a nondenominational prayer.[6] Both the *McCollum* and *Engel* programs were struck down under the Establishment Clause of the First Amendment. A national uproar ensued, and in 1963, the Supreme Court in the *Schempp* case[7] (in which it struck down state laws permitting Bible-reading and recitation of the Lord's Prayer in public schools) took occasion to attempt to a broad rationale for its position and indeed a prescription, or guideline, to the public schools of the nation as to how to deal with religious expression within them.

In *Schempp* (and its companion case, *Murray v. Curlett*) we see the perdurable ingredients of the old case of Master Thomas J. Wall. Instead of Thomas are Roger and Donna Schempp and William Murray, III—all children. Like Thomas, they carry into the public school some sort of commitment with respect to religion. This commitment is in conflict with school policies. The Schempps testify on trial that there were concepts conveyed by the Bible-reading "which were contrary to the religious beliefs which they held and to their familial teaching." William J. Murray, III, contends that, since he is an avowed aetheist, the Lord's Prayer practice "threatens [his] religious liberty by placing a premium on belief as against non-belief." As in the case of Thomas J. Wall, the school contends that its policy is non-religious and neutral. And, as in that case, back of the children stand parents (here, the parents having actively involved themselves as parties in the cases). Finally, although the Court does not resolve the case on an issue of coercion, it notes that the children were in attendance pursuant to the compulsory attendance laws, and it points out trial court testimony that, if the Schempp parents had sought a permitted excusal for their children, the children might be labeled "odd balls."

The decision leaves us with two unanswered questions related to religious liberty in education. First, while conceivably the Court might have ruled in favor of the children on the ground of coercion, it did not. Nor did it use the occasion of this case to vindicate the rights of the parents. While the Court had before it a valuable opportunity to decide the case on the basis of interference with the free exercise of religion, it chose to decide it on the ground that the programs in question represented an establishment of religion. Thus, while in a broad sense the religious liberty claimed by the children and parents was recognized, the recognition was in fact narrow; the governmental imposition was voided only

[5]*McCollum v. Board of Education,* 333 U.S. 203 (1947). Compare *Zorach v. Clauson,* 343 U.S. 306 (1952), wherein the Court upheld off-the-school-premises released time programs.

[6]*Engel v. Vitale,* 370 U.S. 421 (1962). The officially formulated prayer was: "Almighty God, we acknowledge our dependence on Thee, and we beg thy blessings upon us, our parents, our teachers, and our country."

[7]374 U.S. 203 (1963).

because it officially promoted religion and *not* because it got in the way of individual beliefs and commands of conscience.

A second and related question is this: From the point of view of values, what kind of public school is left as the result of *Schempp?* Clearly a school in which no religion is permitted. Now defenders of the Court's decision, and the Court itself in rendering it, stoutly deny that conclusion. How? By a famous statement found in the Court's opinion. Noting that some were insisting that the Court had now established a "religion of secularism," the Court replied:

> We do not agree . . . that this decision in any sense has that effect. In addition, it might well be said that one's education is not complete without a study of comparative religion or the history of religion and its relationship to the advancement of civilization. It certainly may be said that the Bible is worthy of study for its literary and historic qualities. Nothing we have said here indicates that such study of the Bible or of religion, when presented objectively as part of a secular program of education, may not be effected consistently with the First Amendment.[8]

But that statement does not disprove the conclusion that the public school must now be a school in which no religion is permitted; it nails the conclusion down. For when the *believer* speaks of religion, it is meant as the ground of being; and when the believer speaks of his or her exercise of religion, it means the exercise of religion in its fullness and integrity. When Fundamentalists and some Catholics have commented that the Court's decision has "driven religion out of the public schools," they should not be dismissed as having made what Professor Freund has called "intemperate outbursts." Religion, in the believer's understanding of religion, *is* plainly out. Indeed, utterly offensive to the believer is the Court's prescription with respect to the religion that may be left in. That—and some other things that may or may not ultimately be left in—becomes my subject as I discuss one more group of successors to Master Thomas J. Wall.

These are public school children in Northport, New York, or Howell, Michigan, or Fresno, California. In composite, I will call them Robert and Mary. There are many, many Roberts and Marys around the country. Their parents pay taxes for the support of the public schools. The parents have not selected private education for them (none may be available or affordable), and the child attends public school under compulsion of law. The parents, let us assume, are Christian believers: there are religious mandates in their lives, and prohibitions, and the sure religious sense of what is to be valued and what cannot be abided. Robert and Mary come from that household of belief into the public school. Suppose now that they are confronted with all or some of the following in their school's program:

-a course (under whatever label) in comparative religion or the role of religion in civilization,

<hr/>

[8]Ibid. at 225.

-the presentation of the Bible as literature,
-"objective" instruction in religion as part of a secular program.

The foregoing are the areas of permissible "religion" as given in *Schempp*. Not only, as we have pointed out, are they not "religion" in the sense believers have in mind; they almost certainly *confront* religion in that latter sense. Comparative Religion presupposes a teacher who can compare. It is all but impossible to eliminate normative judgments in the process. But at best it also involves the introducing of the child to the broad range of choices in religion. Is it the function of the public school to introduce the child to a series of choices of religions? Not remotely.

But let us shift to the next adjective by which the concept, "religion," is to be modified according to the *Schempp* prescription—the "objective" study. If the "objective study" is honest and real, then the most basic doctrines of the religions must at least be spoken of—in the Christian religions, for example, the Incarnation, salvation by faith alone, predestination, the infallibility of the Bible. How could these be left out? But how can they be usefully presented without discussion? And, if there is discussion, what is to be the teacher's response to the whys of some children and the reticences of others? But if the basic doctrines and historical crises of the religions are not to be presented, then does not the "objective study" become no study at all? Instead there may be—and no one should knock it—offerings on tolerance and good will—what good people were the Pilgrim Fathers, Roger Williams, Christopher Columbus, Al Smith, Robert Morris, and Justice Brandeis. But this promotion of intergroup goodwill has its fragile peripheries, as words such as "Belfast," "Israel," and "abortion" come off the headlines and into the classroom.

How about the Bible as literature? Parents in a case now in the Ohio courts were asked concerning that very point. Here follows the colloquy between counsel and a witness, who was a Fundamentalist:

Q. Now, you are aware that the Bible is taught as literature in the public schools. Is this acceptable to you?

A. No, because I believe it must be taught as the word of God.

Another witness in the same case stated that he felt that the Bible should be read with express understanding that it is the word of God. And here is posed well the very point which the Supreme Court has refused to face. The religious liberty issue is *not:* What is belief to the non-believer, to the neutralist, the relativist, the pagan, the deist, the comparer of ideas, the seeker after mere secular knowledge? The religious liberty question centers on: "What is belief to the believer? And that is a burning question indeed.

I should point out that the Court itself did not take its own religious prescription very seriously, because, in the closing paragraph of its opinion, it pulled the rug out from any illusion which some might entertain that religion was any more to enjoy meaningful existence in the life of the public school. It said:

> The place of religion in our society is an exalted one, achieved through a
> long tradition of reliance on *the home, the church and the inviolable citadel
> of the individual heart and mind.* We have come to recognize through bitter
> experience that it is not within the power of government to invade that
> citadel, whether its purpose or effect be to aid or oppose, to advance or
> retard.[9] (Emphasis supplied.)

Shades of Ulysses S. Grant! The ghosts of Bismarck and the French laicists of
1904! Let religion be confined to house, to sacristy, or to the keeping of the
individual mind. Half of a child's waking time and most of his or her learning
time is spent in school—but school is not a place for religion. Public educators
claim it is one of the glories of the public school that it shapes and develops the
whole person—but it must do so without religion.

But what I have described up to now is only a little part of what Robert and
Mary meet. I had mentioned that, in our earlier American education, the natural
domain of religion had been the full life of the student. Most knowledge was
related to religion. Civic virtues were inculcated as being dictated by the Commandments and the Gospels. Behavior, the emotions, the wellsprings of
conduct—and thus the social person—were profoundly affected by the religious
beliefs which were instilled, beliefs which were intended to have consequences.
Now that religion is out of the public schools, the vacuum left in its old domain is
rapidly being filled. It is natural that this should happen. The questions and needs
to which religion once supplied the answers have not gone away. They are
insistently a part of people, and since the state is now left to answer the questions, it is trying to perform its duty. But some of the state's answers are now
proving to be answers which Robert and Mary and their parents cannot—before
God—accept, and which they must indeed reject.

Myriad examples in a tidal wave of these could be shown. Let me pause with
but one, however, a fairly typical one. Here is a program which is entitled
"Sexuality and Family Life." The aim of this state program is recited to be "To
produce a *mature person* capable of fulfilling his sexuality in the broadest
sense." It states that it is imperative that the child develop "*sound attitudes and
values* to guide his sexual conduct." How? By imparting "a *scientific* knowledge
of all aspects of human sexuality." This, says the state, will enable the child "to
communicate with others in a *mature manner* and will provide the basis for a
successful adjustment in marriage and family living." The state program (called
a "health program") then proceeds to take up the mechanics of sex in very
complete mechanical detail. Described are fetishism, transvestites, sadism,
masochism, sodomy, pre-marital sex, and "the meaning of marriage." Mastur-
bation is described as a harmless source of pleasure, practiced by almost everybody. Fellatio and cunnilingus are taken up, and the children are referred to
reading sources where they can acquire more of all this scientific knowledge.

There are many Christian parents to whom this is profoundly offensive and

[9]*Schempp,* at 226.

religiously utterly unacceptable.[10] At the outset there is the use of broad terms packed with volatile value implications. And parents rightly ask questions about what is under these broad-blanket terms and regulatory fog. After all, it is *their* children who will be wrapped up in these. Who is a "mature person"? Shall the state define it? Is it the state's job to "produce" him or her? What is meant by fulfilling sexuality "in the broadest sense." The state says that those "attitudes and values" which are to guide sexual conduct must be "sound." According to what norm? What does the state recognize as a "sound" attitude or a "sound" value? Is the norm of "soundness" of sexual conduct based upon lack of harm to others? Upon freedom from disease? Upon personal satisfaction? Upon the Ten Commandments? These only get to the threshold of the problem confronting these parents. If the threshold is disturbing, what is inside is forbidding—or forbidden. Christian parents whom I know cannot suffer their children to be exposed to programs such as I have just described. They also may not allow their children to be involved in discussions of these matters—especially in groups or especially where conducted by public teachers who are prohibited, under the law, from expressing Christian moral judgments as guides to the children. By any standards their claims are as real and substantial as those asserted by the parents in *Engel* and *Schempp*.

But the courts before whom these cases have come have been as unsympathetic to these claims of conscience and religious liberty as have the education departments and supporting groups which have imposed them. (The Supreme Court has not yet decided a case fully in point.) Of course there is no difficulty in identifying many of these programs as Secular Humanist, and it is well settled that Secular Humanism is a "religion" within the meaning of both the Free Exercise and Establishment Clauses.[11] And since these programs are supported by public funds extracted from the pocket of every taxpayer, they may be found to violate the Establishment Clause. But their offense to constitutional rights rests in fact upon far broader grounds. Ignored as though non-existent are those First Amendment standards which are applied with such exquisite sensitivity in free expression cases. Seriously failing of recognition are rights of familial privacy and of the sexual privacy of children. The use of state coercion to mold the minds and behavior of children is sanctioned in the face of Supreme Court decisions which define and sharply discountenance such coercion. We should keep in mind how ridiculous it would be to hold that there is no state power to sponsor, on a non-required basis, a twenty-two word, non-denominational prayer, but at the same time to hold that the state has a free hand to impose teachings and values which go to the very vitals of the child's emotions, spirit, mind, conduct, attitude toward the family, and sexuality, and his or her life and destiny.

[10]I do not refer to non-Christian parents simply because no cases of protest by them have come to my attention.

[11]*Torcaso v. Watkins,* 367 U.S. 488, 495 (1961); *Everson v. Board of Education,* 330 U.S. 1, 31 (1946) (dissenting opinion of Rutledge).

What hope have we for religious liberty in the public schools? The hope lies in the firm will to resist the impositions and to arouse public recognition of the problem. Solutions lie in several directions. One is the elimination of the heavily-value-related programs. The doctrine of *parens patriae* is clearly misapplied when, in the name of "child rights," the child is made to become (in the great phrase in *Pierce v. Society of Sisters*) "the mere creature of the state." *"Parens patriae"* then becomes all *"patria"* and no *"parens."* Another—but this is the bare minimum protection—is to require parental consent for *all* instruction in such value-dominated areas as sex education. And in connection with that, it is very important that public officials be made responsible for clear definitions and proper labeling, so that the parent may know what in fact is being offered. In Michigan sex education programs were offered under such a variety of interesting heads as "Practical Arts," "Home Economics," "Human Growth and Development," "Hygiene," and "The Pleasure of Your Company." One of the weaknesses in exemption, however, is, as we saw in *Schempp,* the fear of the child of being labeled by his peers as an "odd ball."

A third partial solution is affirmative rather than negative. It calls for the overruling of the decision in *McCollum* in order to permit real religious instruction on a released-time basis on the public school premises.

III

For many parents—perhaps soon an increasing number—the solution will be found in the separate religious school. It is in respect to that school that we see the second area in which freedom of religion in education is being constricted. Decisions of the Supreme Court from *Pierce v. Society of Sisters*[12] through *Wisconsin v. Yoder*[13] vindicate the freedom to afford one's children separate religious education. The constriction of which I speak lies in their ability to do so. Their decreasing ability to do so lies, in turn, in economics and in state regulation—and sometimes these are interrelated.

The economic factors are inflation and taxation. For most American wage earners a crisis has gradually come home. I know that it can be pointed out that the Catholic people of the nineteenth century—despised immigrants and often the lowest of wage earners—nevertheless by heroic sacrifice built thousands of religious schools which continue to this day. They not only built them, but staffed them for generations with people who gave their generous lives to the Christian education of youth. If those people, in their desperate situation, would make such sacrifice, why not the American of today?

The first approach to answering the question addresses itself to those parents who formerly supported religious schools (or who come from families which did)

[12]268 U.S. 510 (1925).
[13]406 U.S. 205 (1972).

but who today do not. They are intent in their desire to have their children move up in the mainstream of society, and want them to be able to support themselves in accordance with very high material standards. Many of these parents likewise desire to live according to those standards. And for most of those parents the more obvious incidents of religious bigotry directed against their immigrant forebears have disappeared and thus too has their own religious militancy or will to religiously survive. Indeed—and as notably seen both in suburbia and in once-religious colleges—it has been their manifest desire to blend blandly with the religionless community. Then, too, there has been the impact of affluence and the saturating materialism of our society. Who today does not hear, louder than did Matthew Arnold at Dover Beach, the Sea of Faith's

> ... melancholy, long, withdrawing roar
> Retreating, to the breath of the night wind... ?

But, happily, there are millions more parents who not only remain faithful to religion but who, in the teeth of the onslaught of pagan and secular humanist values, are also manifesting an intense radical renewal of their religious sense.

The second approach to answering the question relates to social justice. We now live in a substantially socialized society. In our now heavily welfare-oriented society, massive governmental spending is dominant, and individual men and women, even when banded together in associations or institutions, no longer possess the economic resources with which to maintain diverse, non-state endeavors in education and welfare. Education is plainly the most important aspect of voluntarism and that which is most meaningful in terms of a free society. One question that all private religious schools (except those, if any, maintained by the rich) must ultimately face is whether, in the face of increasing inflation and personal taxation, the per-pupil operating costs can be met. Perhaps for very small units this will temporarily be possible. For larger units the outlook is not bright. But sooner or later parents are bound to ask the question:

> I am paying my taxes for a public education which, solely for reasons of conscience, I cannot utilize for my children. I pay a great many other taxes at the local, regional, state, and federal levels. For reasons of conscience I help maintain a private religious school. That school provides quality education. Out of it comes a better-than-useful citizen. Due to it, the cost and burden of educating the children who attend it is saved to the public. Is it really fair that I must pay twice for education?

This parent brings us to look at what is known to constitutional lawyers as the doctrine of "unconstitutional conditions." It has been well stated by Alanson H. Willcox:

> Whenever a state imposes a choice between... receiving a public benefit, on the one hand, and exercising one's constitutional freedoms, on the other, the state burdens each course to the extent that abandonment of the other is unpalatable. The deterrent to exercise of first amendment freedoms when

public benefits are at stake is a real one. . . . Infringement of constitutional rights is nonetheless infringement because accomplished through a conditioning of a privilege.[14]

The parent asks, "Is it really fair?"

The Supreme Court has never passed on that question. Fairness has not been the point in its numerous decisions blocking most forms of meaningful relief to parents on grounds of church-state separation. It is not my point to reargue those cases here. Rather I would join with Mr. Justice Rehnquist who, in the latest of these cases, put the matter exactly:

> I am disturbed as much by the overtones of the Court's opinion as by its actual holding. The Court apparently believes that the Establishment Clause of the First Amendment not only mandates religious neutrality on the part of government but also requires that this Court go further and throw its weight on the side of those who believe that our society as a whole should be a purely secular one.[15]

As the Chief Justice in the same case said:

> "One can only hope that, at some future date, the Court will come to a more enlightened and tolerant view of the First Amendment's guarantee of free exercise of religion, thus eliminating the denial of equal protection to children in church-sponsored schools, and take a more realistic view that carefully limited aid to children is not a step toward establishing a state religion—at least while this Court sits.[16]

I do not at all think that all forms of aid to parents or children imply state controls. They would be worse than useless if they did. If we could but dry out our brains from their besottedness with bureaucratic concepts, we could see possible means of aid which would involve only minimal controls or assurances. Statists express both a fallacy and a bugaboo when they say that the state must control any entity that it aids. Heaven knows, this does not hold true in foreign aid, and it need never be the case in forms of assistance to parents or in the providing of useful services to children.

But now let me come to a matter closely related to economics and just as basically related to religious liberty in education. I refer to the astounding fact that, in state after state, suffocating governmental regulation is being imposed on religious schools. And we are seeing the possible beginnings also of similar federal regulation. Let me give you some cases in point, some of which I will identify but others of which I dare not identify lest word get back to the governmental administrators involved and more trouble be made for the religious school in question.

[14]41 *Cornell L. Q.* 12, 43–44 (1955).
[15]*Meek v. Pittenger*, 44 L. Ed 2d 217, 250 (1975).
[16]Ibid. at 245.

In Ohio a number of Christian people of modest means but high religious spirit started a Bible-oriented religious school. The state education department then presented the school with a volume of 600 regulations (drafted, not by the legislature, but by the department), interestingly labeled "Minimum Standards." Although the students at this school performed above average in nationally standardized achievement tests the school could not comply with all of the standards. Some of the standards called for unbearable costs—such as the requirement that every non-tax-supported school have a multi-media library in charge of a certificated multi-media operator. Other standards could not be complied with because they were gobbldegook that (so it turned out) the state officials themselves could not explain—such as the requirement which simply read that "educational facilities, pupil-teacher ratios, instructional materials and services at the elementary level" must be "comparable to those of the upper levels." But also there were a series of requirements which plainly invade religious liberty. Some dealt with secular humanist philosophic prescriptions in the content of the Social Studies, Health, and Citizenship curricula. Another said that "*all* activities" of a school must conform to policies of the board of education. Still another provided that the school must have community cooperation in determining its purposes and planning. The school said that, because of these requirements, it could not comply. The state instituted criminal prosecution of all of the parents who had their children enrolled there. They were indicted, tried, and convicted. At the trial the prosecution repeatedly pointed out that the school was "unchartered"—i.e., was not in compliance with the 600 "minimum standards." Reverend Levi Whisner, the pastor-principal, on the stand, again and again tried to explain that he *did not* want a charter since a charter would signify the school's agreement with all of the standards, some of which were religiously unacceptable. (Here we should pause to note the high caliber of his citizenship in rendering unto Caesar the simple candor that is due to Caesar.) The defendants then went to an intermediate appellate court which dismissed their religious liberty claims with the amazing statement that the pastor's testimony

> ... reflects the subjective attitudes of the members of his congregation, and
> his reasoning is based essentially upon a subjective interpretation of biblical
> language.

Here is an example of court establishment of religion through its homemade definition of religion. The case is now on appeal to the Ohio Supreme Court.[17]

There are a number of states whose statutes or regulations are similar to those of Ohio. The harsh and impudent will to remake every private school in the image of the public school is more and more evident. When this is connected to the criminal law process, it becomes frightening. Not all the signs are bad,

---

[17]Since this paper was delivered, the Supreme Court of Ohio reversed the conviction and, in a 37-page opinion held that the regulations had violated their religious liberty. *State of Ohio v. Whisner*, 47 Ohio St. 2d 181 (1976). (Ed.)

however. *Pierce* and *Yoder* still provide the high and commanding principles ultimately to be followed. And on April 6, 1976, came good news from Vermont.

In Vermont some believers had started Life in Holiness Christian School. Vermont's compulsory attendance law requires that if a parent does not enroll his or her child in a public school, the parent must afford the child "equivalent education." The state in 1972 launched a criminal prosecution against parents who had sent their children to the Life in Holiness school, then it dropped the prosecution. The next year it started another and then dropped that. The fourth time that it caused the parents distress and notoriety of being charged with crime, the state decided to stick with its harassment. It based its case on two things: (a) that the school was not an "approved school" (note: the compulsory attendance law does not mention "schools" at all—only "equivalent education"), and (b) that the *parents* had failed to prove that their children were receiving "equivalent education" (i.e., the burden of proof in this criminal proceeding was supposed to be on the parents).

The trial court upheld the parents. But—like the Wisconsin state education department in the Amish case—the state had not had enough. It appealed to the Supreme Court of Vermont. I am happy to say that, on April 6, that court unanimously upheld the position of the parents. I am happy to be able to quote to you the following from the opinion:

> The United States Supreme Court in *Pierce v. Society of Sisters,* 268 U.S. 510, long ago decided that a state could not compel all students to be educated in public schools. As recently as *Wisconsin v. Yoder,* 406 U.S. 205, that court has also stated that compulsory school attendance, even on an equivalency basis, must yield to First Amendment concerns. In the light of what is involved in "approval" the state would be hard put to constitutionally justify limiting the right of normal, unhandicapped youngsters to attendance at "approved" institutions.[18]

At the beginning of this paper, I spoke of the enthusiasm of Americans but warned that some enthusiastically propagandized views in our midst may mask "a grimly deliberate purpose to impose." Perhaps now I have put some flesh on the bone of that statement. Or you may agree that, conversely, we have gotten down to the bone of some matters affecting our religious freedom in education. Platitudes about "better education," "sound attitudes and values," "successful adjustment," and "quality standards" may in fact be cudgels of conformity. 1976 should mean to lovers of religious liberty the year in which began an effective rebellion against growing governmental restriction on religious liberty in education. In that rebellion, they may be called "divisive" by those who demand conformity to their own views. Fears will be expressed over "religion intruding into the political arena." Such repressive counselings have not been

[18]*State of Vermont v. LaBarge, et al.,* Vt., (slip op. 4) 1976.

heard in campaigns by religious groups with respect to Vietnam, welfare rights, prohibition, gambling, capital punishment, aid to Israel, trade with South Africa, or racial discrimination. Neither should they be heeded in respect to religious liberty in education.

RELIGIOUS LIBERTY AND SOCIAL INEQUALITY

John C. Raines

In New York harbor on the base of the Statue of Liberty we find the familiar inscription:

> Give me your tired, your poor,
> Your huddled masses yearning to breathe free,
> I lift my lamp beside the Golden Door.
> . . .
> . . .

Notice that it was a golden door, not a wooden one.

The "shot heard round the world" was not the one fired at British troops at Concord, Massachusetts. It was, instead, the promise of the Land of Promise, the promise of the American Dream. And it was heard round the world! Millions came to our shores seeking freedom from religious and economic oppression. In the hundred years between 1800 and 1900 our population grew more than ten times, from three million to over thirty-five million people. In that hundred years we became a nation of many nations, held together by a dream.

The American Dream began as an explosion of self-confidence. It was the boisterous and proud proclamation of a New World. Unlike the old world, where privilege came with birth, and everyone knew where he or she belonged, in America people were to be unshackled from the bondage of previous generations. Ours was to be a land not of family fate, but of individual freedom. People were not to have the unfair advantage of simply being who they were by birth, by name, or by the accident of parental status. In America everyone was to be only what he or she *could become*.

This set loose an amazing expansion of self-esteem. It broke through the sedentary and determined quality of old-world societies, where heart and vision were tamed early. It set loose the energy of a vast yearning—the promised chance for everyone to find a place in the sun. Yes, there was a freedom to our land which in the eyes of much of the world made us, and still makes us, vastly appealing. Yet, it was an ironic freedom. Permitted to be only what we could become, we were never secure with who or where we were. We pursued our hopes. But in some curious way we were also pursued by our hopes of what someday we might yet become. There was a nervousness in it all which swelled our need to consume, billowing and bulging our economy.

Indeed, it was only this rapidly expanding economy that made the Dream work. The truth is that the Land of Promise sought to keep its promise not by a relative equality of belonging. No, over the years the shares of wealth remained

Dr. John C. Raines is as Associate Professor of Religion at Temple University, Philadelphia, PA.

highly concentrated and essentially unchanged. Rather, we made room for our restless millions by expanding the field of economic opportunity. We enlarged the pie; we didn't change the way the pie was divided, which is to say we were never so much an open society as a wide-open society, consolidated not by distributive justice but by expanding the field of available opportunities.

In a way, this worked well enough. Over the years and generations people improved their life styles. But it also didn't work. As a nation it led us into this fundamental contradiction. Our expanding economy provided relative decency for the many. But this same economic growth amassed immense wealth at the top of our society. The pie grew for everyone—not just those in the middle—and the top two percent had about the same size piece to divide up as the middle seventy percent of us. Meanwhile, we average citizens lived up into our slowly rising incomes. Over the generations we bought a house, moved to the suburbs, got a second car, and started sending the children to college. But a very few got wealth beyond their need to consume, wealth that could be used massively to beget more wealth.

The result is that today the top one percent of our population holds fully twenty-eight percent of all the personally-owned wealth. The top two percent owns forty-four percent, and the top ten percent own fifty-six percent of all the wealth. The Land of Promise has become a land where 1.6 percent of us leave estates averaging $185,000, while the rest of us leave an average estate of $7,900. We have become, you can see, an immensely unequal society. I draw our attention to these figures not to beget pecuniary envy, not to berate the wealthy. No, many of the wealthy got their wealth by hard work and, often enough, by lucky timing. Rather, my purpose is to sound a warning about our threatened democracy. Concentrated wealth translates easily into concentrated social power—power that can be, and has been, used to pay for elections, to buy "friends" in Washington, and to purchase income tax and estate tax laws that benefit the few at the expense of the many.

This is the message of Watergate—not the personal moral failure of certain individuals. No, Watergate displays the massive "you-scratch-my-back-and-I'll-scratch-yours" that goes on routinely between big money and big politics. Officers of International Telephone and Telegraph Company offered $400,000 to help finance the Republican Convention in 1972, hoping thereby to buy-off a Justice Department probe—and they succeeded. The American Dairyman's Association promised millions in campaign contributions if favored by legislation that would line their own pockets while gouging the American housewife—and they succeeded!

As a nation we have purchased decency for the many by expanding our economy, but without attending to the just distribution of its fruits. The result is that today we have nearly lost our democracy. In 1966, forty-five percent of us agreed with the statement, "the rich get richer and the poor get poorer." By 1973, seventy-six percent of us agreed with that statement. And still the politicians do nothing, except, of course, to help themselves to the gravy.

Yet some might ask, "What does all this have to do with religious liberty? So long as we can gather to praise the God of our choice, so long as we can come together to air our complaints, aren't we still free?" "Yes," I answer, "we are free to say. We are free to sing and pray. The only thing We The People are not free to do is to govern."

As originally conceived, religious liberty had to do with religion; but it also had to do with politics. Like the right to free speech and free assembly, originally religious liberty said something about how we chose to govern ourselves as a people. Today, it is fast becoming simply a pious sentiment, a private practice dwelling upon the outskirts of society, with little of what was once its immense social impact and importance. At one time religious liberty did have public power. In fact, it was the very cradle of our public freedoms. Church and synagogue were where we formed and protected that pluralism of conscience which guarantees lively public discourse. Church and synagogue—the companionship of fellow believers—broke open society, encouraging that inner dialogue of conscience, that *complexity* of loyalty, which alone produces a vital people and a vital democracy.

All this is now threatened. To talk about religious liberty and the rights of a free conscience means, necessarily, to address the underlying social fabric within which these rights must take hold if they are to be real. Where that underlying social fabric, because of concentrated wealth and power, is effectively closed to the participation of the people, religious liberty becomes a kind of shadow of its intended meaning. It loses its foothold in the world of human affairs.

That is our situation today. Concentrated wealth and power move effectively behind the scenes to undermine and fictionalize the people's participation in electoral politics. Influential interests advance their cause through the insider's game, through the pressure system, a system of organized interest groups to which ninety percent of us have no access. The result is that religious liberty suffers a profound deformity. It loses its social referent.

This was not how it was meant to be. Like freedom of speech, religious liberty was viewed by our Constitution makers as essential to our other public freedoms, to our whole way of governing ourselves. As the cradle of the dissenting conscience, religious liberty, our founding fathers believed, required a sufficient distribution of social power for that dissent, if persuasive, to take hold and become politically effective.

Today, the concentration of decision making power—both economic and political—undermines all this. It leaves religious liberty a kind of abstraction, a fertile seed without receptive ground to fall upon. It makes religious liberty into something merely private and religious. Of such an eventuality, the prophet Amos has warned us.

> I take no delight in your solemn assemblies,
> . . .
> Take away from me the noise of your songs;
>   to the melody of your harps I will not listen.

> But let justice roll down like waters,
> and righteousness like an ever-flowing stream (Amos 5:21 ff.).

Religious liberty and political liberty are inextricably intertwined. Without religious liberty, there is no complexity of loyalty, no dialogue of conscience. Everything becomes a monologue. And as Albert Camus has seen, the very essence of tyranny is to "reduce everything to a monologue," to establish the rule of the single voice. On the other hand, without political liberty, religious liberty is reduced to a sideshow. It is tolerated, indeed even encouraged, only because it has ceased to be politically significant. Religious liberty then becomes only a private consolation, while all around it the public disaster continues.

And what is that disaster? Are we not told that Watergate proves our Constitution still works? Well, I am here to say that Watergate is in fact alive and well in Washington today. The big-time flim-flam of buying political influence continues. And it flourishes as well among Democrats as among Republicans. Let us make no mistake. Let us take no false comfort. Our Constitutional crisis lies not behind us, but ahead. We are far along the path to becoming a nation of the few, by the few, and for the few. In the Land of Promise we were promised "the chance to become somebody." But we purchased that chance at the price of our public freedom. We expanded our economy without attending to the just distribution of its fruits, with the result that we have come perilously close to the destruction of our political democracy.

Religious liberty has to do with religion. But it also has to do with the way we have chosen to govern ourselves as a people. Those of us who prize and would preserve our heritage of religious liberty have been drawn into a time of fundamental testing. We are back where we were 200 years ago. We have yet to secure our right to be free.

THE CIVIL RELIGION: IS IT A VIABLE CONCEPT?

Elwyn A. Smith

The debate about the "civil religion"—Rousseau devised the term and Robert Bellah re-minted it nine years ago[1]—is no ordinary academic cavil. It is the form in which some very worried scholars are expressing belief in the necessity and possibility of a "reconstruction of the American reality," as Richard Neuhaus puts it.[2] The best way of accomplishing this, they argue, is to bring to light and revitalize this democracy's civil religion.

The Matrix of the Civil Religion Concept

The notion of the civil religion is conspicuous today because of a bewildering succession of social distresses that has eroded American unity and self-confidence. This destructive period began with the Depression and was followed by the Second World War. There was a period of artificial stimulus and quick affluence during the fifties; then came the creeping catastrophe in Vietnam and the social disturbances and public murders of the sixties. Then, in the seventies, "Watergate." At one point during this time it seemed that unbroken economic ascent had supplanted economic ebb and flow, and we were well launched into the affluent society. John Kennedy was the symbol of great expectations, but this only worsened frustration under Johnson and deepened disappointment in Nixon.

The American people has been casting about rather confusedly for the means of grasping all this and recovering its poise. "One analyst returns to majority indifference and ignorance as the rock upon which a new America can be constructed," writes Neuhaus, reflecting on some recently published books; "another returns to the ethnic passions and prejudices of contrived nostalgia, yet another returns to the revivalist fundamentalism of Billy Graham, and [Arthur] Schlesinger [Jr.] returns to tinkering with the machinery of New Deal liberalism...." Neuhaus then states: "There is yet another alternative and I believe it to be discovered in the civil religion of the American symbols of hope....We must project a new definition of national purpose capable of enlisting American consciousness and conscience in the continuing trek toward the new community for which this 'almost chosen' people... was ordained; ordained, if not by God, at least by men prepared to gamble in hope unpon divine intentions within history."[3]

If it is a bit breath-taking to hear a modern scholar speak *sotto voce* of a new

---

[1] "Civil Religion in America," *Daedelus,* 96:1 (Winter, 1967), pp. 1–21.
[2] "Going Home Again: America after Vietnam," *Worldview,* 15:10 (October, 1972), pp. 30–36.
[3] Ibid., p. 33.

Dr. Elwyn A. Smith was Provost of Eckerd College, St. Petersburg, FL, and is now pastor of Garden Crest United Presbyterian Church in St. Petersburg.

American theocracy, it is perhaps no more remarkable than the fact that this threatened Union once gave its vote to a president who could formulate the kind of judgment on the agony of civil war that Lincoln articulated in his Second Inaugural Address. Virtually no article on the civil religion can afford to omit the quotation that follows, and we shall have something to say about the reason for that.

> The Almighty has His own purposes. "Woe unto the world because of offenses, for it must needs be that offenses come, but woe to that man by whom the offense cometh." . . .Fondly do we hope, fervently do we pray, that this mighty scourge of war may speedily pass away. Yet, if God wills that it continue until all the wealth piled by the bondsman's two hundred and fifty years of unrequited toil shall be sunk, and until every drop of blood drawn with the lash shall be paid by another drawn with the sword, as was said three thousand years ago, so still it must be said, "The judgments of the Lord are true and righteous altogether."

The heart of the Jew or Christian who is deeply pained by this nation's modern distresses responds to the moral splendor of that address and we ardently wish to believe that the soul of the nation did truly speak in the voice of Lincoln.

A number of questions arise around the very complex idea of the "civil religion," and we shall be able to deal only with certain of them. For example, any concept designed to reconstitute the national spirit must be shown to be relevant to the precise nature of the present social crisis, but we cannot undertake a general social analysis preliminary to discussion of the civil religion. That would be useless in any case because the civil religion has still no determinate form. The particular phenomena brought together under the rubric "civil religion" are real enough, but it is altogether possible that these data would become more intelligible if arranged according to quite another concept than the civil religion. That, too, is a question we cannot penetrate here. What is crucial for any concept of the civil religion is whether it *is* in reality what it professes to be, and indeed must be, if it is to function effectively in the midst of present American distresses.

What the civil religion professes to be and must be, we shall argue, is a purveyor of the sanction of the transcendent. The question raised in this article is whether the civil religion possesses the integrity required to bring the sanction of the transcendent to bear on the American situation. Implicit in that question, in turn, is the question of whether it honors or damages the notion of religion itself.

The Civil Religion

The civil religion is a "social construction of reality," concedes Professor Bellah, commenting in 1973 on his earlier article:

> It was an interpretation, to some extent a new interpretation, of various pieces of evidence many of which were themselves first-order interpreta-

tions, first-order social constructions of reality.... The very currency of the notion of civil religion is the earnest of its reality.... Its reality depends less on the existence of certain things out there than on a consensus that it is a useful way of talking about things that are indubitably out there.... If another interpretation, another social construction of reality in the same general area, replaces the one I have offered... then the civil religion will cease to exist.[4]

At first Professor Bellah was somewhat less epistemological in his definition of the civil religion. "Few have realized that there actually exists alongside of and rather clearly differentiated from the churches an elaborate and well-institutionalized civil religion in America," he wrote in 1967. "This religion—or perhaps better, this religious dimension—has its own seriousness and integrity and requires the same care in understanding that any other religion does."[5] In 1967, he said, in effect: "Look! It has been there all the time and we didn't see it." In 1973, with more reserve, he said: "Look! Here is a concept that helps us understand," to which Neuhaus and others add: "Whatever it is, the country can be reconstituted by it."

What are the constituent elements of the civil religion? Preeminent among them is transcendence. If the civil religion possesses, captures, and communicates this, the term "religion" is justified. Sidney Mead has written: "The essential dogma of what I call the Religion of the Republic [is] that no man is God.... A concept of the infinite seems to me to be necessary if we are to state the all important fact about man: that he is infinite."[6]

In the terminological thicket that obscures this subject, no American value system which excludes the notion of the transcendent may be identified with the civil religion. For example, consider Professor Herberg's notion of the American way of life.[7] Herberg cites a uniquely American congeries of commitments—to democracy, to a vaguely defined Supreme being, progress, idealism and moralism, affluence—that go to make up the "American way of life"—and there is no end of dispute about just what that is.[8] In any variation, does that notion incorporate transcendence? The sort of transcendence most proponents of the civil religion have in mind is not a hard-working American's freedom to transcend himself or herself by making good in a generally religious capitalism, but the sort Lincoln was talking about in the Second Inaugaural Address: a really transcendent transcendence, if you will. There is no shortage of religious rhetoric in American letters glorifying this country's great experiment, but it may be

[4]"American Civil Religion in the 1970's," in Russell E. Richey and Donald G. Jones, eds., *American Civil Religion* (New York: Harper and Row, 1974), p. 256.

[5]"Civil Religion in America," p. 1.

[6]"In Quest of America's Religion," *Christian Century,* 87:24 (June 17, 1970), pp. 752–756.

[7]Will Herberg, *Protestant, Catholic, Jew: An Essay in American Religious Sociology* (Garden City: Doubleday, 1960), passim. Cf. "America's Civil Religion: What It Is and Whence It Comes," in Richey and Jones, *American Civil Religion,* pp. 76–88.

[8]Cf. John Dewey, *A Common Faith,* Terry Lectures, Yale University (New Haven: Yale University Press, 1934), passim.

doubted whether this confers upon democracy anything more sacred than the emotions of a patriotic holiday.

A most serious question arises here, which we shall discuss in this article: What are we to make of the difference between a romantic or philosophical vision of human and national possibilities (which may be regarded as transcendent by some) and that transcendent righteousness of an autonomous God who judges nations, condemns sin, invites repentance, and promises redemption?

Notions of transcendence are articulated and conveyed through specific vehicles, and the formative period of American culture is rich in myths affirming the destiny of the new settlements and a new-born nation. Some early literature turns on the "Adamic myth"—the notion that the American is a new Adam, essentially innocent, called to implant a garden in a wilderness held empty through the ages for God's new purpose.[9] The theme of transcendence is embedded in the notion of a special divine destiny—in this case, concentrated upon the American; in other myths, upon the nation. The new beginning conferred upon humankind in the American Adam is a gift of God comparable to the act of creation itself. It is something to be confirmed or lost according to those biblical laws that governed and eventually punished the first Adam.

Far more comprehensive, not only in concept but in its greater influence on American thought, is the myth of "God's new Israel."[10] On the model of ancient Israel, the American people are perceived as specially appointed to found a commonwealth essentially conformable to divine law. It will teach a corrupt and confused Europe the true will of God. The kinetic theme of this myth is the covenant: divine blessing contingent upon human obedience. The people must be constantly alert to the subtle intrusion of sin. The dangers of the Atlantic crossing, the strangeness of the new land, the threat of starvation, the savage inhabitants—against these God actively defends the people in this latter-day covenant drama. Thus the transcendent sanction of the divine will reaches every aspect of life, not only law and government. While the Enlightenment introduced less theological views of American destiny, the language of the Old Testament remained conspicuous in, for example, Jefferson's utterances; and notions of natural law and self-evident truth were functionally analogous to the role of revelation in the biblical mythology. Thus the transcendent dimension was preserved as another faith began to permeate the American mind.

The myth of the New Israel has had an important function in North America whenever depravity has threatened to corrupt the people of the covenant. This was the weight of the Puritan jeremiad of the late seventeenth and early eighteenth centuries. Lincoln saw slavery as an American incubus, and one may say that crass commercialism obscured the obligations of the covenant once again

---

[9]Cf. R. W. B. Lewis, *The American Adam* (Chicago: The University of Chicago Press, 1955), passim.

[10]Conrad Cherry, *God's New Israel* (Englewood Cliffs, NJ, 1971).

when, after the Civil War, Lincoln's vision of the ways of God was lost in rampant economic advance. The problem, however, was that the myth could be construed to justify worldly success as well as to recall the nation to obedience. What was the lesson of America's prosperity? Was it not that God approved and rewarded its obedience? Then ought the will of an obviously blessed people be resisted? Certainly not by Spaniards in Cuba and the Philippines!

In its American epiphany, therefore, the myth of the new Israel is not solely prophetic, as early notions of manifest destiny testify. Each American generation must decide what use it will make of the national mythology, and the notion of the New Israel may be corruped for lack of a prophet of divine transcendence. Without a Lincoln, it seeks a Carnegie.[11]

There are other myths that operate in the American mind with great force, and some have little or no religious rootage or history. Such is the concept of progress. The conviction that change is bound, on balance, to be for the better may be harmonized with some of the cruder interpretations of the myth of the New Israel, but that is not its origin. The social gospel movement had an unblinking view of the crimes of industrial urbanism, yet it never doubted that these disgraces would be removed once the conscience of the nation was aroused, since progress itself was divinely ordained.

While a certain religious aura can be borrowed from the myth of the New Israel to enhance and legitimate the notion of progress, it represents a purely humanist commitment to humankind's potential for self-transcendence that contrasts markedly with Lincoln's sense of the all-righteous God judging the nation's deeds.

Civil religion also depends very critically on its forms of expression. Without them, neither notions and feelings of transcendence nor myth and belief can become the property of the populace. The studies of Lloyd Warner, Robert Bellah, and others have concentrated on the ceremonial and verbal expression of the civil religion. Bellah concluded from his observation of religious allusions in public ceremony that they contain enough consistency and functionality to justify their generalization as a civil religion with a distinctive history. He called it a "public religious dimension . . . expressed in a set of beliefs, symbols, and rituals. . . ."[12]

Public ceremony cannot be separated from belief, and the myths that appear in presidential speeches are rich in specific belief content. God is the Creator, human beings are subject to God's will; Christ is redeemer; this land is a garden; the people are God's chosen; and the covenant is the metaphysical structure of American experience. Jeffersonians affirmed God as ultimate principle, nature as ground of law, truth as self-evident to reason, etc. All of this is widely varied as well as very specific and makes it difficult for the analyst of civil religion to establish its belief system. In the folk system, the beliefs that have traditionally

[11]Andrew Carnegie, "Wealth," *North American Review* 148 (June, 1889): 653–664.
[12]Bellah, "Civil Religion," p. 4.

bulwarked the American social system are the doctrine of a personal God who knows what human beings are doing, belief that consequences of wrongdoing are ultimately inescapable, and belief that oaths are broken only at the risk of divine vengeance. These are not the principal points of the Christian religion, but they occur within its system. There are other beliefs that Americans have generally considered to rest on transcendent grounds: government may not expect obedience to "laws" that violate nature; majorities must prevail, but not at the expense of the natural rights of dissenters; the right of revolution is inherent, but only when basic rights are violated. In their own way, these beliefs articulate commitment to the transcendent as conceived by eighteenth-century republicanism.

The civil religion is as substantially a world of belief as it is of tradition or ceremony. Bellah spells out a detailed theology in analyzing the Inaugural address of John Kennedy, and Mead does the same with Lincoln's addresses.[13] While presidents usually refer to God without introducing blatantly sectarian notions, their invocations of deity are futile if they do not motivate citizens to efforts constructive for the nation and deter them from actions hostile to it. For this there must be belief content in the civil religion. Nothing more vividly illustrates the union of definite belief with public motivation than the "Battle Hymn of the Republic." A sort of scripture of the civil religion of the North, it invoked God as judge and identified the northern armies as divine avengers. Without this kind of quality and content, civil religion cannot function as public motivator, controller, and guarantor.

Critique of the Civil Religion

The question of the viability of the civil religion as a concept is principally a question of the adequacy of its grasp upon the transcendent. Clearly there are dangers. A nation's understanding of the transcendent must never be developed so that the nation sees itself as transcendent or sets national values in conflict with the interests of citizens (statism). Nor can we impose American values and interests on non-American peoples (imperialism).

While there exists no stable taxonomy of civil religions, we perceive distinct types. The first of these clearly identifies democracy as religion. J. Paul Williams in *What Americans Believe and How They Worship*[14] first cites the precept of Robin M. Williams that "every functioning society has to an important degree a *common* religion" and that "a society's common-value system—its 'moral solidarity'—is always correlated with and to a degree dependent upon a shared religious orientation." He then calls upon the positive religions of the United States to recognize that "the spiritual core [and] heart of [America's] national existence" is a "democratic faith," and states: "democracy must become an

[13]Bellah, "Civil Religion"; Sidney Mead, "Abraham Lincoln's 'Last, Best Hope of Earth': The American Dream of Destiny and Democracy," *Lively Experiment,* pp. 72ff.

[14]*What Americans Believe and How They Worship,* rev. ed. (New York: Harper and Row, 1952), pp. 484ff.

object of religious dedication.'' Further: ''government agencies must teach the democratic ideal *as religion*.'' There must be ''an open indoctrination of the faith that the democratic ideal accords with ultimate reality . . . that democracy is the very Law of Life. . . .'' Recognizing the need for supporting public ceremonial, he cites the Nazi mass meeting as an effective model and equates communism, fascism, and democracy as ideologies ''equally suited to religious devotion.''

The principal instrument for teaching the religion of democracy is, of course, the public school, which in Williams' system assumes the role of an American ''state-church.'' Its principal doctrines Williams cites from A. Powell Davies:

> . . . belief that man . . . can raise the level of his life indefinitely, making the world increasingly more happy, more just, and more good; no fate has made him prisoner of his circumstances, no natural weakness has condemned him to be ruled by tyranny. He is meant to be free. Through the power of reason he can form intelligent opinions, and by discussion and debate can test them. Knowing that truth is precious above all things and the only safe guide to purposes and aims, the right to seek it must be held inviolate.
>
> The democratic faith declares that human rights are by their nature universal: that liberty is such a right, and that without liberty there cannot be justice; that, to ensure justice, the people should make the laws under which they live; that besides justice there should be benevolence and sympathy; that those doctrines of religion which beseech mankind to practice brotherhood are right; that love must expel hate, and good will take the place of malice; that as well as zeal there must be patience and forbearance, and that persuasion is better than coercion; that none should hold the people in contempt, or profane the sacredness of conscience, or deny the worth of human life; and finally, that God and history are on the side of freedom and justice, love and righteousness; and man will therefore, be it soon or late, achieve a world society of peace and happiness where all are free and none shall be afraid.[15]

Professor Williams has done what his philosophy calls for: identified the right beliefs. He does not recoil from the need to suppress beliefs and attitudes thus recognizable as hostile to the national values. This country has had its bouts with such problems, and they have always been the test of liberty: the Mormon cases, refusals to salute the flag, the debate about religion as a basis for conscientious objection. Precisely this debate over the right religion forced England to opt for religious toleration in the seventeenth century. And toleration was adopted in the name of one of Professor Williams' cardinal values, freedom of conscience.

Williams seems not to have understood Lincoln. During the Civil War, both North and South held specific doctrines which they believed had transcendent sanctions, and soldiers on both sides proved willing to die for them. To this conflict of religiously-held civil values, Lincoln spoke: ''Both read the same Bible, and pray to the same God; and each invokes his aid against the other.'' But both prayers could not be answered. Lincoln concluded that the ''Almighty has

---

[15]*Man's Vast Future* (New York: Farrar, Strauss, and Cudahy, 1951), pp. 27ff.

his own purposes." Worshippers of an autonomous God do not dictate to God. To take God seriously is precisely to seek God's will and obey it, not announce its correspondence with national or sectional cause. The powerful civil religions of the 1860's did not grasp the reality of God. God is not the guarantor of one side or another, but the judge of both and the vindicator of the oppressed. The paradox of the modern civil religion debate is that the supreme invocation of God in American public history precisely denied the civil religions then prevailing. Lincoln stood very much alone when he divorced himself from the clashing cause-religions and spoke of the divine on quite different grounds.

Robert Bellah, working from sociological assumptions, seeks to avoid the gross establishmentarianism of Williams. Bellah wrote in 1973:

> Herbert Richardson argues persuasively for the importance, indeed the indispensability, of a notion of transcendence in a democratic polity. Such a notion provides the highest symbolic expression and legitimation for the openness of a genuinely participational political process. But it is essential that the transcendence which is a constitutive part of the democratic process remain symbolically empty, for particularity of content would operate to prevent precisely the openness it is meant to guarantee.[16]

Bellah commends Martin Marty's distinction between civil religion and "public theology"—the latter comprising varying beliefs expressed by specific religious traditions about national affairs which, notwithstanding their differences, are good for the country.

Bellah attempts to deal with the intolerable implications of Williams' government religion by denying it all specific content. Against his background of oriental studies, Bellah remarks that the Mahayana Buddhist concept of *sunyata* (emptiness) might serve America better than the symbol of the biblical Jehovah. President Eisenhower is much congratulated by proponents of the civil religion for his presumed view that religion is important to the country but what people choose for religious doctrine is not. Such talk simply does not correspond with American historical reality. The American civil religion expounded by those who discern it is very much a matter of content. No civil religion can exist in a liberal democracy without at a minimum affirming that, God being God and man being infinite, no authority can exist in human affairs for curbing free discourse.

The civil religion is built on the notion that religious beliefs have positive cash value for civil life. The Eisenhower principle means simply that any belief is acceptable provided its cash value for public affairs conforms to the national interest as judged, presumably, by existing custom, law, opinion makers, judges, and prosecuting attorneys. For example, belief in God cashes out to "democracy is sacred"; human finitude cashes out to "free speech is sacred"; God's justice cashes out to "minority rights must be vindicated."

---

[16]Richey and Jones, *American Civil Religion,* p. 258.

American social history demonstrates, however, that numerous beliefs cash out negatively. The doctrine of creation has been more than once cashed out to a ban on the teaching of evolution. The Genesis story of the creation of Eve out of the body of Adam has been cashed out to the precedence of man over woman. Belief that slavery is taught in the Bible was once cashed to justify southern secession, and the northern doctrine that slaveholding is sin converted General Sherman's scorched earth policy into God's vengeance on southern slaveholders. One must conclude that since not every belief held among Americans is subject to politically favorable interpretation, government must define correct doctrines and repress teachings, even those of churches and sects, that foster harmful effects. The fantasy of contentless civil religion provides no refuge.

Any viable concept of the civil religion involves establishment. Williams candidly advocates curbs on religious freedom for the sake of the benefits of a civilly-oriented religion. Worse, from the point of view of religion itself, is the debasement of transcendence itself. What Lincoln rebuked in North and South, advocates of the religion of democracy do: having decided what is true religion, they call down the fires of transcendence upon it. But "the Almighty has his own purposes." God is autonomous, or God is not transcendent.

Professor Sidney Mead makes a more sensitive case than either Williams or Bellah, and his choice represents a second major option for civil religion:

> These then are the fundamental beliefs on which the democracy rests: belief in God, belief in "the people," belief in the voice of the people as the surest clue to the voice of God, belief that truth emerges out of the conflict of opinions.... The only safeguard against [trespass of the majority on the rights of the minority] is the conviction that under God truth and right are not matters of majority vote. It is for this reason that democracy without faith in God is likely to sink into demagogic mobocracy.[17]

Mead denies Williams' proposition that "governmental agencies must teach the democratic idea as religion." Democracy is not itself human destiny; it is good because it enables free people to "fulfil their destiny under God." Furthermore, democracy "rests upon faith in the God who is the only object of religious devotion—the Christian [sic] God of mercy and of judgment—the God of creation, of providence, and of history."[18]

Mead notes that the reverence accorded the European state-church was directed by many immigrants toward the nation itself, since they could clearly not revere the congeries of religions that made this nation different. This reverence, together with its referent, Mead prefers to call the "Religion of the Republic": the generally Christian religiousness which came to be associated with notions of American peoplehood and destiny. This must be clearly distinguished from the

---

[17]*The Lively Experiment*, pp. 83, 86.
[18]Ibid., p. 83.

"civil religion" insofar as that term is equated with the views of Williams and, to a lesser degree, Bellah. Mead repudiates the consecrating role of civil religion; his religion of the Republic is prophetic, and Lincoln is its archetype.

There is, however, a problem in Mead's concept, which touches the central issue, transcendence. For Lincoln, the God who is above all gods, including the disputing sections of the American people, is the Transcendent, whereas for Mead the transcendent is a dynamic national ideal operating in the minds of the people. It is no less prophetic on account of its immanence.

> The "worlds above the given world" are pictures in the great mythologies or dramas of the religions, which hold before the people the ideals and aspirations which define their sense of destiny and purpose.... The religion of this, our Republic, is of this nature. Therefore to be committed to that religion is not to be committed to this world as it is, but to a world as yet above and beyond it to which this world ought to be conformed. The "American religion," contrary to Will Herberg's much popularized misunderstanding, is *not* the American way of life as we know and experience it.... Seen thus the religion of the Republic is essentially prophetic, which is to say that its ideals and aspirations stand in constant judgment over the passing shenanigans of the people....[19]

The risks of public religion are clear to Mead: we must "assure ourselves that our attitude toward the nation does not become idolatrous; that the state does not become God; that the Republic does not become heteronomous vis-à-vis other nations."[20] Mead speaks explicitly of a theology of the nation: "the theology of the synergistic and theonomous religion of the Republic stands against this idolatrous tendency equally with Christianity...." Nevertheless, Mead's own version of the theology of the public religion is derived from Whitehead, Tillich, and earlier republican views. In its own way, this reveals a characteristic of public religion in any form: it is a social and evolutionary phenomenon; it is a child of the American soul; it is not a child of revelation. Lincoln himself blended biblical insights with republican commitments. It is certainly true that idealism may function to create powerful tensions in the mind of a people distressed with contemporaneous reality, and this may be called "prophetic." The fact remains that there is a very wide difference between the Jewish and Christian critique of idolatry of all sorts and that transcendence which proceeds from philosophical idealism. "Transcendence" is not exempt from the general truth that words can be given any meaning their users choose; but a religion with a reasonably stable "theology," even a religion of a Republic, cannot equate the God of the Old Testament with the creatures of the republican age.

One cannot but return to Walter Lippmann with a certain sense of relief. Long distressed by the deterioration of public morale and polity, Lippmann analyzed and regretted the infidelity of America to its own "public philosophy":

---

[19]Richey and Jones, *American Civil Religion*, p. 60.
[20]Ibid., p. 70.

his concern was with "the inner principles of [American democratic] institutions." He never spoke of religion; for him, these principles had a power base of their own. Indeed, their power arose in part from their very immanence in the human mind. First among these immanent principles is the natural law and America's belief, derived from both the Enlightenment and medieval traditions that passed largely unquestioned into the Puritan heritage, that reality contains imperatives and sanctions which human beings violate at their peril. A sort of "relative transcendence" characterizes this view of reality. Lippmann remarked that political ideas obtain legitimacy as they bind conscience. "Then they possess, as the Confucian doctrine has it, 'the mandate of heaven.'" Lippmann is here a semantic breath away from contemporary expositions of the public religion, minus their claim on the sort of transcendence of which Lincoln spoke.

Lippmann is surely right in believing that the dissolution of an ennobling common philosophy of humanity and society puts any nation in danger of falling to pieces. But for all his steady telling of this truth, he awakened no power in the national soul to cure its sickness. A new generation of scholars proposes to tap a traditional power source: the sense of transcendence that moved the New Model Army, Cromwell himself, and their successors in North America. The power of the transcendence they knew lies precisely in its "otherness" than anything known to human philosophy. For all the currency of early republican ideas in the New Model Army, its behavior was profoundly shaped by the notion that God disposes among the ambitions and whimsies of human beings.

This great mystery the proponents of the civil religion are attempting to recapture and apply on behalf of American national restitution. Such is the nature of the commitment, however, that it cannot be done by elevating the public philosophy of Lippmann or any version of the civil religion to that plane of holiness which is required. If it were done, it would be a deception of ideas, and it would betray what we have learned from English and American history about the essence of religious liberty.

Public ceremonies may truly touch the mystic chords of American idealism, but neither they nor the noblest public philosophy can be equated with the transcendence that stands forth in Lincoln's Second Inaugural Address: none other than the autonomous God who judges nations, causes, and religions in accordance with a will which, though often inscrutable, is always just and always vindicates the oppressed.

The transcendence for which the proponents of the public religion are reaching cannot be a characteristic of anything, whether doctrine or ritual. It is futile to promulgate something old or new and declare it transcendent. Transcendence is not "made in America." Noble themes and evocative ceremonies there are, but they are religion only as sociology defines it and they possess a purely relative transcendence at best. But God is not put to the uses of peoples and nations. All civil religions are intrinsically flawed because they would make use of God. Such an intention extinguishes the fire that gives them life. The discipline of religion, if not sociology, anthropology, and philosophy, is able to know that it is God

who makes use of nations and that it is the part of the people to humble themselves.

I am fully aware that I speak from America's earliest Christian myth, as
Lincoln did. On a sociological basis it is certainly possible to discern, devise, and
even promulgate something that may be called a civil religion. The idea is
postulated by that discipline. Sidney Mead's thinking is finely tuned to the
history of American Christianity and its traditions of civility and liberty. But
even he draws away from the religion that undergirded Lincoln's interpretation of
the civil war and prefers, as civil religion inevitably must, the national idealism
whose claim to transcendence is grounded in the theory of an immanent natural
law. Yet between the notion of natural law and the Creator and Judge of all law
there is fixed a great gulf. If American national restitution can be accomplished
by a return of respect for the theory and myth of the natural law, well and good;
that is not a matter of religion, insofar as transcendence is constitutive of religion. But if it is true that the power to move nations lies with a God of ultimate
and unconditional transcendence, it would be more useful for scholars who seek
the national restitution to help this not-yet-chosen people understand the judgment of God on the United States for its countless offenses against righteousness,
rather than promulgating the ritual and dogma of a religion of American democracy.

RELIGIOUS LIBERTY—A GLOBAL VIEW

Philip Potter

It is a daunting task to be the only foreigner to speak at what is a national celebration. Americans have every reason to be proud of their history of religious liberty. Indeed, it can be said that historically this country was the testing ground of religious liberty, which is now universally accepted as a basic human right. I do not have to go into the history of the Pilgrims and of the Roman Catholic settlers, not to speak of those who, like Tom Paine, found in America a place where they could propagate and practice religionless freedom. We could also mention those remarkable men such as Washington, Jefferson, Franklin, Madison and Hamilton, who arrived at the principle of religious liberty from the prevailing philosophy of the Enlightenment in a Europe which had grown weary of religious wars and was bursting with new life as it discovered the ordered laws which governed nature and, therefore, human beings. All this has been brought out during these days or written in numerous books and articles.

My assignment is to take a global view of religious liberty and to suggest ways in which the USA is involved. I take it that Father Hesburgh will concentrate on American responsibility for the questions raised by religious liberty abroad. Naturally, I will be speaking from the perspective of the ecumenical movement and in particular from the experience of the World Council of Churches.

I

First I would like to refer to the way in which religious liberty has been developed in ecumenical perspective. Reference has already been made in this Conference to the statements of the World Council of Churches and to the Declaration of Vatican II on Religious Freedom.[1] But I want to take this opportunity to pay a warm tribute to one person who made an outstanding contribution to ecumenical and international discussions and declarations on religious liberty. I refer to the late Dr. Frederick Nolde, who was for many years professor in the Lutheran Theological Seminary here in Philadelphia and Dean of its Graduate School, as well as being a lecturer at the University of Pennsylvania. From 1943 to 1968 he worked tirelessly and with extraordinary knowledge, ingenuity, and wisdom to persuade the churches and the United Nations to adopt adequate safeguards on religious freedom within the general framework, and as an integral part, of human rights. He has told his own story, with his usual dedicated verve,

---

[1] *Dignitatis Humanae;* cf. Walter M. Abbott, ed., *The Documents of Vatican II* (New York: Guild Press/America Press/Association Press, 1966), pp. 672–700.

Dr. Philip A. Potter is General Secretary of the World Council of Churches, Geneva, Switzerland.

in a little book, *Free and Equal* (published by the World Council of Churches in 1968). It is therefore most appropriate that the organizer of this Conference is his widow, Nancy Nolde. Indeed, this Conference is a fitting memorial to the outstanding work done by Frederick Nolde in the field of human rights, and especially of religious liberty.

We can properly start with the famous Four Freedoms speech of Franklin D. Roosevelt to Congress in January, 1941, and the subsequent Atlantic Charter in August, 1941. I well remember listening that August Sunday afternoon to the voice of Roosevelt enunciating those Four Freedoms. It was for us young people in the Caribbean a word of hope. Let us listen once more to Roosevelt's unforgettable words:

> In the future days which we seek to make secure, we look forward to a world founded upon four essential human freedoms.

> The first is freedom of speech and expression—everywhere in the world. The second is freedom of every person to worship God in his own way—everywhere in the world. The third is freedom from want—which, translated into world terms, means economic understandings which will secure to every nation a healthy peacetime life for its inhabitants—everywhere in the world. The fourth is freedom from fear—which, translated into world terms, means a worldwide reduction of armaments to such a point and in such a thorough fashion that no nation will be in a position to commit an act of physical aggression against any neighbor—anywhere in the world.... Freedom means the supremacy of human rights everywhere. Our support goes to those who struggle to gain those rights or keep them. Our strength is our unity of purpose.

The Federal Council of Churches and the Foreign Missions Conference (which together later became the National Council of Churches of Christ in the U.S.A.) established a Joint Committee on Religious Liberty in 1943, of which Dr. Nolde was the Executive Secretary. In 1944 a statement was issued which included the following paragraphs:

> The right of individuals everywhere to religious liberty shall be recognized and, subject only to the maintenance of public order and security, shall be guaranteed against legal provisions and administrative acts which would impose political, economic, or social disabilities on grounds of religion....

> Religious liberty shall be interpreted to include freedom to worship according to conscience and to bring up children in the faith of their parents; freedom for the individual to change his religion; freedom to preach, educate, publish and carry on missionary activities; and freedom to organize with others, and to acquire and hold property for these purposes.

That statement was shared with a similar British Joint Committee which produced a "Charter of Religious Freedom."

The representation of the churches, under the leadership of Dr. Nolde, at the

San Francisco Conference in 1945 ensured that one of the principal purposes of the new U.N. would be "to achieve international cooperation . . . in promoting and encouraging respect for human rights and fundamental freedoms for all without distinction as to race, sex, language or religion" (Art. 1, Sec. 3). The churches also pressed for the setting up of a Commission on Human Rights for "promoting and encouraging respect for human rights and for fundamental freedoms." By 1946, the World Council of Churches, then in process of formation, and the International Missionary Council established the Commission of the Churches on International Affairs under the directorship of Dr. Nolde. This brought into the discussion leaders of many Orthodox and Protestant churches around the world. The CCIA called for an International Declaration of Human Rights, for Covenants spelling out in greater detail those rights, and for measures for implementing the Covenants. When the First Assembly of the W.C.C. met in Amsterdam in 1948, it passed a resolution appealing to its constituent member churches to press for the adoption of an International Bill of Human Rights. It also adopted a Declaration on Religious Liberty, in which the following points were made:

(1) Every person has the right to determine his own faith and creed.
(2) Every person has the right to express his religious beliefs in worship, teaching and practice and to proclaim the implications of his beliefs for relationships in a social or political community.
(3) Every person has the right to associate with others and to organize with them for religious purposes.
(4) Every religious organization formed or maintained by action in accordance with the rights of individual persons, has the right to determine its policies and practices for the accomplishment of its chosen purposes.

It was therefore with great satisfaction to the churches that the U.N. General Assembly meeting in Paris soon after the Assembly did pass a Universal Declaration on Human Rights. Dr. Nolde tells us of the concerted effort of Orthodox, Protestant, and Roman Catholic leaders, as also of Jews and Muslims, to secure the passage of Article 18 of the Declaration: "Everyone has the right to freedom of thought, conscience and religion; this right includes freedom to change his religion or belief, and freedom, either alone or in community with others and in public or private, to manifest his religion or belief in teaching, practice, worship and observance." This is important because it indicates the recognition that "freedom of thought, conscience and religion" was considered an inalienable right of all members of the human family regardless of confession or religion or ideology. The next task was the production of the International Covenants on Human Rights—the Covenant on Economic, Social and Cultural Rights, and the Covenant on Civil and Political Rights—which were adopted in December, 1966. The first was ratified last year and the second is in process of being ratified.

During these years the World Council has again and again spoken on human rights and religious liberty. On December, 1965, the Second Vatican Council produced its strong Declaration on Religious Freedom, which says, *inter alia:*

> This Vatican Council declares that the human person has a right to religious freedom. This freedom means that all men are to be immune from coercion on the part of individuals or of social groups and of any human power, in such wise that no one is to be forced to act in a manner contrary to his own beliefs, nor is anyone to be restrained from acting in accordance with his own beliefs, whether privately or publicly, whether alone or in association with others, within due limits.

> The Council further declares that the right to religious freedom has its foundation in the very dignity of the human person as this dignity is known through the revealed Word of God and by reason itself. This right of the human person to religious freedom is to be recognized in the constitutional law whereby society is governed and thus it is to become a civil right.

This in itself was a great step forward, because at long last the whole Christian world had ranged itself on the side of promoting religious liberty for all. For centuries the churches had been in conflict over this fundamental human right. It is no secret that Protestant concern about religious liberty was partly directed at the Roman Catholic Church which in many countries, notably in Latin Europe and Latin America, had up to the 1950's been somewhat hostile to the presence and activity of Protestant witness.

I have tried to outline the role of the churches and of the U.N. in calling for international recognition of religious liberty for three reasons. First, the Christian churches around the world and people of other living faiths have now accepted religious liberty as a basic human right everywhere and relate it integrally with the other human rights. Secondly, the U.N.O. itself has rendered a great service by promoting human rights and religious liberty so persistently during these thirty years of its existence. In view of the prevailing negative attitude toward the U.N. in the western world and especially in this country, it is important to hail this remarkable achievement on what has been one of the most sensitive and divisive issues facing the nations and peoples of the world. Thirdly, American religious leaders—Protestant, Catholic and Jewish, and both clerical and lay— have played a considerable part in bringing about this achievement. One could say that this was a natural outcome of a long American tradition, enshrined as it was in the Declaration of Independence. But it also implies a very heavy responsibility on the American people to help implement these human rights, both here and abroad.

II

What then is the situation of religious liberty around the world today? What is the responsibility of religious groups in promoting effective religious liberty? What in particular is American involvement in this field? In facing these questions we must keep constantly before our minds the radically changed character of the relations of nations and peoples, and therefore of religious liberty, since 1945.

First, during these years a large number of countries have gained their independence from colonial rule. The self-determination of peoples has become an accepted fact. Many countries which have been independent in a formal political sense are seeking to rid themselves of economic and cultural imperialism. Minority groups are claiming their rights to preserve and express their particular ways of life and are resisting what they call "ethnocide." In all these situations religions—and especially Christianity—have played an ambiguous role in promoting religious liberty. For example, Christianity during the colonial period had secured for itself a position of dominance along with the imperialist powers of the West. While demanding for itself religious liberty, it was by no means consistent in respecting the religious liberty of those with whom it had to do.

Christianity has itself become a minority almost everywhere, if not in numbers, certainly in status. Even in those countries which have been traditionally Christian, there has been an influx of people coming as workers who have different religious allegiances and demand the right to practice religious liberty, including the propagation of their faith. The situation in our world has become one of pluralism—a pluralism which the founding fathers of the U.S. were seeking to establish and foster in the name of religious liberty. This has now become a worldwide phenomenon. There is a sense in which the concern of the churches and other religious groups to secure the recognition and implementation of human rights, including religious liberty, demonstrates their acceptance of the present reality.

How can this pluralism be affirmed, maintained, and allowed to be fruitful for the benefit of the human family? A significant development during these years has been the dialogue between people of different living faiths and ideologies. Dialogue is seen not as an intellectual exercise, but as an expression of the meeting of life with life in mutual respect, trust, and caring. It is, as the Jewish philosopher Martin Buber taught us, the way of recognizing and furthering the otherness of a person, group, or culture, which is mutually enriching. Such dialogue presupposes and indeed makes a reality of all that is implied in religious liberty, as described ecumenically and internationally. Christians have recently been promoting dialogue with people of other living faiths. This has facilitated the discussion of specific issues of the violation of religious liberty in particular countries. There are examples of this in traditionally Muslim-dominated areas of the world, where the problems of religious liberty have even in the recent past been acute.

Dialogue between people of different religious faiths takes place in the context of the search for community in justice and peace. Confronted with the violations of human rights, especially economic and social oppression, there is opened up the possibility of sharing faith convictions for facing these violations and working for a more just society. This is a clear example of the interaction of religious liberty with other fundamental human rights.

There are cases where cultural and religious minorities are now making their voices heard against the assault on their identity. In the last ten years or so there has been a big debate about mission to the Latin American Indians, who have felt that their culture has been despised and that they are being forced to accept a Christianity under missionary effort which is destructive of their beings and makes them a prey to political and economic exploitation. There is growing sensitivity about situations like this which involve not only religious liberty but also other human rights.

Even among Christians there is considerable questioning in what were once called "mission lands" of the pressure to maintain a western style of expressing the Christian faith, whether in confessions or worship or ways of making decisions. Many Christians in Asia, Africa, Latin America, and the island world consider western missionary power an infringement of their religious liberty and human rights, and are calling for a moratorium on western presence in their midst. Moreover, while in the past Christians in their philanthropic help to peoples in need were tempted to use this as a means of subtle coercion, of evangelizing or proselytizing, this is no more the case. Christianity has in the process gained in credibility as a faith which is disinterested in its goodwill towards all persons.

Secondly, during these thirty years there has developed a clear realization of the interdependence of peoples around the world. Thanks to the technological revolution, which has conquered space and brought the economies of peoples and nations so closely together, there is no way of being isolated in today's world. The U.S.A. has played a major role in this process as the nation which has, in the last thirty years, become the most powerful state in the world with its tentacles, whether economic or military, all over the globe. It is at this point that the interrelation between religious liberty and the other fundamental human rights becomes most acutely patent.

In this connection, at the Fifth Assembly of the W.C.C. in 1975, this interrelation was brought out in the statement on human rights and on religious liberty in particular. It says:

> By religious freedom we mean the freedom to have or to adopt a religion or belief of one's choice, and freedom, either individually or in community with others and in public or private, to manifest one's religion or belief in worship, observance, practice or teaching. Religious freedom should also include the right and duty of religious bodies to criticize the ruling powers when necessary, on the basis of their religious convictions. In this context, it was noted that many Christians in different parts of the world are in prison for reasons of conscience or for political reasons as a result of their seeking to respond to the total demands of the Gospel.

I want to illustrate what is implied in this statement in different parts of the world, because it raises a fundamental question of the nature and implication of religious liberty.

In the Republic of Korea, which is closely allied to the U.S., Christians have been expressing their religious liberty by identifying themselves with those who are deprived of their human rights, who are economically and socially exploited, and who are hardly able to express their religious freedom. These Christians are drawing out the implications of their faith to expose this situation and to challenge the government to respect human rights and to be more just in its dealings with its citizens. The result has been harassment, imprisonment, and the deprivation of the rights of such Christians. Efforts have been made to get teams of Christian leaders, including Americans, to visit Korea and also to make representations to the U.S. government on this matter. One crucial element here is the dependence of the Korean government on U.S. military and economic aid which are being used to violate human rights.

In Latin America today there is a tragic struggle going on among people who, though politically free in a formal sense, are under the grip of foreign economic power. All over the continent local oligarchies are ganging up with foreign powers, especially the U.S., to develop quickly economically, but at the expense of the vast majority of the people. In the past the churches have been active or passive supporters of these violations of human rights. But in the last fifteen years there has been a radical change in outlook among the churches. The result has been that Christians have expressed their religious liberty by drawing out the implications of the Gospel for the recognition of the basic human rights of people, as enshrined in the Covenants on Human Rights adopted by the U.N. They have in the process developed a "theology of liberation" which is in fact an exposition of what the Universal Declaration of Human Rights and the Covenants mean from the viewpoint of Christian faith. Here again, many Christians have been imprisoned, tortured, and even killed because of the exercise of their religious liberty for the sake of the poor and the oppressed. Here again, the U.S. government and U.S. multi-national and other enterprises have appeared to undergird oppressive regimes which flagrantly violate human rights including religious liberty.

In the U.S.A. itself and in Southern Africa, racism has been institutionalised in a manner which has been a denial of human rights and often of religious liberty. While the situation in the U.S.A. is by no means as desperate as it is in Southern Africa, there are similar elements in both areas. Indeed, the U.S.A. led the way in what was to happen elsewhere. The very Declaration of Independence excluded the blacks and Indians. Religious liberty was not seen as having implications for the conduct of people in the nation to one another. Even churches were and still are segregated. In Southern Africa, and particularly Rhodesia and South Africa, the system of racial oppression has again been considerably strengthened by economic investments and the sale of arms through secret military deals. The U.S.A. has played a not inconsiderable role in this. In response to this denial of human rights, black Christians have been articulating a "black theology" which exposes the violation of fundamental freedoms in both the U.S.A. and Southern Africa.

There are other situations which can be mentioned briefly. In the Middle East, we have the continuing conflict between Israel and neighboring Arab states and especially the Palestinian Arabs. There are religious elements in the ideology of Zionism which make it difficult to envisage a sharing on equal terms of a state in Israel between Jews and Arabs, just as there have been religious elements in the prevention of Jews by Muslim Arabs from worshipping at the "wailing wall" before the 1967 war. These elements have to be faced sooner rather than later if any lasting solution is to be found in that festering conflict. Similarly, in the present conflict in Lebanon, while the main factors making for such wanton destruction of human life are political and economic, there is no doubt that the historic divisions between Christians and Muslims and among Christians themselves have greatly exacerbated the conflict. In Northern Ireland, we see the result of English colonialism which was Protestant in religious allegiance against a people who were Roman Catholic. While the main causes of the continuing conflict have been political and economic, the very meeting of these peoples has created a climate in which it has been the Catholics who, as a religio-cultural group, have found their human rights being denied. It is correct to say that the conflicts in the Middle East and in Northern Ireland are not, strictly speaking, religious, but they do have their roots in the denial of human rights, including religious rights, in the past.

To return to Africa, there are two interesting situations which raise questions of religious liberty. Mozambique was for over 400 years a province of Portugal. Such was the religious colonialism in Mozambique that one Roman Catholic order, the White Fathers, felt compelled to withdraw in 1971, because they considered that they were being denied the right to exercise their religious duties to the people in anything more than formal ways. All the bishops were Portuguese and were paid by the state. Now that Mozambique is independent, the new government insists on taking responsibility for educational, medical, and other social work which was the bastion of foreign missionary power. A delicate situation has arisen with the churches, though reports that religious liberty is being curtailed have been denied by Mozambiquan Christians. However, this is a clear example of a reaction to the denial of human and religious freedoms in the past. In Ethiopia we have a situation where the ancient Orthodox Church had been part of the imperial system of oppression of the peasants. With the change in the regime, the Church failed to go beyond statements of intent to actual reform of its life in a manner which would respect basic human rights. In the process the military government has improperly deposed the Patriarch, though it is allowing the Church to appoint a new Patriarch in July, 1976. Curiously enough, this military government is also endeavoring to follow the declarations of the U.N. in devising a constitution which would recognize all religions as having equal rights.

The above examples are indications of the ways in which religious liberty and the other human rights are intertwined. This Conference has been discussing issues in this perspective for the U.S.A. It is no less true for other parts of the world. What is important here is that we become aware how, one way or the other, the American state and American economic involvement have a profound influence on whether human rights, including religious liberty, are observed or not, especially in the Third World.

In recent years, a particularly acute example of the relation of religious liberty to other human rights has been seen in the socialist states. Here we are dealing with a quite different ideology from that of the West, with its tradition of individual rights as the basis for all other rights. Marxist ideology insists that social rights must take precedence. In its analysis of capitalist societies, it has concluded that religion was an oppressive factor, or at least a passive supporter of the oppressive powers. While these states allow religious liberty in the form of religious worship and association, they are, in varying ways, hostile to people's using their religious liberty to draw out the implications of their faith by being critical of aspects of the system. The knowledge of the suppression of such people has greatly increased lately. The Helsinki Agreement, with its restatement of the observance of religious liberty in accordance with the declarations and covenants of the U.N., makes it possible to challenge the socialist states to liberalize their practices regarding religious liberty. It must, however, be admitted that there is considerable truth in the fact that before these states were set up, the churches had not been officially conspicuous in maintaining basic human rights, especially social rights. Even religious liberty was not often observed. These churches are now going through a radical change in their attitudes to religious liberty and to issues of social justice.

Another comment which needs to be made on this matter is that while it is proper to challenge socialist states about the religious liberty of those who, because of their faith, feel compelled to question aspects of the life of their countries which they consider to be a denial of human rights, we should also ask ourselves whether in the western world there is much sympathy or tolerance for those who, on the basis of their religious liberty, challenge their societies and governments about the denial and violation of human rights and especially social rights. This is a question which the U.S. needs to face. A further comment here is that experience in the ecumenical movement has shown that the way forward in having a fruitful dialogue with people from the socialist states about religious liberty is to discuss both individual and social rights in their inextricable relationship. If such a dialogue is to lead to the implementation of the Helsinki Agreement, then all the signatory states will have to learn to do the same. From a Christian point of view, human rights are indivisible. That is the challenge for all of us, and not least for the U.S.A.

Finally, the issue of religious liberty is being raised in a new way all over the world. The challenge of secularism in a technological culture has been to emphasize those values which downgrade the spiritual dimensions of life. Consumerism, the emphasis on having rather than being, the brutal destruction of nature in the interests of economic growth—all these and more are having a dehumanizing and alienating effect on people everywhere. Even in socialist states, religious hunger is expressing itself in ways which the authorities did not anticipate and seem unable to cope with. Everywhere there is a search for spiritual sources and resources for living. One interesting sign of this is the way in which western young people are submitting themselves to Asian gurus and to new charismatic movements, some of which are not very respectful of the liberty of persons. The only comment I would make here is that this is a clear indication that religious liberty is not an end in itself. It is a means whereby people may be enabled to draw from the depths of spiritual wisdom and revelation in order to become fuller persons expressing and being all that they were intended to be. The problem as I see it is that, for example, in this country religious liberty has become an ideology rather than a means for people to seek to fulfil the purposes for which this nation was proclaimed.

Speaking as a Christian, I would say in conclusion that religious liberty is God's way of enabling us to explore all the implications of our faith for the whole of our lives and for all persons of whatever race, sex, or religion. It is in this perspective that we are involved in questions of human rights and religious liberty in the ecumenical movement. I hope that in the period following this Bicentennial, the religious groups and the nation as a whole will make religious liberty a reality—a reality of wholeness for all here and abroad.

THE AMERICAN RESPONSIBILITY FOR FOSTERING RELIGIOUS LIBERTY INTERNATIONALLY

Theodore M. Hesburgh

It is a curious paradox that America is one of the most criticized countries on earth, especially if one listens to U. N. debates, and yet, at the same time, America is the country which most people would prefer to live in, if they were free to choose. The reason for the worldwide criticism is, I believe, that our political ideals are so high, so universally human, so transcendent that any betrayal of these ideals in our national life is considered by all the world to be a kind of global sin—a sin against the hopes and aspirations of all humankind for human freedom, justice, and dignity. The reason that so many peoples of every nation would like to live in America is that, whatever our national faults, there is a true opportunity here for everyone to enjoy life, liberty, and the pursuit of happiness, unlike other nations on earth.

When one considers this paradox of fierce criticism and obvious envy of America, it should be clear to all Americans that we have a special responsibility before all the world. In a sense, we always have had such a world responsibility because we had such a great opportunity to create, among other things, the greatest haven of religious freedom that the world has ever seen. America was, in its very birth, an answer to religious intolerance, prejudice, and persecution. Whether one considers the Puritans in Massachusetts, the Quakers in Pennsylvania, or the Catholics in Maryland, they all came to America to get away from a human condition that was inimical to their deepest religious beliefs. They came here to create a new human condition, and indeed they did. The amazing fact is that what they created far transcended both their wisdom and insights and their needs at that historical moment. What they did is still valid today, not only for us, but for the world situation as well.

Over a century later, the American Catholic Bishops, meeting for their Third Council in Baltimore, said: "We consider the establishment of our country's independence, the shaping of its liberties and laws, as the work of a special Providence, its framers building better than they knew, the Almighty's hand guiding them."

What was written in their Declaration of Independence spoke to the whole world, in solemn tones, and with a majesty of language that truly speaks, even today, to the heart of humankind, everywhere in the world. What they said changed the world then, and is still capable, as an idea, of changing the world today. "We hold these truths to be self-evident, that all men are created equal, that they are endowed by their Creator with certain inalienable rights, that among

The Rev. Theodore M. Hesburgh, C.S.C., is president of the University of Notre Dame, Notre Dame, IN.

these are life, liberty, and the pursuit of happiness. . . . that to secure these rights governments are instituted among men, deriving their just powers from the consent of the governed.''

Note that when these words flowed from the pen of Thomas Jefferson in the final draft, the fifty-six signers had no idea what kind of a government they would create to elicit the support of the governed and to secure these rights. Thank God, Jefferson changed the usual version of states' rights, life, liberty, and *property,* to life, liberty, and *the pursuit of happiness.* There are great human aspirations stored up in that pregnant phrase, "pursuit of happiness.''

While the promise of religious freedom brought early settlers to America, and ultimately to this day of independence, what the founders really legislated was far beyond religious liberty, and yet not uninspired by the religious liberty they now enjoyed. It has perhaps been the grateful role of free religious leaders, in all the futures of America, to help enlarge human dignity and human rights beyond the religious base to that more complete panoply of total human rights to which all people fundamentally aspire.

It is no chance event that many years later, following World War II, it was a Christian and a Jew, a woman and a man, an American and a Frenchman— Eleanor Roosevelt and Réné Cassin—who wrote the United Nations' Universal Declaration of Human Rights for the world.

What I would now like to focus on is how, in a most unique fashion, religious liberty was established in America by disestablishment. Secondly, I would like to trace, in the context of religious freedom, the enlargement of human dignity and rights in America, from the Declaration until today, and to indicate finally what this means to all the world.

It all began with a special sense of Governor John Winthrop of the Massachusetts Bay Colony, a key person in the quest for religious liberty, who saw his little band as a city "set upon a hill,'' not a light hidden under a bushel. The writers of our Declaration were conscious of the opinions of humankind regarding their actions. When later the Constitution was written, in a brief seventeen weeks, the founders took eight weeks to consider all existing governments in Europe and finally rejected all of them as potential models for America, because in the words of Benjamin Franklin, "They all carried with them the seeds of their own dissolution.'' How right he was! By some great providence, these fifty-six men, whose average age was only forty-two, devised a new and unprecedented form of government which was best characterized later by Abraham Lincoln as being "of the people, for the people, by the people.'' The whole world watched as the American experiment grew and prospered under the new Constitution.

With all of the genius of that discovery, I am convinced that the new Constitution would not have survived 200 years until today, had not that great American, Thomas Jefferson, put his finger on its fatal flaw. Jefferson was our Minister to France in 1787, and thus was absent from the Constitutional Convention in Philadelphia, the city where thirteen years before he had drafted the Declaration of Independence. When he read the new Constitution, he admitted

that it was a remarkable instrument of governance—especially in the checks and
balances of powers—his fellow Virginian, James Madison, had devised, faithfully following the political theory of Montesquieu, to solve the dilemma created
by the extreme and opposing Constitutional views of Alexander Hamilton and
George Mason. But Jefferson pointed to the missing element, the lack of a bill of
particulars regarding human rights, including the precise situation of religion and
religious liberty in America. Jefferson specified twenty such human rights and
declared that unless the Constitution were amended to include them, these rights
for which the signers of the Declaration of Independence had pledged their lives,
their liberty, and their sacred honor, he would see to it that the Constitution was
defeated, at least in Virginia and probably New York, too.

Such was the enormous prestige and leadership of Jefferson that they gave
him his Bill of Rights that included all of the rights he specified, and even more,
included the power to further amend the Constitution to secure an even broader
scope of rights, yet unmentioned. Thus, we were provided with the instrumentality to solve eventually the many ambiguities still unaccounted for in the Constitution, which largely looked to the rights of white Anglo-Saxon males. More of
this later. For the moment, I would like to call your attention to the interesting
fact that the very first of the Ten Amendments looked to religious freedom and
solved that fundamental problem in a most unusual and ingenious way in its first
two Articles.

For 1400 years, since the action of Emperor Constantine constituting Christianity as the official religion of the Roman Empire, religion had been established
by civil law, thus enjoying special status and favor within the state. While most
of the Colonists were dissenters who came to enjoy a new religious freedom,
soon enough they and their particular dissenting religion became a new
establishment—as Roger Williams found out when he dissented from the
newly-established religion and had to move to Rhode Island, then called Rogues
Island, to enjoy freedom for his particular beliefs.

Nine of the thirteen colonies soon had established religions, but soon enough
they also had their quota of drop-outs and dissenters. How were they to achieve
peace and freedom for all in the new nation, since no one church was strong
enough to prevail, and multiple establishment of multiple faiths seemed unworkable? Again, James Madison came up with an unique solution: depart from the
centuries-old, Augustinian theory of establishment, and cut off all churches from
legal and fiscal support by civil authority. Madison called this "a line of separation between the rights of religion and civil authority." Practice of religion and
fiscal support of religion would become voluntary under the disestablishment
clause of the First Amendment. They would also grow as never before.

This surprising innovation was immediately accepted with a sense of relief in
all but three of the Colonies. Eventually, it became so thoroughly accepted,
despite its dramatic departure from the governmental practice of fourteen centuries, that in 1888 Lord Bryce could write: "It is accepted as an axiom by all
Americans that the civil power ought to be not only neutral and impartial as

between different forms of faith, but ought to leave these matters entirely on one side. There seem to be no two opinions on this subject in the United States.''

Madison's solution linked together the problem of religious and civil rights and illuminated the problems of the latter that we still face. In his words: ''Security for civil rights must be the same as that for religious rights; it consists in the one case in a multiplicity of interests and in the other, in a multiplicity of sects.'' In either case, the nation needs peace and justice and freedom. If at that period in history you happened to be one of the 20,000 Catholics in America, or a Jew whose co-religionists were one-twentieth of one per cent of the population, the First Amendment came as a special blessing in a world of great religious conflict and dissension.

The interesting point is that with this new formulation and system of religious freedom, religion flourished and grew and became increasingly respected throughout the nation. While there was legal non-establishment of a particular religion, religion as such became established in the life of the nation in a very unique way by the ethos, customs, and practices of popular government, as well as by the pronouncements of its leaders who were never loath to call on God for help. Even so, starting with a largely Protestant religious background, it would be almost 200 years before America would have a Catholic President, and we still have to break new ground with a Jewish President.

The religious clauses of the First Amendment may well be seen as an ingenious invention of what Crevecoeur calls, ''this American, this new man'' to create a situation, a social environment protected by law, in which men and women of different religious faiths could live together in peace and with tolerance, a great civic virtue for Americans. However, I believe that John C. Calhoun really described the event more modestly when he said: ''This admirable federal Constitution of ours is superior to the wisdom of any or all of the men by whose agency it was made. The force of circumstances and not foresight or wisdom induced them to adopt many of its wisest provisions.'' I am inclined to add, though, that it was precisely the phenomenon of America, the attraction of a free religious situation for dissenters, that brought so many different religious and non-religious groups to America. Thus were the circumstances created that called for this very special solution contrary to all the political wisdom of almost a millenium and a half.

What should be of special interest to us today is that the world at large faces many of the tensions that faced a burgeoning America. New solutions, geared to peace, freedom, and justice are needed just as much for the world today as they were desperately needed by the new nation being born between 1776 and 1787. As they then faced the problem of creating one nation from thirteen widely diverse colonies, we now face the larger problem of creating one world from widely diverging nations and nationalities. Something valuable might be learned from the American experience in this same context.

John Courtney Murray has, in my judgment, best described the meaning of American peace and unity, despite the widely divergent faiths of its people:

The unity asserted in the American device, "E pluribus unum" . . . is a unity of a limited order. It does not go beyond the exigencies of civil conversation [such as we are having today] . . . This civil unity, therefore, must not hinder the various religious communities in American society in the maintenance of their own distinct identities. Similarly, the public consensus, on which civil unity is ultimately based, must permit to the differing communities the full integrity of their own distinct convictions. The one civil society contains within its own unity the communities that are divided among themselves; but it does not seek to reduce to its own unity the differences that divide them. In a word, the pluralism remains as real as the unity. Neither may undertake to destroy the other. Each subsists in its own order. And the two orders, the religious and the civil, remain distinct, however much they are, and need to be, related. All this, I take it, is integral to the meaning attached in America to the doctrine of religious freedom and to its instrumental companion-doctrine called (not felicitously) separation of church and state. I use the word "doctrine" as lawyers or political philosophers, not theologians, use it.[1]

And later,

From the standpoint both of history and of contemporary social reality the only tenable position is that the first two articles of the First Amendment are not articles of faith but articles of peace. Like the rest of the Constitution, these provisions are the work of lawyers, not of theologians or even of political theorists. They are not true dogma but only good law. That is praise enough.[2]

And lastly,

In the science of law and the art of jurisprudence the appeal to social peace is an appeal to a high moral value. Behind the will to social peace there stands a divine and Christian imperative.[3]

At this point, and on the note of religious imperative to social peace, both within the nation and across the world, I would now like to trace briefly the evolution of those other freedoms and rights that were left ambiguous in the noble words of our Declaration and Constitution. I take it that one cannot understand or imagine religious freedom in a vacuum of human rights. While religious freedom does facilitate human development on the highest spiritual level, those who enjoy religious freedom must work for the totality of human freedom, dignity, and rights. This is precisely what endears to all humanity such diverse religious leaders as Gandhi, John XXIII, and Martin Luther King, Jr.

Now whatever good example America gave the world in the stirring words of the Founders, there was that fatal flaw of slavery—the utter negation of human freedom and human rights. Both Northern shippers and Southern slaveowners

---

[1] 1*We Hold These Truths* (New York: Sheed and Ward, 1960), p. 45.
[2] Ibid., p. 56.
[3] Ibid., p. 60.

headed off a strong negation of slavery proposed for the Declaration and later for the Constitution. Unfortunately for America, it took a bloody Civil War, almost a century later, to bring the matter to a head and give birth to a provisional solution to slavery. That enormous reluctance to face the full realization of the ideals we expressed about "inalienable rights" explains why Lincoln called us "an almost chosen people." His own Cabinet voted unanimously against his "Emancipation Proclamation," forcing him to cast the single ballot "aye" and to declare with a courage that obliterates his former moral ambiguities on the subject of slavery, "The 'ayes' have it."

Unfortunately, the nation also shared his moral ambiguity, and this was all too evident in the days following the freeing of slaves and the end of the Civil War. Despite the 13th, 14th, and 15th Amendments to the Constitution, despite the initial good efforts of the period of Reconstruction, it seemed almost inevitable that a man like Hayes would arrive on the scene to gain the support of the South and the Presidency against Tilden by selling out the blacks. His remarks in Atlanta, returning the problem of the former slaves to those who had created it, assured America of almost another century of apartheid. *Plessy v. Ferguson* was the Supreme Court's shame in legally enshrining as separate and equal that which other later and better Justices in *Brown* would declare, more than half a century later, to be inherently separate and unequal. In the area of civil rights, the peace and justice of *E pluribus unum* did not come as easily as it did in regard to religious liberty.

Even after *Brown,* little happened until the middle 1960's to make the promise of the Declaration and Bill of Rights a reality for the now more than twenty million descendants of the former slaves. Perhaps it took that long to condition our people for a massive change of heart. Certainly, great religious leaders such as Martin Luther King, Jr., and his black and white comrades in the struggle were willing to face death daily to speak prophetically for racial justice. The death of a President also helped set the stage. To his credit, it was a southerner, President Lyndon Johnson, who voiced the famous refrain, "We shall overcome," before a joint session of Congress and led them to overcome racism, legally at least, by passing the great civil rights laws of 1964, 1965, and 1968. The laws responded to a change of heart that was largely religious in its inspiration: that all men and women indeed are children of God and should be equal and should have equal access to those realities that are an important part of the pursuit of happiness—education, employment, housing, public accommodations of all sorts, political participation, voting and standing for election, and especially equal treatment in the administration of justice.

Long is the list of those who fought this crusade for equal justice under the law in America. No one will deny that, in this battle for human rights, important factors in the ultimate victories were religious freedom to speak out, religious leaders to proclaim justice, and religious conviction to sustain the effort and accept the new laws. Religious martyrs also played their part.

It was not lost on all the world during the 1960's that American was engaged in a massive internal struggle to make its political ideals come true at long last. It is a shame that the ill-begotten war in Vietnam and the seedy Watergate episode distracted the world from what I consider a much more important event: the legal abandonment of more than three centuries of apartheid. Not that the battle for human rights was completely won. It never is. But there was a victory unmatched in any modern or ancient nation—the sad, shameful customs and mores of three centuries were abandoned almost overnight, and it happened in a nation more variegated than any other on earth—in fact, a kind of microcosm of all the world, with Americans of every color, religion, culture, race, and nationality involved. Foreigners who are accustomed to Sweden being populated mainly by Swedes and Switzerland by Swiss forget that America has more blacks than there are Canadians in Canada, more Spanish-speaking than Australians in Australia, more American Indians than when Columbus arrived, two or three times more Jews than Israel, several times more students from every country on earth than found in all the universities of Europe. More than a quarter of the Irish nation came to America after the potato famine and, in the first two decades of this century, 14,000,000 immigrants arrived in New York from every country on earth.

If a nation this varied can come to a conviction about the importance of full human dignity and full human rights for the most depressed and deprived part of its population, then one may begin to have hope for the future of human rights in all the world. This is, I take it, what Lincoln had in mind about America when he praised, in his first inaugural address, "the struggle for maintaining in the world that form and substance of government whose leading object is to elevate the condition of men; to lift artificial weights from all shoulders; to clear the paths of laudable pursuit for all; to afford all an unfettered start and a fair chance in the race of life."

It was this kind of promise that brought so many millions of oppressed, poor, and homeless people to America with hope. It was and is the fulfillment of their hopes that gives hope to the world. When the lights were going out all over Europe, the French philosopher, Jacques Maritain, wrote from America:

> There is indeed one thing that Europe knows well, and knows only too well; that is the tragic significance of life.... There is one thing that America knows well, and that she teaches as a great and precious lesson to those who come in contact with her astounding adventure: it is the value and dignity of the common man, the value and dignity of the people... America knows that the common man has a right to the "pursuit of happiness"; the pursuit of the elementary conditions and possessions which are the prerequisites of a free life, and the denial of which, suffered by such multitudes, is a horrible wound in the flesh of humanity; the pursuit of the higher possessions of culture and the spirit.... Here heroism is required, not to overcome tragedy, but to bring to a successful conclusion the formidable adventure begun in this

country with the Pilgrim Fathers and the pioneers, and continued in the great
days of the Declaration of Independence and the Revolutionary War.[4]

I should like to take as my concluding theme those words of Maritain, "to
bring to a successful conclusion the formidable adventure begun in this country." My point will be that the adventure must now be worldwide, that it may
have begun in this country, but it will not be really successful unless human
dignity and human rights are vindicated worldwide, for all humans have this
God-given dignity and deserve these inalienable rights, be they religious or civil
or, most fundamentally, just human.

What happened in 1776, what we are celebrating today, was a Declaration of
Independence, something that gave voice to a yearning for freedom and rights in
thirteen small and weak and very different colonies. What they voiced and what
we have been trying to achieve and enlarge upon more and more ever since then
was and is important to every human being, everywhere in the world. If there is
any worldwide meaning to the Bicentennial, it is this.

During this Bicentennial Year, there have been many pessimistic voices
raised, saying that America is a burnt-out case, that those primordial dreams and
this form of democracy are the wave of the past, now finished. According to
these prophets of doom, the future is already foreclosed for freedom, human
dignity, and human rights in most of the world. I simply do not subscribe to this
pessimism, although neither do I believe that the future is automatically bright
and promising. We do live in an age of violence, inhumanity, and widespread
deprivation of human rights and human dignity, even in supposedly highly-
developed and civilized countries. There is a Gulag Archipeligo, torture in Brazil
and Chile, massacre in Ruanda, genocide in Bangladesh. There is even a sophis-
tication to human torture, an escalation of terror, a nightmare of possible global
destruction already in place, waiting for the finger to touch the bottom.

Still I agree with Maritain that, from all those who cherish religious and other
freedoms, we need a new heroism to bring the American experience to a successful conclusion, not only in America where the brave words were first uttered, but
worldwide. To this end, both prophecy and martyrdom will be needed in the
present and future, as in the past.

One would hope that America—the nation most varied in population, most
endowed by the perennial promise of its founding documents, most affluent in
resources, most powerful in arms, and most committed to world peace and
freedom—might find some new expression to inspire and lead the world at our
present sad juncture, just as it did in 1776 when conditions for human freedom
and dignity were appreciably worse, though less widely known and lamented.

I will make two suggestions for action, neither original, but both worthwhile
and needed.

First, I believe that in this Bicentennial Year our President should order and

---

[4]*Reflections on America* (New York: Charles Scribner's Sons, 1958), pp. 194–195. Quoted from
his article, "America's Role in the New Europe," *The Commonweal*, February 26, 1943.

our Senate ratify the two covenants for human rights growing out of the Universal Declaration, the one for civil and political rights, the other for economic, cultural, and social rights. We should declare that we believe in this full panoply of human rights, not just for Americans, but for every man, woman, and child on earth. We should throw the full weight of all that we do internationally behind the complete achievement of these rights, especially today for those suffering persecution and deprivation anywhere in the world, whether in lands of friends or foes, allies or enemies, detente or no detente. This is where the great adventure, begun 200 years ago, succeeds or fails today. Moreover, our country should move for the appointment of a United Nations High Commissioner for Human Rights, a person of highest international prestige and acceptance, who would be, by general consent, empowered and enjoined to go everywhere in the world to investigate allegations of the denial of human rights, and to publish for everyone to see the facts as he or she finds them. This appointment would put the requisite teeth in the Universal Declaration which just about everyone accepted more than twenty-five years ago. It needs to come true as our Declaration did, and in a shorter time span, one would hope.

My second suggestion is that we back, as a nation, a new national Declaration, this time not for Independence, but for Interdependence. The world has traveled many thousands of millions of miles since 1776. We have in our day glimpsed anew the unity of our world and of humankind when for the first time people saw the earth from the moon and recognized what it really is—a spacecraft, limited in size and resources, unlimited in the vision of what we may make of this common globe if we make it reflect the unity of humankind and the many-colored splendor of humanity.

No really important problems facing humanity today are any longer purely national; all human problems are global in their import, only globally understood aright, only global in their solution. There is no purely national solution for peace, freedom, human dignity or human rights, environment, education, health, science, trade, development, law, communications, transporation, basic resources, energy, or crime. One might add that at the heart of all of these problems, so interdependent in their solutions, is the recognition of human freedom, dignity, and rights, equally upheld before God and human beings, with justice under the law. The founders of the nation could not have known how interdependent the quest for life, liberty, and the pursuit of happiness would become among all humankind. But Jefferson had the foresight to write in his last letter, fifty years after his final draft, and ten days before his death:

> May it [the Declaration] be to the world, what I believe it will be (to some parts sooner, to others later, but finally to all) the signal of arousing men to burst [their] chains.... All eyes are opened, or opening to the rights of man.... For ourselves, let the annual return of this day [July 4th] forever refresh our recollections of these rights, and an undiminished devotion to them.

What I am suggesting as the highest form of devotion to these rights, freedom of religion and all the rest, is to declare them the human patrimony of every human on earth.

Henry Steele Commager, under the aegis of the World Affairs Council of Philadelphia, has formulated a Declaration of Interdependence such as I am suggesting. I conclude by reading its Preamble, not unlike the original Declaration, but this time professedly addressing itself to all the world. I subscribe fully to all it says and commend it to all Americans.

A DECLARATION OF INTERDEPENDENCE
(Preamble)

When in the course of human events the threat of extinction confronts mankind, it is necessary for the people of the United States to declare their interdependence with the peoples of all nations and to embrace those principles and build those institutions which will enable mankind to survive and civilization to flourish.

Two centuries ago our forefathers brought forth a new nation; now we must join with others to bring forth a new world order. On this historic occasion it is proper that the American people should reaffirm those principles on which the United States of America was founded, acknowledge the new crises which confront them, accept the new obligations which history imposes upon them, and set forth the causes which impel them to affirm before all peoples their commitment to a Declaration of Interdependence.

We hold these truths to be self-evident: that all men are created equal; that the inequalities and injustices which afflict so much of the human race are the product of history and society, not of God or nature; that people everywhere are entitled to the blessings of life and liberty, peace and security and the realization of their full potential; that they have an inescapable moral obligation to preserve those rights for posterity, and that to achieve these ends all the peoples and nations of the globe should acknowledge their interdependence and join together to dedicate their minds and their hearts to the solution of those problems which threaten their survival.

To establish a new world order of compassion, peace, justice and security, it is essential that mankind free itself from the limitations of national prejudice, and acknowledge that the forces that unite it are incomparably deeper than those that divide it—that all people are part of one global community, dependent on one body of resources, bound together by the ties of a common humanity and associated in a common adventure on the planet Earth.

Let us then join together to vindicate and realize this great truth that mankind is one, and as one will nobly save or irreparably lose the heritage of thousands of years of civilization. And let us set forth the principles which should animate and inspire us if our civilization is to survive.

I would hope that many distinguished Americans would sign this Declaration of Interdependence during this Bicentennial Year. I would further hope that Americans throughout the land, who believe in our country and what it means to the world, would also sign. Henry Steele Commager gives the best reason in the final paragraph of the Declaration:

> We can no longer afford to make little plans, allow ourselves to be the captives of events and forces over which we have no control, consult our fears rather than our hopes. We call upon the American people, on the threshold of the third century of their national existence, to display once again that boldness, enterprise, magnanimity and vision which enabled founders of our Republic to bring forth a new nation and inaugurate a new era in human history. The fate of humanity hangs in the balance. Throughout the globe, hearts and hopes wait upon us. We summon all Mankind to unite to meet the great challenge.

THE PROSPECT FOR RELIGIOUS LIBERTY

Milton K. Curry, Jr.

We are now in the sixth day of The Bicentennial Conference on Religious Liberty. During these days together, we have listened to scholarly lectures; we have discoursed on "The Foundations and Traditions of Religious Liberty"; we have been exposed to a wide spectrum of the "Contemporary American Experience of Conscience and Dissent"; we have considered in some depth and breadth some "Contemporary Issues of Church/State Relations"; and, finally, we have taken time to relate our discussions to "Religious Liberty in the International Scene." In the process, we have witnessed a play which reviewed for us in dramatic form "The First Hundred Years"—a period in which the paradox between our profession of faith and our practices was clearly, if shamefully, demonstrated. I have an idea that most of us would like to reinvent the Genesis story of the Creation and prepare the rest on the seventh day as the record reported God did. But, we have not created what God created, and we have not finished what we have started.

Today, as we prepare to end this conference, in Philadelphia, the city where so much of our history started, we have been asked to take a look at the future and to seek to divine what "The Prospect for Religious Liberty" may be. No time limit on this projection has been set. The period may be ten years; it may be twenty-five years; it may be a century. Some may want to project the prospect another two centuries. Obviously, we know less about the future than we do about the past or the present. Yet, we know we cannot be true to our trust as "doorkeepers" for present and succeeding generations without attempting to sketch what we think may be some alternative futures for humankind and attempting to deduce, from what we have seen happen in the past and what we now experience, some possible and probable prospects for Religious Liberty for ourselves and our posterity.

Since I am honored and privileged to share this hour with Dr. Cynthia C. Wedel, the President of the World Council of Churches, I may presume to think that I shall be expected to limit my remarks in general to what I think the future for Religious Liberty may be in our land, and that she will discuss in proper depth and breadth the possibilities for the world. Nevertheless, I am persuaded to believe that while developments in America will impact greatly what happens in the rest of the world, I am just as impressed that what happens in the rest of the world with regard to Religious Liberty and the other fundamental freedoms will exert profound effects on the nature and quality of all Freedoms, including Religious Liberty, in our own land. Because Dr. Wedel will speak last, I am

Dr. Milton K. Curry, Jr., is president of Bishop College, Dallas, TX, and president of the United Negro College Fund, Inc.

happily in a position "to stand corrected" if any of my suggestions or projections or surmises are immediately seen by her to be inaccurate or incorrect.

James J. Kilpatrick wrote an article for *Nation's Business* for August, 1975, entitled "The New National Nightmare," which was reprinted in *The Freeman* in December, 1975, in which he sought to describe our national predicament as we prepared to celebrate the Bicentennial of our nation's history. What he said provides a somber but provocative starting point for our discussion. Listen:

> The tip point is among the most familiar phenomena of our everyday life. A child discovers the tip point of a tricycle and a teetertotter. A boatman perceives the turning of a tide. A baseball umpire will take so much sass from a player and then no more. At a certain point, matter will boil, freeze, crystallize, or jell. The tip point is the moment at which conditions change not in degree, but in kind, or in direction.

> Two hundred years after our free society began, we are close to such a tip point now. We are within a drop or two of the critical moment at which freedom crystallizes into regimentation, when the people no longer are masters of government, but government is master of the people.

> The dangers are widely perceived, but they are separately and not collectively perceived. It is the occluded vision of the man who cannot see the forest for the trees. Doctors see one part of the picture, educators another, businessmen yet another. We dwell in small rooms, in little shut-off cells, and sometimes we labor to breathe. "It is stifling in here," we complain. And we are not always aware that air is being sucked from the next room also. Yet the atmospheric changes are so slow, so gradual, so apparently insignificant, that we seldom complain at all. We do not understand what is missing: *It is the very air of freedom.*

Then Kilpatrick quotes Thomas A. Murphy, chairperson of the Board of General Motors, who, speaking as a business leader, from his small room, charged that "Our economic system founded with our nation 200 years ago, has come more and more under government control. Very conspicuously in the marketplace, the government, by mandate and edict, is substituting its sovereignty for that of the individual consumer. . . . What is of greatest concern is that each intrusion of government, because it takes decision-making power away from the individual consumer, diminishes his economic freedom." He quotes Dr. Murray L. Weidenbaum, director of the Center for the Study of American Business, as observing a new revolution which is far more subtle than the first managerial revolution in America. And he suggests that "It involves the shift of decision-making from managers, who represent shareholders, to a cadre of government officials, government inspectors, government regulators."[1] And Kilpatrick adds, "The last word is the key word: *regulators*. If we were to give a name to the ominous new age that lies ahead, the age beyond the tip point, we might

---

[1]See "Where Overregulation Can Lead," *Nation's Business*, June, 1975.

well term it the Age of the Regulators. A part of the ominous aspect of the approaching era is that many Americans see nothing ominous in regulation. It is a friendly word. We are favorably inclined toward a regular fellow. We shy from the irregular. . . . A regulated life is popularly thought to be a good life.'' ''This very complaisance,'' says Kilpatrick, ''contributes to the creeping oppression.'' Operating under a delusion, the author says, that ''a little regulation is good, more regulation is better. On the sound premise that freedom cannot exist without order, a fallacious conclusion is erected: the more order, the more freedom. It does not work that way.''

Now, the scholars and the business leaders are not the only Americans who suspect that we may be close to the tip point with regard to our freedoms in America. Last Christmas, I was stunned when I read a Christmas greeting letter sent by someone I did not know, from no listed address, but in America, in which he wished my family and me ''A Merry Christmas in 1975 because certain elements in our nation and outside our nation ''would see to it that we did not enjoy such freedom two centuries from now.''

Now, I do not hold that this ''ominous trend'' is one-sided, namely from the government's activity alone. Rather, I would submit that at least two other factors generated by individuals and by organized religion and by society at large have brought us to what Kilpatrick called ''the tip point.'' One is the erosion of the principle of Religious Liberty as a result of our espousal of the idea of *secularism,* an idea which reads God out of the affairs of human beings and in doing so demeans and diminishes the significance of religion and hence reduces the need to maintain Religious Liberty. The void which is created has opened the door for a substitute for the religion of the founders of the nation which may be called Civil Religion.

The other factor is the gradual erosion of the principle of separation of church and state as organized religion relinquished its prophetic function in the face of moral and ethical issues and either condoned or supported evil actions initiated by the state or sold its soul for ''a mess of pottage'' in order to secure temporary economic relief or to escape assuming its own social and moral responsibilities.

A third factor which might be mentioned is the trend to ''water down'' the convictions of conscience to the point that the stance of the religionist may not be distinguished from that of other religionists or from non-religionists. Under the banner of supporting ''equality'' and tolerance, we have ignored ''quality'' as it relates to integrity and commitment, and we have developed no ''intolerance'' of what is fundamentally wrong and sinful. Hence, there is no tension between good and bad, because we leave it to everyone to determine this for herself or himself without regard to any overarching standards. Drunk on an inadequate definition of democracy, we have forgotten that the rightness or wrongness of some things is never determined by the vote.

In the light of these facts, what can we say about future prospects for Religious Liberty in America? Let us begin by asserting that forecasting the future is a human activity which harks back to the days of primitive humans. Indeed, it is possible that the development of the capacity to differentiate between past and present and to dream of differences between the present and the future was the critical factor which enabled humans to emerge among animals as the masters and rulers of the earth. Will next year be a repetition of this year? Will the next decade duplicate the last ten years? May we conjecture from a study of the actions and trends of the past two centuries, or of the past century, what we may expect to happen during the next century or in the next two centuries? Will manhood and womanhood perpetuate the opportunity for unrestrained play and irresponsible action of infanthood, of childhood, and of youth? Will old age preserve the strength and agility of youth or the beauty of adolescence and early adulthood? Will the professions and trades of one decade be applicable and relevant to the opportunities and needs of the next generation, or even of this generation ten years from now? Will human relations in the family, the community, the state, the nation, or in the world of nation-states follow the same trends and patterns during the next quarter of a century which they did during the past twenty-five years? If our value system changes as much between now and 2001 as it has since World War II, what kind of value system will we have? What kind of men and women will we be producing? If government continues to increase its regulatory powers over individual and private existence, will we have any freedoms? If we lose the freedom to work, can we maintain the freedom to speak? If we sacrifice the freedom to debate, can we preserve the freedom to learn? If freedom to worship is limited to ceremonial and beliefs and is not allowed to penetrate all of life, how much Religious Liberty will we really have? If we deny to some of our citizens the freedom to live, how can they—being dead—exercise the freedom to worship? What will happen if we turn over all the functions of society to the government—the state—and deny to our citizens the freedom to serve in voluntary associations according to their desires and aspirations?

Is it really possible to forecast the future in any realm of human endeavor, whether it be personal, physical, social, economic, political, academic, moral, or spiritual, with any degree of reliability, particularly when we are in a period of extraordinary, even revolutionary change? Well, whether we can forecast reliably and accurately or not, we must admit that forecasting the future has become, in our day, one of the most fascinating games being played by people of all levels. It has also become one of the grimmest and most debilitating exercises of the human mind. In many ways, it is one of the most dangerous exercises with which one can be associated. Many people in this audience are too young to remember the demise of an outstanding magazine a half century ago because it made the wrong prognostication regarding a national election. Even the more mature among us may have forgotten, if they every knew, the forecast of some experts in the late 1890's that in half a century there would be so many horse-drawn carriages in Boston and New York that the lives of every citizen in them would be threatened if they appeared outside their yards! Well, the century did change; the number of people in the cities did increase, but horsedrawn carriages were replaced before the end of the half century with horseless carriages, and those who dreamed of making new fortunes in horseshoeing found themselves without any horses to shoe, and hence without any skills which were marketable.

Wilbert E. Moore, writing in *The Educational Record* for the Fall, 1964, issue, on "Forecasting the Future: The United States in 1980," declared that "The job of the prophet presents unusual occupational hazards, and were it a full-time position, it is probable that life insurance premiums would be very high. Though forecasting is a reasonable and even necessary part of life's orientations in the modern world, there are substantial uncertainties and possibilities of error in predicting the future, and, as we are well aware, some errors could be fatal."

Nevertheless, however dangerous forecasting may be, however uncertain of achievement setting goals for the future may be, more and more people in America and in the rest of the world have been concerned about doing just these things; and every year, more and more money is spent by individuals, organizations, industries, and governmental agencies in research and development and on planning and projecting and forecasting the future.

Back in 1949, George Orwell wrote a novel entitled *Nineteen Eighty-Four* which I am sure most of you have read. Orwell essayed to speculate on what might happen thirty-five years later in our society. The scene is London, where there has been no building of houses since 1950, and where the city slums are called Victory Mansions. Science has abandoned humankind for the state. As every citizen knows only too well, war is peace. To Winston Smith, a young man who works in the Ministry of Truth (Minitru, for short) come two people who transform his life completely. One is Julia, whom he meets after she hands him a slip reading, "I love you." The other is O'Brien who tells him, 'We shall meet in the place where there is no darkness." The way in which Winston is betrayed by the one and, against his own desire and instincts, ultimately betrays the other makes a story of mounting drama and suspense.

But aside from its high literary qualities, *Nineteen Eighty-Four* has profound implications for our times. It points the path which the society may now be traveling and leaves the reader with the shocked feeling that there is no single horrible feature in the imagined world of 1984—now only eight years away—which is not present, in embryo, or perhaps in full bloom, today! George Orwell spells out, for the first time in literature, how the spirit of every person may be broken in Room 101, and how he or she can be made to avow—and believe—that black is white, that two times two equals five, and that evil is good!

Back in 1955, Peter Drucker published his little book on *America's Next Twenty Years* in which he made a number of predictions, only two of which I will mention now. One was that the major problem of the period, 1955 to 1975, would be *inflation,* not unemployment. The second prediction was that while America would make outstanding contributions in the area of technological advancement, in the long run—"in the long view of history, it will be for *social inventions* that Americans may be best remembered!" Unemployment has become a major problem in recent years, but over the two decades no one can dispute that the economic and social loss from inflation has been even greater.

His second prediction gives us ground for hope as we think about the future of Religious Liberty in America.

In 1962, the Council on World Tensions did a study of World Tensions and Development and published its findings in a book entitled *Restless Nations,* which described the plight and promise of emerging nation-states and the efforts of so called "backward" nations to escape from their terrible slavery to the past, to ignorance, and to poverty. Even within the past decade, so many changes have been implemented that it does not take a genius to see that one can predict with reasonable accuracy some things which can happen in the future.

We know the future—the next decade, and the next quarter of a century—will probably be different. The twenty-first century and the years leading to our tercentennial may make the past decade, the past quarter of a century, and the past two centuries look like the dark ages. Now I believe that if we make progress in America that is significant, it will be in the area of human relations. If we make progress in the area of human relations, it will derive in considerable part from a recovery of some values which for a season we have cast aside. If we continue to permit the "creeping paralysis" of private and personal dignity which the "welfare state" and government regulation impose on our nation, the capacity for flexibility, for renewal, for creativity, for innovation will cause us to decay from within, so that little by little, we shall unconsciously give up our freedoms—one by one and then altogether—seeking a false security unworthy of free people. People who give up the freedom to learn cannot protect the freedom to work, for they will have no marketable skills. People who give up the freedom to work, preferring to exist in a "welfare state," will not maintain freedom of speech, including the freedom to debate the issues. People who try to live without a faith in something greater than themselves, and ultimately in a God greater than themselves and the state, will not contend for freedom of religion or Religious Liberty. People who do not maintain Religious Liberty for themselves will have no base from which to contend for the freedom to live!

We may postulate, then, that Religious Liberty does not exist in a vacuum; neither does it exist in isolation from the other freedoms. They all stand together. Religious Liberty is not the monopolistic possession of people who think and believe as we do. It is no longer protected completely by walls of constitutional language, nor is it secure simply because it is engraved in the tablets of the Bill of Rights. Religious Liberty derives its vitality and its permanence from the fact that, as D. Elton Trueblood said in his book, *The Declaration of Freedom,* "The basic ideas of the free society all turn out, upon analysis, to be moral ideas. The free society is, in essence, the responsible society, for responsibility is the one valid alternative to both slavery and license. But responsibility is meaningless unless there is a moral order. . . . Our hope lies in the fact that the free society has ultimate and eternal truth on its side." And he points up the fact that "The heart of the whole view, on which so many of the world religions unite, in spite of particular differences, is that behind and beyond our world of change there is another, the Living God."

In 1976, we are at "the tip point"! Integrity of character in private and public life is in a state of disrepair. Doubt and cynicism are rampart. Regulation by the state has increased and has been all too willingly accepted. License has replaced a sense of responsibility in the home, the church, and the school. "The Politics of Lying" describes accurately the nature of our domestic and foreign policies and practices, but we still have before us the great ideals of the founders of the nation and the Judaeo-Christian tradition which declare human beings to be the "children of God." I predict that we shall raise up leaders, prophets, teachers, seers, and dreamers who will turn us in a new direction and lead us to purify the streams of our culture, so that we can get a new start and build a society of freedom, equality, quality, and human dignity.

Now, the development of a cadre of committed people of deep religious conviction will not of itself insure Religious Liberty. The production of unusually "good" people will increase tensions between them and those who are mediocre and/or poor, and those who do not believe at all. It is possible that if the state is not directed by people so committed, the judgments of the prophets and of the organized religious forces will generate tensions. But it will be possible to make the tensions creative, and through the process of resolution of the new problems there will evolve a new synthesis in which the quality of our life together will be improved.

The explosion of knowledge will intoxicate men and women and excite our human pride so that some may come to think religion unnecessary and God to be an antiquated notion. But we have already discovered that no generation can exhaust what is to be known about God and no expanse of new knowledge will make God irrelevant to increasing human needs. God is in truth the God of succeeding generations!

The explosion of the population in the rest of the world may well place a heavy strain on our ability to provide food for all and to continue to live at the level of abundance we now enjoy, but most Americans who may come to live with more purpose will eat less and enjoy it more as they exercise the freedom to serve.

Technological improvements may provide us with more leisure time before 2001, but improved education may help us learn how to use our leisure time more effectively, and meditation on the opportunity for spiritual renewal may lead us to treat ourselves and others better. Aggressive, organized religion that is willing to lose its life to save the world may well find life more abundant for itself as it provides for others. If it does, it will deserve to live in 2001 and in 2076! If it does not, Religious Liberty will degenerate into license and will have no real significance anyway.

In summary, I agree with Wilbert E. Moore, whom I have quoted earlier, when he says that there are at least four things which we can postulate with regard to the future, and I shall apply them to the future of Religious Liberty. These presumptions are:

1. The persistence of the present and immediate past;
2. The continuation of some orderly trends;
3. The control of the future as a result of planning what we want to happen; and
4. The recapitulation of experience in developing nations in other lands and among developing people in our own land will tend to replicate what has been done in the past.

I would add a fifth possibility. It is that the "golden age" of human existence is ahead of us; the future will be brighter than today. Religious Liberty will be more real to more people in 2001 than it is now. I think this simply because I believe the alternative will eliminate Religious Liberty for all of us if it is not made real to those who do not enjoy it now.

Let us consider each of these presumptions briefly:

1. *Persistence of the present and the immediate past.* It is still true that with all the modern equipment for measuring barometric pressure and velocities, temperatures, and the like, calculations from these factors "still yield less reliable short-run forecasts than the simple assumption that tomorrow will be pretty much like today." For much of our social and political conduct, and our educational and religious endeavors, we can make the same assumption. "Even over considerable periods into the future, customs, organizations, and values may be expected to survive the pressures of other changes." It is not likely that the Constitution, or the Bill of Rights, or any of the Amendments to the Constitution of the United States will be radically changed within the foreseeable future. It is not likely that the character of the membership of the Supreme Court will change radically within the next ten to twenty-five years. With zero-base population growth predicted between 1980 and 2001 in America, and with a trend toward migration to the suburbs, to the small towns and rural areas, and to the South, it is likely that the prevailing mood of the country will be moderate-to-conservative. What this means is that whatever plans we have for improving the prospects for Religious Liberty in the next twenty-five years, we must expect strong head winds to try to slow down the procession of life!

If progress can be made toward winning the "War on Poverty" and a dimiuntion in unemployment, and if the drive toward desegregation and integration in education and in housing is successful, the tensions which might generate extremes should be lessened, so that the spread between divergent political philosophies will be contained within manageable limits, thus minimizing the tendencies toward reduction of forbearance. Our past history appears to suggest that the more that minorities receive quality education, get jobs for which they are prepared, and are able to move upwards as others, the more their political and religious beliefs and practices tend to match those of the majority in the middle class. On the other hand, it is true that the "rise in expectations" increases geometrically rather than arithmetically, once the barriers to hope have been broken and individuals and groups pass from despair and the edge of death to view the dawn of a new day. Hence, we may expect the persistence of present trends and immediate past practices in the protection of Religious Liberty and all the other freedoms which go with it.

2. *The continuation of orderly trends.* Even though we have seen some accleration in the speed of change within the past thirty years in social legislation, and a greater number of cases involving citizens' unalienable rights have been handled by the courts, the rate of change has been predictable. The move to ecumenicity has broken down many barriers between denominations and among world religions. Friendships among the leaders have increased the strength of the bonds which hold organizations and communions together. This leads to increased tolerance of differences between and among peoples of various religious professions. At the same time, the increasing secularization of the society tends to produce a certain relaxation in religious beliefs and a moderation in practice, so that the general mood of religious groups tends to be less intense. Hence, tolerance of other religions becomes easier to realize. I would insist, however, that the tolerance generated by secularization must be considered an "uneasy tolerance" which should be watched carefully. It can be another head wind slowing down the procession of life toward greater ends. Thus, despite Peter Drucker's contention that this is "The Age of Discontinuity," many elements in the society point to a "continuation of orderly trends" with regard to our stance on Religious Liberty.

3. *Control of the future as a result of planning what we want to happen.* If there are changes in the priority we give to Religious Liberty in the future, there is the strong possibility that what we get will be what we shall have planned and worked for. More and more, we are seeking in our individual and collective lives to control the future by planning for it. With increased proportions of the population being educated and coming to participate in all phases of government and economic activity, the impact of the emerging majority, however "new," would appear to support more meaningful insistence on insuring greater freedom for individuals and groups heretofore excluded from the decision-making process. While there is still some danger that freedom of the media will continue to be prostituted by minority control (that is, control by a small group which has cornered power in the past), the new decision-makers may be depended upon to dilute or change the constituency altogether and to impact the influence the media may have on the distortion or diminution of Religious Liberty and the other freedoms associated with it.

As long as the government maintains "neutrality" with regard to Religious Liberty, religious groups and individuals who support their beliefs should remain substantially independent and free to act according to the dictates of their consciences.

4. *Recapitulation of experience will tend to replicate what has been done in the past.* This fourth factor which may be used as a basis for predicting the future is based on the fact that "while precise replication of rates and sequences of change need not always occur, and often will not, still we can go rather far in

reasoning from the Western Experience to major parts of the social organization and personal standards of those nations now seeking to become a part of the modern world.'' In other words, it may be expected that countries which adopt the democratic form of government and which are committed to a capitalist economy, though somewhat controlled (as ours has come to be), may be expected to put a high priority on the basic freedoms just as we have done.

The problem which America must face is what will happen if these emerging nations adopt communism and prefer totalitarianism to the democratic form of government. In this case it may be expected that there will be few, if any, individual freedoms, and the rights of the state will take precedence over those of individuals. Established religions will be the order of the day, or the organized religious bodies will be controlled in the name and interest of the state, as is the case in Russia and its satellites today. If Russia and China are joined by large blocs in Europe, Asia, Africa, and South America, the impact on the freedoms enjoyed now by Americans may well be very adverse.

Now the interaction of these four factors on society would appear to indicate that we may expect conflicting forces to be at work in our nation during the next quarter of a century just as they have been active in the recent past. The capacity and determination of "the committed" to mesh these forces in a creative manner so as to maximize the quality of our life together as experienced by all American citizens may well determine how much progress we make towards guaranteeing the implementation of these rights and freedoms, including Religious Liberty, to every citizen and group in our own land, and also insuring the continued existence of these freedoms for succeeding generations at home and around the world.

I will close with this story:

In the Prologue to his 1927 book on *Tolerance,* Hendrik Van Loon drew a striking picture of human society which aptly summarizes the dimensions of our human predicament as we seek to achieve the better life. The scene was laid in a little valley completely surrounded by rugged mountains which shut it off from the beautiful and prosperous life which lay beyond. A little stream, the meager source of life and knowledge for the villagers, wound its way out of the massive hills, down through their valley. When evening came, the "Old Men Who Know" sat on the banks of the stream and vaunted the venerable traditions of the past. They told the villagers that the little brook within the ranges was the only stream, and that to leave it would be to disregard the work of their ancestors.

One morning a man who had questioned the laws of the "Old Men" came down from the mountain, elated at what he had seen. He was dragged before the "Old Men Who Know" and commanded on pain of death to be silent. But knowing that the "Old Men" lied, Wanderer turned his back and spoke. He told of fresh soils and deeper streams beyond the ranges, and pleaded with the villagers to follow him up the steep ascent, across the mountains to a better home. "The Old Men Who Know" rose in anger. With the villagers nodding their heads in complacent assent, they stoned him till he died, and then they took his bones and placed them at the foot of the mountain path which he had traveled as a warning to any other "rebel" who would question the laws of the "Old Men."

Years came and went. The brook ran dry. The tribe faced starvation and misery. Their only hope lay beyond the ranges, but blind faith in the laws of the "Old Men" kept them from venturing forth. But, finally, a few courageous villagers recalled the dying words of Wanderer. One night, the "Old Men" were cast aside and the hard flight up the tortuous ascent was begun. The trail of the martyred pioneer was rediscovered and followed across the mountain to another valley, to the green banks of a fresh stream. Here they found a newer, better life, and lived peacefully.

As years passed, however, the tribe increased; new desires and new dreams of the race could not be met even in their present home. But a strange thing happened! The villagers failed to cross the ranges towering beyond. For, you see, the "original pioneers" had settled down, and they, in turn, had become "The Old Men Who Know."

Such, in allegory, is Van Loon's interpretation of our social progress, our creative search for the better life. It is my conviction that democratic society provides through its homes, churches, and schools for the continual development of Wanderers in succeeding generations who will break sufficiently with the past to venture forth to catch new visions of the more abundant life beyond the ranges, and will take the time to make the necessary reconnaisance trips to get the facts, and then return to stir the hearts and minds of the complacent and the fearful, the slumbering and the starving, to new, creative, and lifegiving endeavors.

It is rather disturbing to note, however, as the historian, Arnold Toynbee pointed out years ago, that we are susceptible to the "nemesis of creativity"— the danger of becoming the victims of our successes, so that the creators of one crisis experience who become the heroes of the revolutions in history by developing innovative and meaningful solutions to problems which improve the quality of life may become, in the words of Van Loon, "The Old Men Who Know" of the next crisis experience and the leaders of reaction against any further creative response to the new situation! Obviously, then, the major problem facing us with regard to the future of Religious Liberty reduces to our capacity for renewal. We did it in 1776. We did it in 1865. Another generation did it in 1954. Can we do it again in 1976? Will we do it again in 1996, and in 2076?

It is my hope that "The Old Men and the Old Women Who Know" and "The Young Men and the Young Women Who Want to Know" will sit on the banks of the stream of time and plan the roads that are to cross the ranges towering in the distances beyond us today—the still-unsolved problems of human relations which keep us from granting to all others the same freedoms we insist on having for ourselves. We may make mistakes. We may have to retrace our steps to rediscover the trails our martyred pioneers have already made, which are now grown up in weeds. But, in the morning, gladly will other Wanderers return to show us the way to the land beyond. Each generation will have to rediscover for itself the fountains of our strength—the sources of our freedoms. Whenever they do, they will find inseparably tied to those freedoms we cherish so much—and among them at the top, Religious Liberty—the integrity and the sense of personal and corporate responsibility, inseparably linked together. We can never have the one without the other. What therefore God has joined together, let not man or woman try to put asunder!

Bibliography

Bellah, Robert N. *The Broken Covenant*. New York: Seabury Press, 1975.

Drucker, Peter. *America's Next Twenty Years*. New York: Harper & Brothers, 1955.

Hall, Cameron P., compiler. *Human Values and Advancing Technology*. New York: Friendship Press, 1967.

Kilpatrick, James J. "The New National Nightmare," *The Freeman, Ideas on Liberty,* December, 1975.

Leinwand, Gerald, general ed. *The Future*. New York: Pocket Books, 1976.

Mannheim, Karl. *Diagnosis of Our Time*. New York: Oxford University Press, 1944.

Moore, Wilbert E. "Forecasting the Future: The United States in 1980," *Educational Record*, Fall, 1964.

Orwell, George. *Nineteen Eighty-Four*. New York: Harcourt, Brace & Co., 1949.

Roche, John P. *The Quest for the Dream*. Chicago: Quadrangle Paperbacks, 1963.

Trueblood, D. Elton. *Declaration of Freedom*. New York: Harper & Brothers, 1955.

Valentine, Alan. *The Age of Conformity*. Chicago: Henry Regnery Co., 1954.

Van Loon, Hendrick. *Tolerance*. New York: Sun Dial Press, 1927.

THE PROSPECTS FOR RELIGIOUS LIBERTY

Cynthia C. Wedel

We have thought about many aspects of religious liberty during this week—what it means, how it has been enshrined in the laws and practices of this country and dangers to which we must be alert. My assignment is to help us look to the future—to see if we can discern what life and society will be like during the third century of our history, and what place religious liberty may play.

Before looking to the future, I would like to put forward two propositions upon which my thesis depends. The first of these is a theological assumption—that God made us free. As far as we know, human beings are the only part of the creation with freedom of choice. Everything else lives and operates according to built-in qualities or instincts. We alone can choose to do or not to do things. We can even decide to disobey, ignore, or deny God. Since God (in the Jewish-Christian tradition) is both purposeful and good, there must be some reason for this unique gift of freedom. It is my assumption that God took the risk of creating a free being, knowing that we would almost certainly misuse our freedom, because the essence of God is love and God wanted to create love in the universe. Since love is not a "thing" but a relationship, the only way to create it was to create a being capable of love—a being with whom God could enter into a relationship of mutual love.

God knew something about love which we human beings have difficulty learning or accepting. This is that *real* love, in the highest sense, can only exist in complete freedom—when there is not the slightest element of power, force, or coercion. To make a love relationship possible, God had to limit divine power by giving complete freedom to human beings.

With our limited understanding, human beings have always been desperately afraid of freedom. The God who made us and knows us better than we know ourselves trusted us with freedom. But we do not trust one another. All of human history attests to this. From the beginning of time, human society has been organized with the powerful few making decisions and forcing the vast majority of humanity to accept and obey. The assumption that most people could not be trusted with freedom is very deep in most individuals and institutions. I believe that for this reason God has never been very pleased with the way we have structured our common life.

Out of this first proposition grows the second one. It is this—that religious freedom is the basis of all freedom. Human freedom comes from the fact that God made us free. Tragically, through most of history, the forces of religion have been as dominating and fearful of freedom as have governments and other institutions. Since God entrusted to us even the structure of the human-divine

Dr. Cynthia C. Wedel is president of the World Council of Churches, and lives in Alexandria, VA.

relationship, we responded in a typically human way—by a few seizing the power of religion and coercing everyone else through laws and rules, and even through persecution and force, to worship God in one or another specific way. Religion has often been used also to reinforce the power of the state.

The fact that religion itself has been perverted by human beings to limit religious freedom may be responsible for the severe lack of freedom which has marked most societies in history. If and when the forces of religion come to understand and proclaim the God-given freedom of every human being, there may be hope for real liberty. It is not coincidence, but rather the operation of this principle, that the majority of the founders of this country were "believing" people. Many of them were devout Christians. Some—such as Jefferson—could not accept the strictures of the churches of that time, but were strongly deist, believing with certainty that there was a power operating above and beyond the life of this world.

A belief in a supreme being is clearly written into the Declaration of Independence and into the Constitution which grew out of it. Looking back over 200 years, we can marvel at the fact that the often intolerant religious people of the Revolutionary Era could take the bold step of forbidding the establishment of religion in the new nation and of providing for liberty of individual conscience. It is hard for us, at the present time, to realize what a bold action this was. Everywhere else in the world they knew religion and government were the same. The churches were supported by taxes, and clergy and people had to conform.

Through the past two centuries, there have been many efforts by "religious" people to undermine the principle of separation of church and state. Many kinds of legislation have been proposed which would require Americans to conform to one religious point of view or another. Prohibition, prayers in the public schools, and anti-abortion legislation are only a few of such efforts.

As we look to the future, it behooves the leaders of religion to consider carefully the requirements of true religious liberty. If any one of our religious groups had any hope that it might be able to become the established religion of the country, it might be tempted to try to achieve this status. The idea of being supported by tax money, and having special privilege and status, might look alluring, especially in times of economic recession. This is obviously impossible. But I believe that any church with sense would not choose that role even if it were possible.

With our freedom and our almost frightening plurality of religious bodies in the U. S., we have also a far more viable religious sector of the population than any nation with an established church. Even our diminishing church attendance is spectacularly larger than that of other countries. The only places where interest in religion is increasing rapidly today are some of the developing countries which, like the U.S., have freedom of religion written into their laws.

I suggested earlier that freedom of religion is basic to other freedoms. If this is true, we who are part of the religious "establishment" of this country have a major responsibility for protecting and extending religious liberty in order to protect all of our precious freedoms. We cannot expect anyone else to do this for us. Nor—in our pluralistic society—can any one religious group do it alone. We must work together far better than we have ever done in the past.

What can we do to insure that the prospects for religious liberty will be good in the future? I will list seven things which I have thought of. No doubt you can think of others.

1. We need to be very clear that the basis of liberty is the God-given freedom of every individual to act according to his or her own conscience. Conscience—a sense of right and wrong—has to be cultivated, through experience, through the example of others, through teaching. The "content" of conscience depends on some sense of order and reason in the universe—something beyond the rule of might or "the law of the jungle." How are our churches and synagogues handling the religious education of adults, parents, and children to ensure the development of "conscientious" citizens?

2. As religious bodies, we must pay more attention than we have in the past to learning to know and respect one another. We must encourage our diverse religious groups to develop, preach, and practice their own beliefs. We have seen some good examples of this in recent years when churches have come to the aid of other churches in trouble, even when they held strongly contrary beliefs—because of concern for the principle of religious liberty. Many of our churches for whom pacifism is not a matter of doctrine strongly support the "peace churches" in their witness.

3. Because religious liberty is based on the God-given freedom of every human being, the religious people of this country must be the leaders in fighting for the rights of the poor and oppressed in our own and other lands. We had a short-lived moment of glory in the civil rights struggle of the early 1960's. But where are we now as we see educational, health, and welfare programs—which offer hope of freedom to the neediest citizens in our land—being dimantled and destroyed? And where are we as our nation supports oppressive regimes around the world and reduces aid to other countries, except for armaments? If individual religious people and groups of Christians and Jews are not speaking out and acting for freedom and justice for others, we will have no right to claim help if our religious liberties are threatened.

4. We must be in the forefront of those who are working for humane and rational systems to maintain reasonable law and order. Individual liberty, in a mass society, cannot be unbridled license for everyone to do exactly what he or she pleases. There have to be *some* controls, but these must be fair, impartial, and compassionate. What are we religious people doing to improve our systems of justice? How much do we care about children who get into trouble (as long as they are not our children), or people who cannot afford to fight unjust arrest? How vigorous is our ministry to those in prison or—almost more crucial—to those released from prison?

5. Arms and weapons are the basic tools of repression. Recognizing that a case can be made for the carefully controlled use of them by law enforcement

officers or the military, how active are we in working for reasonable gun control laws? And how much is our voice being heard by the Congress as it votes far higher amounts for armaments than were spent in time of war? Surely, for every gun or bomb which may protect freedom, a hundred are used to destroy the freedom of others.

6. The founders of our country gave us a framework of freedom and a remarkably flexible method of keeping our nation up to date. They were people of their time. They could not see, then, the need for freedom for slaves, or for the poor, or for women. We have begun to expand the areas of freedom—and must continue to press on until freedom for these groups is real. And we must realize that we, too, are people of our time. With our religious concern for all of God's children, we need to be ready to stretch the boundaries of our imaginations to encompass other groups now the victims of discrimination or oppression—the physically handicapped, for example, or the mentally retarded and the aged, or those who deviate from traditional sexual roles.

7. We may also need—together—to look critically at our own freedom as religious groups within the framework of our government. We enjoy our tax-exempt status, and like to think of it as a friendly gesture from a benevolent government. I do not question the motives of those who provided this benefit. They knew that churches and synagogues were vital for the moral and religious standards of the country, and wanted to help them. But the law which gives us the exemption also prohibits us—and other voluntary public interest organizations—from any efforts to influence legislation, even though trade associations and other special interest groups have no such restrictions. Some thoughtful legislators are trying to do something about this. Are we aware of their work? Have we decided what we need and want? Should we not be consulting together about this, seeing it as a step forward in our own religious liberty?

Finally—and basically—our task of helping to form the conscience and sense of value of the American people must be taken much more seriously than we have taken it in the recent past. For without such individual responsibility on the part of informed citizens, no liberties are safe. Edmund Burke said it very well two hundred years ago: "There must be a curb on human will and appetite somewhere. The less there is within, the more there must be without. It is contrary to the eternal constitution of things that men of intemperate minds can be free."

Appendix A

THE BICENTENNIAL CONFERENCE SEMINARS

An important dimension of the Bicentennial Conference itself was provided by the leadership and membership of Seminars centered upon special questions arising from the exercise of Religious Liberty. A dynamic concept, Religious Liberty cannot properly be reduced to static dogmas. Moreover, the legal protection of "soul liberty" has been expanded over the generations and in some areas of social life is still expanding.

The purely negative dimension of Religious Liberty—the legal barriers to establishment—is readily reduced to static dogmas, while the positive dimension—the right to free exercise of religion—constantly opens new insights and new claims which must in due course be rejected or affirmed in the public consensus and in the courts.

No attempt can be made here to catch the fullness of Seminar discussion, but readers may benefit from summary of some of the important issues which arose as specialists and delegates argued some of the questions which arise when a dynamic interpretation of the free exercise of religion is pursued.

To implement the work of the Seminars, lists of key questions, accompanied by lists of books and articles, were distributed in advance. The Seminars met three times during the Bicentennial Conference and a summary of findings was drawn up at the end.

Free Exercise of Religion. Moderator: Dr. Bertram Korn, Congregation Keneseth Israel, Philadelphia. Discussant: Dr. Dean M. Kelley, National Council of Churches, New York City.

Findings in summary: deprogramming of persons over 18 is a serious infringement of religious liberty; any efforts of government, by means of tax laws, to inhibit or penalize churches' efforts to influence public policy on moral and ethical issues should be resisted; definitions of "religion" and "church" should come from the religious groups and not from government; the right of religious groups to exemption by reason of conscience from general laws (e.g., vaccination, blood transfusion, attendance at public secondary schools) should be abridged, if at all, only in cases of public health, safety, or the life-rights of others. Unsettled questions: whether churches may set their own criteria for admission or employment, even if conflicting with equal employment or civil rights laws; whether the military chaplaincy as presently organized genuinely provides free exercise of religion. General principles: (1) the free exercise of religion should take precedence over all other considerations except, possibly, survival or self-defense in the event of invasion; (2) in deciding religious disputes, the civil courts should not assess religious doctrines or tenets, but enforce the ruling of the ecclesiastical tribunal having jurisdiction.

Religious and Ethnic Minorities. Moderator: Dr. Dennis J. Clark, Fels Fund, Philadelphia. Discussant: Dr. Murray Friedman, American Jewish Committee, Philadelphia.

Chief points arising from discussion: American society is now pluralistic, with ethnic diversity perhaps more responsible than religious factors for acceptance of that concept; the old line religious structures have generally lacked sympathy for diversity and its articulations; economic power is a vital factor in the achievement of its rights by an ethnic or religious group. Query: to what extent does freedom, or lack of it, within a denomination affect its contribution in the society at large?

Religious Liberty and Public Education. Moderator: Prof. Joyce Bailey, Drew University, Madison, NJ. Discussant: Dr. James E. Wood, Jr., Baptist Joint Committee on Public Affairs, Washington, DC.

Points arising from discussion: the study of religion in the public schools is constitutional and desirable; more attention must be given to train public school teachers and prepare teaching aids in teaching about religion; the public schools cannot be held primarily responsible for removing the "religious illiteracy" which surveys have revealed in the youth; the public schools should teach about religion but avoid advocacy of religion, including secular humanism. An unanswered question: Are not Christians in America now a minority, as Jews have always been, and therefore more dependent upon family and church to implement religious education?

Religious Liberty and Private Education. Moderator: Pres. John R. Coleman, Haverford College, Haverford, PA. Discussant: Monsignor Edward T. Hughes, former Superintendent of Schools, Archdiocese of Philadelphia.

Chief points arising from the discussion: some feel strongly that transmission of values cannot be accomplished without integration with religious principles; opinions differ widely as to whether the civil courts are stifling freedom of speech and freedom of religion and in effect establishing secular humanism as the value system of the public schools; concern was expressed that without some form of tax aid to private schools that option will be denied to low and middle income families.

Civil Religion. Moderator: Dr. Roland R. Hegstad, Editor of *Liberty,* Washington, DC. Discussant: Ms. Elizabeth Bettenhausen, Lutheran Church in America, New York City.

Major points arising in discussion: if the transcendent order stands in judgment over temporal creations of the society, civil religion is a relative good; if the transcendent order becomes an unambiguous justification of the society and its creations, civil religion is a necessary evil. In no case is civil religion identical to the normative claims of Christianity, Judaism, or the emerging varieties of Eastern religions. Some see civil religion providing some integrative force when traditional ideals and myths collapse, but it belongs in any case to the realm of the transitory and temporal. Query: Does the USA have one civil religion or many? Is a civil religion based on a covenant possible in a self-consciously pluralistic society?

Conscience and the Limits of Civil Obedience. Moderator: Rev. William J. Shaw, White Rock Baptist Church, Philadelphia. Discussant: Dr. Richard J. Niebanck, III, Lutheran Church in America, New York City.

Among questions which arose: From whence does authority flow? How is legitimate authority discerned? How are laws judged legitimate or illegitimate? How are religious obedience and civil disobedience related? At what point does violent revolution become an option for persons or groups of conscience? Proposed criteria of legitimacy of laws: all persons equal at law; general applicability of laws affecting life and liberty; illegitimacy of ex post facto laws affecting life and liberty; separation of law-making from law enforcement. The danger to Religious Liberty of retreat by individuals into merely private religion ("privatism") was clearly stated in response to the question, "How does conscience die?"

Rights of Privacy and Clergy Confidentiality. Moderator: Dr. Robert G. Stephanopoulos, Sts. Constantine & Helen Cathedral, Cleveland Heights, OH. Discussant: Dr. Dieter T. Hessel, United Presbyterian Church in the USA, New York City.

Major themes: privacy in associations, in record-keeping, in clergy confidentiality. The forms of abuse, including those by the FBI, CIA, grand juries, etc. are manifold and increasing. Concern was expressed for the sacrifice of the Bill of Rights through increase of illegal surveillance, technical progress (overhearing devices, data banks, etc.), and the decline of protection for the integrity and dignity and liberty of the human person. Privacy includes freedom from interference and intrusion, control of personally sensitive information, and the rights of notification and access for the citizen. For the church, it means the integrity of church records and internal meetings and of clergy-communicant communication.

Women's Liberation and the Rights of Conscience. Moderator: Ms. Judith Ann Heffernan, Philadelphia. Discussant: Dr. Patricia Budd Kepler, Harvard Divinity School, Cambridge, MA.

General themes: at issue is the liberation of *both* men *and* women. The values endorsed by the work institutions of the society are largely the values of men. The values of communal institutions, such as the family and the church, are predominantly those associated with women. The potential for a controlled technocracy in which religious freedom is openly fostered rather than subtly repressed lies in the women's movement, as a force seeking to break down sexist polarities in the value systems of social institutions.

Mass Communication and the Formation of Human Values. Moderator: Prof. Murray S. Stedman, Jr., Temple University, Philadelphia. Discussant: Mr. Don Brewer, KYW-News Radio, Philadelphia.

General problems: the enormous influence of the media, especially TV, coupled with audience passivity; the intellectual and spiritual sterility of the religious ghetto in TV and radio programming; control of news and programs according to a low-level assessment of public taste, compounded by lack of attention to the media by responsible religious leaders.

Genocide as National Policy and Resistance Thereto. Moderator: Dr. Homer A. Jack, World Conference of Religion and Peace, New York City. Discussant: Sr. Ann Gillen, Inter-Religious Task Force on Soviet Jewry, Chicago.

General principles: Genocide has been defined as a crime by a Convention signed by seventy-seven nations, not including the USA. Although it includes assault on minorities short of mass murder, in sheer killing the twentieth century qualifies as "The Age of Genocide." Specically, it has been borne by 1,500,000 Christian Armenians in Muslim Turkey, 6,000,000 Jews in Nazi-controlled Europe, the Bengalis in E. Pakistan, political opponents in Indonesia, and tribal groups in parts of Africa. It threatens Jews in the USSR and Middle East, some Christian groups in the USSR and Middle East, Hindus in Bangladesh, Indians in parts of Latin America, etc. Specific actions: the UN should devise appropriate machinery to implement the Genocide Convention and to rescue the endangered; the USA should ratify the Convention; religious groups should reaffirm and make effective their commitment to dignity and integrity and liberty of the human person and challange government action which threatens recurrence of the crime of genocide.

The Aging and the Rights of Conscience. Moderator: Dr. Alvin Wilson, Gray Panthers Project Find, Inc., Cherry Hill, NJ. Discussant: Ms. Maggie Kuhn, National Convenor of Gray Panthers, Philadelphia.

General issues: Many aged are "locked in a cave," incapable of true humanity let alone true religious life, by reason of poor health care, poor housing, poor nutrition, and lack of social interaction. A time of rampant inflation and corporate irresponsibility threatens the liberties of all citizens, but it afflicts most of all the young and the old. Re-integrating older people into society is a special duty of religious groups, which can also provide interaction between the young and the old. Specifically, older people are the right people at the right time to exercise the rights of conscience in the society and to provide the "watchdogs" of the Good Society—monitoring committees, legislation, projects, and budgets.

Religious Liberty in the International Scene. Moderator: Ms. Alba Zizzamia, Roman Catholic Archdiocese of New York. Discussant: Dr. Richard M. Fagley, Commission of the Churches on International Affairs, New York City.

General issues: religious freedom seldom appears in pure form, but is interrelated with other factors and rights on the world map; an international ethos, implemented by specific standards of behavior, is needed; ratification of the Human Rights Covenants is needed; the churches can help create such an ethos by demonstrating a lifestyle consistent with their teachings and by active concern for those whose freedoms are injured. Agreed: international safeguards are needed; deprivations of liberty in the USSR, Philippines, Chile, etc. are of concern to the churches; the lifestyle of the American churches needs to move away from affluence toward austerity.

The Military/Industrial Complex and the Concerned Conscience. Moderator: Sr. Margaret McKenna, Medical Mission Sisters, Philadelphia. Discussant: Mr. George Lakey, Friends Peace Committee, Philadelphia.

General themes: The basic theme of the military/industrial complex is domination, with a damaging denial of human rights; strategies for waging peace are neglected, for wealth and power rest upon the arms race—both internationally and in the American economy. Opposition to the proliferation of violence needs to be accompanied by education in viable alternatives, such as the "civilian defense" described in Boserup and Mack's *War without Weapons.* Strategies of non-cooperation and the development of resistance unity require a redistribution of economic and political power, which the military/industrial complex secures for a small and practically unaccountable wealthy minority. Religion must "choose life," opposing the support of oppressive regimes abroad and the irresponsible abuse of human life and the environment at home, offering reconciliation in place of fear and justice in place of exploitation.

Medical Ethics and the Rights of Conscience. Moderator: Dr. Bruce Hilton, National Center for Bio-Ethics, Washington, DC. Discussant: Sr. Margaret Farley, Yale Divinity School, New Haven.

The Seminar, after attention to philosophical discussion of moral obligation and the parameters of conscience claims, focused on three areas of ethical decision: (1) choices regarding death, (2) genetics and reproduction (including genetic screening, genetic counselling, *in utero* diagnosis, abortion, fetal experimentation), and (3) questions of distributive justice in health care delivery.

Prophecy. Moderator: Pres. Ira Eisenstein, Reconstructionist Rabbinical College, Philadelphia. Discussant: Rev. David Gracie, St. Barnabas Episcopal Church, Philadelphia.

General issues: six criteria were laid out to determine when a dissenting word may properly be called "prophetic": (1) it must have proper motivation; (2) it must be spoken in the name of a Power greater than oneself; (3) fundamental ethical or spiritual values must be at stake; (4) resistance must be encountered from the environment, hence requiring courage; (5) the act must be related to historical time and place, explaining or interpreting it; (6) it must offer salvation, not some transitory good. Specific attention was given to contemporary prophetic actions: e.g., opposition to the B-1 bomber, to the Arab anti-Jewish boycott, to illegal actions of government agents (wire-tapping, etc.); for amnesty.

Appendix B

CONFERENCE PROGRAM

(most events at Friends Meeting House, 4th & Arch Sts., Philadelphia)

Sunday, April 25, 1976
Reception in the evening, with music by the All-Philadelphia Boys Choir.

Monday, April 26, 1976
First Plenary: Worship (Most Rev. Martin N. Lohmuller); Welcome (Francis G. Brown); Introductions (Rev. William J. Shaw); Keynote Address (Dr. Franklin H. Littell); Addresses on the Protestant, Jewish, and Roman Catholic Traditions of Religious Liberty (Dr. Robert McAfee Brown, Dr. Robert Gordis, Rev. James Hennesey). Following a coffee break, the participants divided into five Sections for discussion. In the afternoon there were either post-plenary discussions with the speakers or a film program, followed by Seminars (described in Appendix A).
Public Session: An historical street play, "The First Hundred Years," by John Welden, examining Pennsylvania's long tradition of religious freedom and its influence on the authors of the Constitution.

Tuesday, April 27, 1976
Second Plenary: Worship (Rabbi Morris V. Dembowitz); Introductions (Dr. John C. Shetler); Addresses on Contemporary American Experience of Conscience and Dissent (Dr. William A. Jones, Professor Janice G. Raymond, Dr. Edwin B. Bronner, Rev. Jesse L. Jackson); followed by Section discussions, discussion with speakers or film program, and Seminars.
Public Session: Yom HaShoa, Official Day of Mourning for Six Million Jewish Martyrs of the Holocaust; Introduction (Rabbi Bertram W. Korn); Address, "Freedom of Conscience—A Jewish Commentary" (Dr. Elie Wiesel).

Wednesday, April 28, 1976
Third Plenary: Worship (Rt. Rev. Silas, Bishop of Amphipolis, Greek Orthodox Archidiocese of North and South America); Introductions (Rev. LaVonne Althouse); Addresses on Contemporary Issues of Church/State Relations (Rabbi Marc H. Tanenbaum, William B. Ball, Esq., Dr. John C. Raines, Dr. Elwyn A. Smith); followed by Section discussions, discussion with speakers or film program, and Seminars. The evening was free.

Thursday, April 29, 1976
Fourth Plenary: Worship (Rev. Joseph L. Joiner); Introductions (Rabbi Charles Lacks); Addresses on Religious Liberty in the International Scene (Dr. Philip A. Potter, Rev. Theodore M. Hesburgh); followed by Section discussions, discussion with speakers or film program, and Seminar Report Groups.
Banquet: Including arts program presented by Affiliate Artists, Inc., in cooperation with the Religious Communities for the Arts, featuring Pauline Domanski, soprano; Stewart Newbold, clarinetist; and Glory Van Scott, actress.

Friday, April 30, 1976
Seminar Report Groups and Coffee Break.
Fifth Plenary: Introductions (Francis G. Brown); Addresses on the Prospect for Religious Liberty (Dr. Milton K. Curry, Dr. Cynthia C. Wedel); Concluding Remarks (Francis G. Brown).

The leaders for the Section discussions included Rabbi M. David Weiss, Germantown Jewish Center, Philadelphia; Dr. Rufus Cornelsen; Sr. Gloria Coleman, Cardinal's Commission on Human Relations, Archdiocese of Philadelphia; Rev. H. Daehler Hayes; and Rev. Elizabeth Miller, Secretary of the Office of Issue Development for American Baptist Churches, USA, Valley Forge, PA.
The film program included "The Emerging Woman," "Yudie," "The Right to Believe," "Chile," "Mr. Nixon's Secret Legacy," "Night and Fog," and "Rendezvous with Freedom."

Appendix C

PERSONALIA OF BICENTENNIAL CONFERENCE

Chairman: Mr. Francis Brown, Philadelphia Yearly Meeting of the Religious Society of Friends
Executive Director: Ms. Nancy Nolde

National Committee

William B. Ball, Esq., Ball and Skelly, Harrisburg, PA
Dr. Eugene Carson Blake, former General Secretary, World Council of Churches; President, "Bread for the World"
Dr. Robert McAfee Brown, Professor of Religious Studies, Stanford University
Dr. Marion de Velder, General Secretary, Reformed Church in America
Dr. R. H. Edwin Espy, Chairman of Project Forward '76
Mr. Richard J. Fox, President, Fox Companies, Philadelphia
Mr. John T. Gurash, Chairman of the Board, Insurance Company of North America
His Eminence Archbishop Iakovos of the Greek Orthodox Archdiocese of North and South America
His Eminence John Cardinal Krol, Archbishop of Philadelphia
Dr. Robert J. Marshall, President, Lutheran Church in America
Mr. Frank C. P. McGlinn, Executive Vice President, The Fidelity Bank, Philadelphia
*Dr. Robert V. Moss, President, United Church of Christ
Bernard G. Segal, Esq., Schnader, Harrison, Segal & Lewis, Philadelphia
Mr. Laird H. Simons, Jr., President, William Amer Company, Philadelphia
Douglas V. Steere, T. Wistar Brown Professor of Philosophy Emeritus, Haverford College
Rabbi Marc H. Tanenbaum, National Interreligious Affairs Director, American Jewish Committee
Mr. William P. Thompson, President, National Council of Churches
Dr. Cynthia C. Wedel, President, World Council of Churches

Conference Planning Committee

The Chairman

Vice-Chairpersons: The Rev. LaVonne Althouse, Pastor, Salem Lutheran Church, Philadelphia

Rabbi Charles Lacks, Immediate Past President, Board of Rabbis of Greater Philadelphia

Bishop Martin N. Lohmuller, Vicar General of the Roman Catholic Archdiocese of Philadelphia

The Rev. William J. Shaw, Pastor, White Rock Baptist Church, Philadelphia

Secretary: Mr. William B. Miller, Director, Presbyterian Historical Society, Philadelphia

Treasurer: Dr. Rufus Cornelsen, Executive Director, Metropolitan Christian Council of Philadelphia

Members: Bishop James M. Ault, Presiding Bishop, Philadelphia Area, United Methodist Church

Dr. Edwin B. Bronner, Librarian and Professor of History, Haverford College

Mr. Albert D. Chernin, Executive Vice Chairman, National Jewish Community Relations Council

Dr. Anderson D. Clark, Senior Vice President, Affiliate Artists, Inc.

Rabbi Morris V. Dembowitz, President, Board of Rabbis of Greater Philadelphia

The Rt. Rev. Msgr. Charles V. Devlin, Executive Director, Cardinal's Commission on Human Relations, Archdiocese of Philadelphia

The Rev. Dr. Charles H. Diamond, Bicentennial Coordinator, Archdiocese of Philadelphia

Bishop Alfred G. Dunston, African Methodist Episcopal Zion Church, Philadelphia

The Rev. Everett Francis, Chairman, Ecumenical Task Force on the Religious Observance of the Bicentennial, New York

Dr. Murray Friedman, Regional Director, American Jewish Committee, Philadelphia

Dr. Charles W. Fu, Department of Religion, Temple University

Rabbi Harold Goldfarb, Executive Secretary, Board of Rabbis of Greater Philadelphia

The Rev. Joseph L. Joiner, Minister, Mother Bethel African Methodist Episcopal Church, Philadelphia

The Rev. Dean M. Kelley, Executive for Religious Liberty, National Council of Churches

Rabbi Bertram W. Korn, Senior Rabbi, Congregation Keneseth Israel, Elkins Park, PA

Dr. Robert Kreider, former President of Bluffton College, Lima, OH; Member of Executive Committee, Mennonite Central Committee

The Rev. John A. Limberakis, Archpriest, Greek Orthodox Community of Philadelphia; Pastor, Church of the Annunciation, Elkins Park, PA

Dr. Franklin H. Littell, Professor of Religion, Temple University

Dr. Frederick E. Maser, Executive Secretary, World Methodist Historical Society

Mr. William R. Meek, Associate Professor, School of Social Work, University of Pennsylvania

Dr. John M. Moore, Editor, *Quaker History,* Swarthmore, PA

The Rev. High J. Nolan, Professor of Theology, Immaculata College, Immaculata, PA

*The Rev. Bernhard E. Olson, Director of Inter-Religious Program, National Conference of Christians and Jews, Inc., New York

Dr. John C. Raines, Associate Professor of Religion, Temple University

The Rev. F. Lee Richards, Rector, St. Peter's Episcopal Church, Philadelphia

Mr. John H. Sardeson, Executive Director, Greater Philadelphia Region, National Conference of Christians and Jews

Dr. John C. Shetler, Chairman, Metropolitan Christian Council of Philadelphia; Conference Minister, Pennsylvania Southeast Conference, United Church of Christ

The Rev. Grant Spradling, Director, Religious Communities for the Arts, New York

Dr. Murray S. Stedman, Professor of Political Science and Chairman of the Department, Temple University

Dr. Frank H. Stroup, Executive Secretary, Philadelphia Presbytery, United Presbyterian Church in the U.S.A.

Dr. Margaret B. Tinkcom, Executive Director Emeritus, Philadelphia Historical Commission

Dr. Cynthia C. Wedel, President, World Council of Churches

Dr. Don Yoder, Associate Professor, Department of Folklore and Folklife, University of Pennsylvania

Deceased

Conference Committees, Staff, and Consultants

Program Committee
Dr. Rufus Cornelsen, co-chairman
Dr. Franklin H. Littell, co-chairman
The Rev. LaVonne Althouse
Dr. Edwin B. Bronner
The Rt. Rev. Msgr. Charles V. Devlin
The Rev. Dr. Charles H. Diamond
Dr. Murray Friedman
Rabbi Charles Lacks

Mr. William R. Meek
The Rev. Hugh J. Nolan
Dr. John C. Raines
The Rev. William J. Shaw
Dr. Murray S. Stedman

Protocol Committee
Dr. Frederick E. Maser
Dr. Margaret B. Tinkcom

Interns/Volunteers Program
Mrs. Marion Wilen, National Vice
   President, American Jewish Congress

Religious Liberty Sabbath/Sunday Program
The Rev. Gerald W. Gillette,
   Historian, National Presbyterian
   Historical Society, Philadelphia

Conference Speakers Bureau
Dr. Howard G. Hartzell, Minister,
   First Baptist Church, Philadelphia

Press Conference Chairman
The Rt. Rev. J. Brooke Mosley,
   Assistant Bishop, Episcopal
   Diocese of Pennsylvania

Conference Staff
The Executive Director
Mrs. Therese Dymski,
   Administrative Assistant
Ms. Marlene Crowder
Ms. Diane Dymski
Mrs. Joan Shipman

Ways and Means Committee
Dr. Frank H. Stroup, Chairman
Rt. Rev. Msgr. Charles V. Devlin
Rabbi Morris V. Dembowitz

Finance Committee
Mr. Frank C. P. McGlinn
Mr. Richard J. Fox
Mr. Laird H. Simons, Jr.

Conference Hospitality
Rev. H. Daehler Hayes, Pastor,
   Old First Reformed Church, Philadelphia

Films
Thomas Swain, Associate Secretary
   for Religious Education, Young
   Friends, Philadelphia Yearly
   Meeting of Friends

Press Room
Dr. Erik Modean, Director of
   News Bureau, Lutheran Council
   in the USA, New York
Mr. William Epstein, Director
   of Public Relations, Jewish
   Community Relations Council,
   Philadelphia
Mrs. Eve Stedman, Director of
   Public Relations, Metropolitan
   Christian Council of Philadelphia
Ms. Dorothy Rensenbrink, former
   staff member, Department of News
   & Information Services, National
   Council of Churches
Mr. Donn Mitchell, free lance
   journalist and environmental
   consultant

Consultants—Arts Program
The Rev. Grant Spradling
Mr. John Skelton, Appointment Services,
   Affiliate Artists, Inc., New York

Consultant—Sections/Seminars Program
Mrs. Carman St. J. Hunter,
   Director, Project Worldview,
   New York